1st Bedfordshires

1ST BEDFORDSHIRES

PART ONE: MONS TO THE SOMME

STEVEN FULLER

Published in 2011 by Fighting High Ltd,
23 Hitchin Road, Stotfold, Hitchin, Herts, SG5 4HP
www.fightinghigh.com

British Library Cataloguing-in-Publication data.
A CIP record for this title is available from the
British Library.

ISBN – 13: 978-0956269652

Designed and typeset in Monotype Baskerville
11/14pt and Monotype by Michael Lindley
www.truthstudio.co.uk

Printed and bound by Toppan Printing Co. (SZ) Ltd.

Contents

Foreword

In August 1914 the 1st Battalion the Bedfordshire Regiment (the Bedfords) was mobilised and sent to fight with the British Expeditionary Force as it clashed with the German army at Mons. They went on to confront the Germans in all the major actions, from the steadfast resistance at Mons, through to the ferocious hand-to-hand combat at Ypres, and then they endured the appalling attrition during the 1916 Somme offensives.

Their months of training meant that they were highly regarded both by their commanders and also by the enemy. General French, the Commander-in-Chief, declared that the Bedfords 'have always done what was asked' and in April 1916 it was said that 'the Bedfords and the Norfolks are considered two of the best battalions in the Army'. A captured German prisoner said 'the Russians can't shoot at all, the French are good shots but the British shoot and kill'. British rifle fire was the fastest and most accurate in the world.

The Bedfords were outstanding in their resilience to the appalling conditions in the trenches and the heavy toll of casualties. At the infamous Hill 60 (or 'Murder Hill' as it became known), out of 630 Bedfords who went forward on 17 April 1915, only around 200 marched or limped back four days later. One sergeant had thirty out of his thirty-five men killed or wounded. And yet the battalion was largely left out of the accounts of the vicious struggle for Hill 60, despite having held firm against all the odds and suffered such a dreadful, long list of casualties.

Steven Fuller has drawn on numerous eyewitness accounts and expertly and vividly brought to life the history of this battalion in perhaps its finest hour.

Sir Samuel Whitbread, KCVO

President – The Bedfordshire and Hertfordshire Regiment Association

Chapter 1

The Bedfordshires' Call to Arms

'Our one wish was to get at the Germans.
Little did we know what we were in for.'

The history of a British infantry regiment of the line can be followed through a lengthy series of garrison duties throughout the British Empire, laced with battles, campaigns and any number of specific events, all of which meld together to form their own, unique and fiercely proud regimental traditions. The Bedfordshire Regiment was no different and being the sixteenth most senior regiment of the line, had 226 years of service to the country behind it by the time the First World War erupted.

Initially raised in October 1688 as a regiment of pikemen and musketeers, the first three decades of its existence had seen the regiment engaged in more European combat than any other single battalion of foot in the British army. By the end of Queen Victoria's reign, it had stood in the battle lines during some of the most famous engagements in British military history, including Walcourt, Steenkirk, Landen, Blenheim, Ramilies, Oudenarde and Malplaquet. Present during major events such as the American War of Independence and the South African wars, in addition to many of the Empire's 'small wars' and skirmishes with other dominant European powers, the regiment had forged a fine history of faithful and reliable service. Garrison duties had taken it from the Far East to the New World, with long tours spent in the Fever Isles, the Indian subcontinent and the North-West Frontier over and above many years posted throughout England, Ireland and Scotland.

Before 1751 the regiment was known by the names of a succession of ten colonels until standardisation of the British army that year saw the title of the 16th Regiment of Foot introduced. The year 1782 saw a further change, intended to encourage enlistment within specific geographical areas, the regiment becoming the 16th (Buckinghamshire) Regiment of Foot. In 1809 the regiment exchanged titles with the 14th Foot, becoming the 16th (Bedfordshire) Regiment of Foot, finally being renamed the Bedfordshire Regiment in 1881, although it was still referred to as the 16th for decades afterwards.

In 1908 the 1st Bedfordshires returned home, having been stationed in India, the Far East and Africa for almost thirty years. The last year of their 'grand tour' had seen them based in Aden, leaving for home on 8 December 1908, 18 officers and 670 'other ranks' strong. As their transport ship, the HT *Rohilla*, passed Gibraltar where the 2nd Bedfordshires were based at the time, they signalled their greetings to the garrison and were sent the reply: 'Welcome home and a Merry Xmas to you all.'

Five years of parade grounds, manoeuvres and retraining based at Aldershot followed, under the command of their fearsome but highly respected Lieutenant Colonel De Gex and former Grenadier Guards Regimental Sergeant Major Wombwell.[1] They raised the battalion's condition to nothing short of impeccable and, as a result, June 1911 saw them selected for duty at the coronation of King George V and Queen Mary. That September a detachment of 13 officers and 329 other ranks was also chosen for duty at Chelsea Barracks, relieving the Scots Guards in guarding Buckingham Palace, St James's Palace and the Bank of England. During 1912 and 1913 they further enhanced their reputation and added to the regimental silverware considerably, winning many of the army's competitions, including bayonet fighting, rifle meetings and Young Soldiers' trophies among many others. Army manoeuvres in the summer of 1913 were held in the Midlands, in the countryside between Buckingham and Rugby, after which the 1st Bedfordshires were issued orders to proceed to Ireland in the autumn.

That September Lieutenant Colonel De Gex was promoted to a post in the Irish Command and the following month Lieutenant Colonel Charles Griffith was transferred from the 2nd Bedfordshires to assume command of the 1st. On arrival in Ireland, half of the battalion was based in Mullingar in Co. Westmeath, with detachments posted at various locations throughout the surrounding countryside, and the other half was based in Belfast. There it earned itself a reputation as a good battalion to be involved in policing the unsettled countryside, following the introduction of the unpopular 'Bill for Home Rule'. Nevertheless, despite the goodwill shown, Lance Corporal Herbert Spencer recorded how 'we were not even allowed to go about alone; one could always see groups of British Tommies together in case of accidents'.[2]

The date of 20 March 1914 saw the battalion posted further north, with Headquarters, B Company, under Captain Cecil ('Johnnie') Ker and D Company under Captain Francis Edwards posted to Enniskillen. A Company under Captain John McMasters Milling was based at Omagh and C Company under Major Walter Allason at Armagh. Although their move north was in response to the growing unrest in the region, the men of the battalion were not called upon for any duties over and above policing their area of command, which in the event proved a comfortable posting before the trying times they would be subjected to in the coming years. Herbert Spencer remarked that on arrival, they 'received a very hearty welcome. There were flags flying, bands playing and a cavalry regiment to meet us ... we soon became on good terms with the new army and made many friends amongst the inhabitants, some even marrying the girls.'

War is declared – August 1914

Up until May 1914, Captain John Macready,[3] who was serving as the battalion's adjutant, had been inundated with telegraphs and instructions from the War Office regarding the unrest. Every imaginable bureaucratic detail had been incorporated into the messages, but for two months not a single one had been thrust upon him. On the evening of 31 July 1914, he sat alone in the officers' mess and was bemused to receive the first wire for a long time, delivered on a silver plate by one of the waiters. There had been no trouble in their area for many months and no news had reached him from Omagh or Armagh of any events so, curious, he opened it. It simply read, 'take precautionary measures'. Macready was none the wiser for some time, having run through their deployments, measures and orders for each company and its station, but then it hit him. The warning did not relate to Ireland but to Europe.

Following the assassination of the Austrian archduke and his wife in Sarajevo, events had been boiling away in Europe and all countries were posturing in readiness for the war that many expected. Austria demanded to be allowed to 'police' Serbia following the outrage and Serbia refused, calling on their ally Russia. Russia announced they would have little choice but to declare war on Austria if they invaded Serbia, thus causing Germany to remind Russia they were Austria's ally. In their turn,

France would be forced to join Russia – and so the string of alliances went on. Technically, Britain was neutral, but had promised Belgium its protection should it be needed. This guarantee would drag Britain and its Empire into the European war that was on the verge of breaking out, as the tiny Belgian army would soon be overrun by the mighty German military machine.

Captain Macready was the only officer around, the others having gone into town looking for amusement. Before orders were even issued recalling his fellow officers so the battalion could concentrate at Mullingar, as was the plan, the official order came to move. The next day saw the companies, detachments and various other elements gather quickly and smoothly at Mullingar and the battalion waited on tenterhooks for further orders. Several long days later, on the afternoon of Tuesday 4 August 1914, the British army was mobilised and entered the First World War.

Macready expected pandemonium to break out once the order was issued, yet he, along with many of his fellow officers, found they had little to do as the battalion was so well organised. The reservists were even gathered from England over the next week to join them, and RSM Wombwell called what would be the final roll on the battalion's parade square on 13 August. When he called the very last name of the final batch – 'Basham' – roars of laughter filled the air, adding to the surreal atmosphere. Doubtless Private Arthur Basham[4] from Biggleswade had already heard the jokes many times before, but laughed along with his chums nonetheless.

As the men trained hard while waiting for the anticipated move to the fighting front, and packed up what Lance Corporal Spencer called their 'reds and whites' (dress uniforms) for shipment back to the depot, their thoughts naturally turned to home. Affairs were put in order, wills were completed ensuring their loved ones received something in the event of their death, and bags of letters were shipped to England. Among the deluge of mail leaving Ireland was a letter from Private Edwin Bywaters of Henlow, Bedfordshire.[5] Eddie, as he was known, was a 'tall, handsome lad' and the eldest of ten children who had joined the battalion nine months earlier. His letter to his mother sent the usual assurances but quietly affirmed his strong sense of duty. The 22-year-old spoke fondly of the Henlow Cricket Club, of which he was a regular first-team player and how his keen sense of right and wrong inspired and braced him for what was to come. Eddie's thoughts, wishes and opinions were mimicked thousands of times over in the literary mountains making their way across the Irish Sea as the troops made their final preparations for war.

The entire brigade was ready by 9 August, but due to a few minor administrative issues, the men were not shipped out immediately. Blenheim Day was celebrated as regimental tradition demanded on the 13th (being the 210th anniversary of the 16th Foot's involvement in said battle), which proved to be their final day before leaving for war. That evening soldiers of the battalion waited in the parade square in full marching order, rifles and two bandoliers of ammunition by their sides. From his position on guard duty, Lance Corporal Spencer noted how some of 'the boys slept out all night by their rifles and equipment and the band played a good time in the square during the night and livened us all up. Large numbers of people came to say "Goodbye" and there were many tears from sweethearts.'

With rations handed out, the battalion assembled and marched to the station accompanied by the band, which played 'very cheery tunes and the favourite "It's a long way to Tipperary"'. Herbert Spencer was among those on the 'lively march' who welcomed the local 'girls running amongst the men, kissing them and wishing them luck. Our battalion was well liked in that district.' The battalion boarded trains at Mullingar with the HQ section, A and B Companies leaving at 1.30 a.m. on the 14th and C and D Companies following on another train at 2.15 a.m. The men were flattered that, despite the unsociable time of day, most of the town saw them off from the station as the band played 'The Girl I left Behind', leaving Lance Corporal Spencer and many of his chums 'rather depressed'.

By 8.30 a.m. the entire battalion was at Belfast and after a breakfast of 'tea, cakes and anything we wanted' in the railway siding the band led the battalion as the men marched through cheering crowds before starting to board the SS *Oranza* at 11 a.m. Two hours later the ship was loaded and the men just had time to send their last letters home before leaving the Belfast dock at 3 p.m. Lance Corporal Spencer was on deck as the transport left harbour, remembering that 'opposite us a large boat called the "*Gigantic*" was being built, she was the sister ship to the "*Titanic*". Thousands of men were working and gave us a very cheery send off.' The troubles of the past year appeared forgotten, as the entire port was full of people waving flags and handkerchiefs, giving the soldiers an unexpectedly fond and appreciated farewell.

According to the diary of Lieutenant J.S. Davenport,[6] the officers who mobilised with the battalion from Mullingar on Friday 14 August 1914 are shown below. Just Lieutenant Colonel Griffith, Captains Newington and Hanafin (the Medical Officer), Lieutenants Corah and Duke, and Lieutenant and Quartermaster Peirce were not casualties by the time Christmas 1914 arrived.

Lieutenant Colonel Charles Richard Jebb Griffith, DSO,
Commanding Officer
Major Cranley Charlton Onslow, Second in Command
Major Edward Ivan de Sausmarez Thorpe,
Officer Commanding B Company
Major Walter Allason, Officer Commanding C Company
Captain John Cassells Montieth, Officer Commanding D Company
Captain John McMasters Milling, B Company
Captain Cecil Howard Ker, C Company
Captain Robert James McCloughin, D Company
Captain Francis Hyde Edwards, D Company
Captain Claude Newington
Captain John Macready, Adjutant
Lieutenant Joseph Herbert Mayne, Machine Gun Officer
Lieutenant Hugh Courtenay, B Company
Lieutenant William Wynter Wagstaff, D Company
Lieutenant Charles Edward Gowran Shearman,
Scout Officer and C Company
Lieutenant Alfred Geoffrey Corah, Cyclist Platoon
Lieutenant James Salter Davenport, D Company
Lieutenant Sheldon Arthur Gledstanes, C Company
Lieutenant Cyril Pope, D Company
Lieutenant William St John Coventry, Transport Officer
Lieutenant William Alexander Charles Duke, C Company
Lieutenant Charles E. Goff, B Company
(attached from the 1st King's Liverpool Regiment)
Second Lieutenant Leonard William Rendell, A Company
Second Lieutenant Walter Arthur Beaumont Walker, A Company
Second Lieutenant Villiers Chernocke Downes, A Company
Honorary Lieutenant and Quartermaster Alfred Ernest Peirce
Captain Patrick John Hanafin, Medical Officer (attached from
the RAMC)

The British Expeditionary Force arrives in northern France

When mobilised, the 1st Bedfordshires were part of the 15th Infantry Brigade, commanded by Brigadier General Count Gleichen, and served alongside the 1st Norfolks, 1st Cheshires and 1st Dorsets. Along with the 13th and 14th Infantry Brigades, they formed the 5th Division under Major General Sir Charles Fergusson and served in II Corps, which was initially commanded by Lieutenant General Sir James Greirson.

Other than an overnight thunderstorm, Lieutenant Davenport described the journey from Belfast as 'a fine journey' on a 'flat, calm sea'. On board was Sergeant Leonard Godfrey from Royston,[7] who had been with the battalion from the age of 15 and served in India and Ireland. He was one of the professional soldiers who was on the deck around midnight and wrote home of how their ship was steaming ahead with all lights out when it 'tried to knock a tramp steamer out of the water', remarking how lucky they were not to have come a cropper. After previous near misses when, on manoeuvres in 1909 their train just missed a furniture van on a level crossing and when the following year's manoeuvres saw them 'come off second best' when they mischievously decided to charge a cruiser during an invasion scheme, Godfrey was convinced they were a 'lucky regiment'.

As battalion orders were sealed, no one was certain of their direction, but most expected their destination to be England initially. Passing Land's End at 11.30 a.m. and Southampton that afternoon, the transport convoy hugged the English coast until darkness fell.

Despite rampant speculation, no one knew for sure where they were headed in the dark night, so it was a surprise when the battalion landed at Le Havre around 6 a.m. on 16 August and started to disembark in the damp morning air. The men were held in huge sheds at the dockside while the transport was unloaded, before being moved to Rest Camp No. 8, 10km away in the hills above Le Havre.

During the march through Le Havre, a mixture of Boy Scout troops and local musicians playing the penny whistle 'escorted' the battalion with enthusiastic variations of 'God Save the King' and the 'Marseillaise'. The French civilians lining the streets were 'beside themselves' to see the professional British battalions marching in long columns, and it was not long before souvenirs were being exchanged between the British soldiers and local French girls. As Lance Corporal Spencer recalled, 'this is where Tommy started to learn French ... plenty of beer, wine and fruit was given to us'. The rear platoon soldiers were covered in flowers when they made it through the town and their officer remarked that 'they were practically naked', having lost just about every badge and button from their uniforms and many left without their caps. Even the veteran Orderly Room Sergeant Charles Kennedy[8] was exhausted by the amount of hugging and kissing the French girls bestowed upon them! Later in the month some generals would complain that they were unable to identify which battalions men came from due to the lack of cap badges and shoulder titles, most of which were adorning French maidens' dresses by then.

The night came and all civilians were ordered from camp, outposts were placed, and as hardly any of the transport had made it to the camp due to the slippery roads, most of the battalion camped on sheets on the damp ground. At 2 a.m. the brigade's horses slipped their pegs and stampeded, causing a sleepless night – not helped by the general mixture of amusement and foul language that pervaded the campsite.

The following day – 17 August – was spent in a mixture of tidying up fatigues, and rest, with many of the men going into the town to look around. The 5th Division was still concentrating, with units arriving throughout the day, so the men of the battalion amused themselves through various activities; one group suddenly found the sight of a local funeral fascinating enough to hold their attention for over an hour and some even helped the local farmer harvest his oats and corn. Naturally rumours found a welcome home in the camp too, with stories of British units being badly mauled in ferocious fighting further east, but considering they were the first wave to arrive all such stories proved untrue.

Just before midnight on the 17th, the battalion left camp and marched to Le Havre train station, arriving around 3 a.m. After spending two hours in a large shed by the docks the train arrived, being made up of carriages and open cattle trucks. Lance Corporal Spencer voiced the general opinion of the British troops as they restlessly waited to move: 'Our one wish was to get at the Germans. Little did we know what we were in for; not many of us knew what "active service" meant.'

Thirty minutes later the train left with the battalion crammed onboard. Passing through Rouen on a gloriously hot day, the overloaded train headed for Le Cateau, where the British Expeditionary Force was concentrating. After a twelve-hour ride there was a twenty-minute pause at Arras, where they were met with the news that General Greirson had died from a heart attack on the journey. Many of the officers were unsettled by the news, as they saw him as the most knowledgeable man there was when it came to the German army and its tactics. As he had been in command of the Bedfords' II Corps, General Smith-Dorrien was rushed from England to take over, just in time for the opening engagement of the war.

After a day-long train ride the battalion arrived at Le Cateau late on the 18th and marched through the peaceful countryside to Pommereuil, some 4km away. None of the men could possibly know that several days later they would be back at Le Cateau under completely different conditions to those in which they had arrived. They spent two hot summer days of route marching to harden them up while waiting for the small British army to gather, until orders finally came and they moved north on the 20th. The weather was fine, clear and warm and the men marched through a green, ripe countryside filled with crops ready to harvest. Locals smiled warmly as the battalions passed through clean, neat villages and were offered fruit and local drink by the villagers. Yet all through the march no one really knew what was happening further east, such as where other brigades were, if British divisions were over the next crest, or perhaps French units, or maybe even German ones. The small British army tramped obliviously northward, with the surreal feeling of being alone in the sprawling countryside.

On the road north to Mons, the soldiers of the battalion found themselves marching along the very same road their military ancestors had covered on the way to the Battle of Malplaquet in September 1709. Later on that morning, curious heads craned to the east as they passed the field their forebears, the 16th Regiment of Foot, had lined with their musketeers and pikemen.

During a break in the middle of 21 August a curious sound was heard coming from the army's right flank. Closer inspection found it to be the massed artillery of French and German armies blasting away, and the word rippled along the column that the French were attacking. In hindsight, they were actually retreating, having lost over 200,000 men in the first few days alone, a figure that was much larger than the entire British army at the time. However, for the time being these facts were unknown to the tiny British army, which was unwittingly marching into an already exposed salient.

That night while in billets, a group of officers found themselves listening to the sound of rifle fire growing nearer. Straining to try and establish whether or not it was really a firefight between an advanced

German guard and a British picket, the group grew 'quite windy' in the darkness and were on the verge of raising the alarm as the noise grew louder and nearer. When one finally went to investigate he returned with the news that the German assault was in fact a dog-drawn milk cart trundling noisily down the cobblestoned road.

At dawn on Saturday 22nd, C Squadron of the 4th Royal Irish Dragoon Guards, commanded by Major Tom Bridges, pushed out two patrols north from Mons towards Soignies. Here they met the Germans for the first time and the cavalry skirmishes started. During the day and in the rear of the cavalry screen, the British infantry of the 1st, 2nd, 3rd and 5th Divisions marched ever northwards, and the men noted the countryside was changing. Greenery was replaced by a more industrial landscape littered with slag heaps; heavy iron machinery grumbled constantly and the people somehow looked 'more dour and less inviting'. Major Onslow recorded[9] that when the battalion crossed into Belgium near Autreppe around midday the distinctive sound of cannon fire could be clearly heard coming from the north-west.

Rumours started to reach the marching columns that both their own cavalry and local civilians were reporting that enemy troops were not far to the north, and orders to assume a defensive position followed. After marching through Dour, the battalion stopped at Boussu late on the 22nd with the plan for II Corps to advance across the Canal de Conde around Mons the following day. However, late that night two unwelcomed pieces of news reached the tiny army. To their right the French had been pushed back in complete disarray and to the left there were no Allied troops whatsoever, leaving the British army as the only intact flank guard for the larger, retreating French forces. Furthermore, a wide German flank march far to the west had exposed the British and left them in a difficult position.

In response, the cavalry was moved out to cover the open left flank, I Corps was staggered in a defensive stance on the right flank, and II Corps held the main line of resistance in the middle. It was decided that if pressure grew on the outposts along the canal, II Corps would evacuate Mons and take up a defensive position among the pit villages and slag heaps a little way to the south, along the line that the Bedfordshires and their comrades in the 15th Brigade were hurriedly preparing. Through all this, the Germans were apparently unaware of the presence of the British Expeditionary Force in this area until the skirmishes on the 22nd, and even then neither side really knew much about their adversaries' strength.

The II Corps took up their thin line of roughly entrenched positions along the Mons canal that day and overnight, following it around the pronounced salient to the north of the town. They lined the canal bank with the 3rd Division in front and the 5th Division in support. The Bedfordshires' 15th Brigade was to be the 5th Division's reserve and spent a sleepless night preparing the best defensive positions possible.

Chapter 2

The Battle of Mons
23 and 24 August 1914

"The Russians can't shoot at all, the French are good shots
but the British shoot and kill.'

The first battle fought by the British army against the Germans came about simply because pre-war plans had unintentionally placed the British Expeditionary Force in the way of the German advance towards Paris. In the preceding three weeks, German troops had entered Luxemburg to the south on 2 August and moved into Belgium, near Liège, the next day. The British government had declared war on 4 August 1914, and the Bedfordshires had landed in secret with the rest of the British army on 16 August. By 22 August the relatively tiny force of four infantry divisions and one cavalry division, which comprised the British Expeditionary Force, had disembarked in France and taken up their positions according to plan, just across the Belgian border, some distance south of Mons on the extreme left of the Allied line. Estimates vary, but it seems reasonable to state that they faced odds of at least seven to one along most of the battlefront, although they did not initially know that. Ironically, the last time a British force faced an enemy in open European battle was ninety-nine years earlier near a village called Waterloo, when, in alliance with the Prussians, they faced the French.

The German army's contempt for the 'puny' British forces was apparent, as they openly laughed at the prospect of meeting them on the field. Their initial disregard was to prove fatal in the coming weeks, as years of practice and warfare meant that all soldiers in the British ranks could fire fifteen accurate shots a minute. Many soldiers could fire even faster without losing their accuracy, making the small British

Expeditionary Force something to be reckoned with.

At 5.30 a.m., Sir John French (the British Commander-in-Chief) met with Generals Haig, Allenby and Smith-Dorrien at his advanced HQ at a chateau in Sars-la-Bruyère, where he ordered the outpost line on the canal to be strengthened and the bridges prepared for demolition. They recognised that the British position was not good, for the canal salient was badly exposed on three sides, while 'the selection of positions by the 5th Division was causing great difficulties'. The ground was nothing more than a wilderness of deep ditches, with occasional buildings sited here and there, punctuated with meandering roads and tracks. Irregular slag heaps littered the scenery, being an inconsistent mixture of heights and stability.

The morning of Sunday 23 August broke in mist and rain, which cleared around 10 a.m. There were some early exchanges between German cavalry and British infantry outposts around 6.30 a.m., near Obourg, Nimy and Ville Pommeroeul, but the main German focus was on the units of II Corps, thinly spread along and behind the canal.

Before 9 a.m. German heavy guns were in a position on high ground north of the canal, and opened fire on the positions of the 4th Middlesex and 4th Royal Fusiliers. German infantry assaults began from across the canal and increased in strength all around the salient from Obourg to Nimy. The 84th Regiment from Schleswig launched the first assault on the positions around Nimy, but the British infantry's professional and highly concentrated rapid rifle fire mowed down the regiment as they advanced towards the canal in their tightly packed waves.

Captain Walter Bloem's book, *Vormarsch*,[10] describes the German losses. He commanded the 12th Brandenburg Grenadiers as they assaulted the area around Tertre, west of Mons. After the first day of battle, his proud battalion had been 'smashed up, shot down – only a handful left'. He was horrified to learn that 25 officers and more than 500 of his men were dead, with most of the rest wounded. The Germans were convinced they had faced a 'wall of machine guns' but, in fact, the British only had two per battalion. Their rifle fire was simply the fastest and most accurate in the world at the time, as a result of many years of policing the Empire and extra pay for marksmen. Bloem and his Grenadiers had been laughing heartily at the thought of fighting what they saw as the amusingly dressed British Tommies in their 'grey-brown golfing suits with flat topped cloth caps' before the battle. After the day's bloody business was over he wrote: 'Our first battle is a heavy – unheard of heavy – defeat against the English. The English we laughed at.'

A Gordon Highlander who was among those in the front firing line said:

Poor devils of infantry! They advanced ... in files five deep and our rifle has a flat trajectory up to 600 yards. Guess the result. We could steady our rifles on the trench and take deliberate aim. The first company were simply blasted away to Heaven by a volley at 700 yards and in their insane formation every bullet was almost sure to find two billets ... they had absolutely no chance. ...

The highly trained British infantry were starting to inflict a heavy toll on the advancing waves, yet they came on time and time again.

The bridges at Nimy were being held by the 4th Royal Fusiliers, the advanced company being under Captain Ashburner with two of the machine guns commanded by Lieutenant Maurice Dease. As the German attacks increased, Dease's gunners were all killed or wounded so he took over a gun himself. He was wounded five times and eventually taken to the dressing station, where he died from his injuries. Private Sidney Godley assumed control of Dease's gun and kept it firing. He covered the withdrawal from the overwhelming German advance despite being wounded, and eventually dismantled and threw the gun into the canal just before being taken prisoner. Both men were awarded the army's first Victoria Crosses of the war.

The troops in the canal salient had orders for 'a stubborn resistance', and they held their positions despite being hard pressed until after 11 a.m. At Nimy a brave German private called Niemayer jumped into the canal under fire and closed the swing bridge, which enabled the first German troops to cross. He was killed in the act, with many of his comrades following soon afterwards, but his actions released the Germans onto the southern bank where their sheer weight of numbers forced the thinning line of defenders back.

The Bedfordshires' HQ was in Pâturages, with their companies digging a defensive line to the north that morning. As the Bedfords' brigade continued digging among the slag heaps to the sounds of battle, the attack spread westwards along the straight canal and previously unengaged battalions came into action around Jemappes, 3km west of Mons. The forward post of the Scots Fusiliers north of the canal was withdrawn and gradually the Germans advanced to within 180m of the bridge at Lock 2, where they were brought to a standstill by the accuracy of the British fire. Further to the west, the Brandenburg Grenadiers fought doggedly through Tertre and were only stopped by the maze of wire fences, boggy dikes and the crossfire of the West Kents and Scottish Borderers on the canal bank. By noon fighting was continuous along the canal and the British battalions to the west began to fall back in the early afternoon.

Just after noon in the canal salient, the Germans succeeded in crossing the canal west of Obourg and reached the village railway station. Taught by their recent experiences, they abandoned their massed formation and deployed in extended order. The Middlesex and Royal Irish battalions in this sector were under growing pressure, being under observation from the high ground north of the canal and with advanced German patrols pushing through Mons to their rear.

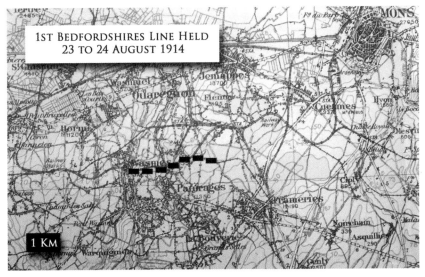

1ST BEDFORDSHIRES LINE HELD
23 TO 24 AUGUST 1914

1 KM

At 2.30 p.m. the Bedfordshires and other battalions in reserve were shelled for the first time and by 3.15 p.m. the last of the British front-line units had retired from the canal, with the lead German troops so close behind that only one bridge was successfully blown. Some small parties, either not receiving orders to withdraw or ordered to defend to the last man, were engulfed as the Germans swarmed across the canal, through Nimy and along the straight road into the city. In spite of the efforts of the staff to co-ordinate the withdrawal to the planned defence line, there was no uniformity of movement from the outpost line on the canal and parties of infantry began to get mixed up. Effective command fell to the captains, subalterns, and senior NCOs on the spot.

Around the same time, the Bedfordshires' A and B Companies were digging trenches north of the railway line at Wasmes, as advanced parties of the C and D Companies fired their first shots from their defensive line north of Pâturages, having been rushed there to plug a gap between the Dorsets and the 3rd Division to the east. Private William Pigg of Royston[11] was known as Bob and was in D Company during the battle. In a letter home,[12] he wrote of the battle:

It was a fight I shall never forget. On the Sunday we stayed at Dewar [sic] and advanced onto Mons at night. At 5 o'clock Monday morning a few shells came at us and by 6 o'clock nearly all the houses were blown down. About 20 of us laid in a garden where we were all laughing at the fact the German bullets were flying about. To see us one would think we were on a field day but all at once a shell burst near us wounding two of my section. We then had an order to retire. A Corporal and myself ran in front of a railway bridge and laid down flat, not daring to move and we heard our mates say that Bob and Golding were shot. I think we should all have been shot had it not been for some long grass in front of us which gave us a little cover from the sight of the Germans.

Shelling of the Bedfordshires' A and B Companies around Wasmes increased so the digging stopped and the battalion took its first casualties, including A Company's 'tall, handsome lad' Private Eddie Bywaters, who was the battalion's first combat death of the war. Men literally lay on top of one another for hours on end, pinned into their shallow, half-dug trenches by the endless rain of shells. One of the 77mm German field batteries found a position enabling them to fire almost point blank onto a section of the prone soldiers, which it continued to do all afternoon. Around 5 p.m. the Bedfords saw German infantry appear about 600m to their front and opened fire. However, Major Saunders from the Dorsets to their right said it was the French retiring, as he had seen French uniforms, so the order to cease fire was given. Lieutenant Mayne, the Bedford's Machine Gun Officer, watched carefully and remarked that it was an odd way to behave if they were French, as they marched as if attacking rather than retiring. Major Onslow wrote that 'a large body, about 1,000 men, of Germans advanced against our line and when they were fired at, put up a French Tricolour and came to within 200 yards of our trench without being fired on. Then our people saw their uniforms and they prepared to charge, when of course, they got it hot!' Realising it was the Germans' first 'dirty trick' of many, the Bedfords opened fire again and a firefight started. Around dusk the suspect French troops retired, waving a French Tricolour, and a relative quiet descended over the area.

That evening the battalion held a small salient with half the men around Wasmes facing north and half, near Pâturages, facing east. They had expected to connect the line between the Dorsets on their left and the 3rd Division to their right, although the latter were not where they should have been when contact was attempted.

As dusk arrived on the 23rd German buglers were heard to sound the ceasefire. A and B Companies were still exposed north of Wasmes and overnight received orders to rejoin the rest of the battalion once relieved by the West Ridings. Their wait would last all night. Meanwhile, C and D Companies had been preparing themselves for another defensive battle the next day, but news would arrive early the following morning to change their plans.

Although the men digging their defensive 'scrapes' and rifle pits were oblivious that night, the French Fifth Army HQ got a message to the British force during the early hours of the morning that Tournai had fallen, long columns of the enemy had broken through, and a wide gap had opened up on the right between the British and French armies. Sir John French had little choice but to order a general withdrawal on the 24th, in the direction of Cambrai, and to try to re-establish contact with his allies. The Old Contemptibles were mystified by the orders to retire as they knew that they had fought the Germans to a standstill.

British casualties for the day amounted to around 1,600, while the German army lost around 5,000, with some estimates reaching 10,000 for the first day alone. Practically half of the British casualties were from just two battalions: 400 from the 4th Middlesex and 300 from the 2nd Royal Irish in the canal salient.

After the first day of battle the Bedfordshires and their comrades of the 15th Brigade kept a watchful eye overnight, as those units which had been heavily engaged gathered their men and retired to positions further back. The line was stretched thinly and, with little happening to their front, men took it in turns to rest or talk quietly among themselves in their shallow pits and behind natural shelters.

Around 9 p.m. on the 23rd, Captain Macready was with A and B Companies, who were waiting for their relief to show up, and noticed a distant figure running towards him from the rear areas. The person held something reflective and ran short distances before dropping to the ground. The item must have attracted the attention of German gunners as shells exploded above and around him, yet he was not deterred. Having picked himself up, he would start running again, and continued this peculiar behaviour, all the while grasping the shiny object, until finally reaching Macready's shallow trench. On arrival the captain realised it was Corporal West from the officers' mess. He gasped for breath, still clutching what Macready could now see were two tin plates stacked one on top of the other. Lifting the inverted plate on top, he simply remarked between intakes of breath, 'Your dinner, Sir', before moving back to the rear and returning with the next officer's meal, repeating the same process. Macready watched in amusement and admiration as the determined corporal continued his cat and mouse game with enemy shells and snipers late into the evening.

Overnight the Bedfordshires held their lines as some British troops made their way back through them in singles and small groups, having hidden until darkness could cover their escape. Every church steeple in sight was ablaze and artillery fire had damaged a factory whistle in Wasmes, which blared on all night in its monotonous tone. Patrols were sent into the night to establish where the enemy were and what they were doing, one of which comprised Lieutenant Charles Shearman, the battalion Scout Officer from C Company and around eight men. They started from Pâturages station at around 11 p.m. on the 23rd and moved eastwards to try and find the flank of the 3rd Division, who should have been on the Bedfordshires' open flank yet had not been seen. In the pitch black night they moved along the Pâturages to Frameries railway line expecting to find their neighbours, but after around 500m stopped. They listened to the noise of a large column marching a few metres away along the north–south road to Frameries and, hearing voices, realised they were Germans. The patrol quickly moved back towards Pâturages and after a brief firefight with what was presumed to be an enemy patrol, reached the station again. Shearman broke into the station and used the telephone system to try and relay the urgent news to anyone he could reach in the British command structure. Having spoken to several French operators, they eventually put him through to General Haking, who hurriedly sent the 5th Brigade into the gap. The brigade arrived soon after, sweating heavily, having been force marched there with full packs and in fighting order.

At the same time, Captain Edwards from D Company had been sent east along the road towards Frameries with another larger patrol, with

Lieutenant Davenport out in front with an advanced guard. They also had the objective of finding the 3rd Division's flank, so set off initially with a group of locals who were to lead the way and interpret. In no time at all their guides had faded into the darkness, having thought better of putting themselves in danger, and Davenport's group probed further and further into the night without meeting a soul. When they passed houses, the locals would lean out of their windows calling 'Vive L'Angleterre' which, while being appreciated, was warning any listening German patrols of their presence. After several instances of the same behaviour, Davenport rushed ahead to every new house they came across and politely asked them to stay indoors and close their windows.

After around 1,000m they heard the sound of running feet, but no gunfire spat at them from the darkness and nothing further happened. Continuing on their way, an English voice unexpectedly challenged them from the pitch black night. Standing perfectly still they responded and figures emerged to see who they were. With a pistol held to Davenport's head and a bayonet pressed against his stomach, an officer questioned him to establish whether he was who he said he was. Once satisfied, the officer relaxed, saying 'Thank God! We nearly shot you!' His orders had been specific: to shoot anything moving from that direction, as it would not be 'friendly'. The patrol had found the flank of the 3rd Division, being a crossroads picket from the Northumberland Fusiliers.

When Captain Edwards arrived with the rest of his patrol, he sent Corporal William Tucker[13] back to Pâturages on a bicycle to relay the news to his commanding officer. He returned with orders to guard every crossroads between the two divisions, which was impossible given the sheer number of points to guard along the 2km stretch of road and the relatively small patrol he had. An English general soon arrived and countered their orders, telling them to stay where they were and, shortly after, the 5th Brigade arrived to take the gap over, courtesy of Lieutenant Shearman's exploits further north-west.

The patrol and elements of the 5th Brigade set off in the direction of Pâturages and Lieutenant Davenport formed the advanced guard, who placed the 5th Brigade's posts along the way. By the time they returned to battalion HQ in Pâturages, it was around 2 a.m. and the night's events were over, for the next few hours at least.

The Bedfordshires around Pâturages were still only at half strength, with A and B Companies waiting north of Wasmes for the West Ridings. As a result they were spread very thinly and their left flank was similarly devoid of troops. Small parties from the Bedfords and their neighbours in the Dorsets were strung out to counter the threat of German troops penetrating their dangerously fragile lines. The other two battalions from the 15th Brigade were held in reserve, leaving just the Bedfordshires and Dorsets holding almost the entire front line for a time. When Captain Edwards returned to D Company, they were the only ones not in position along the front lines. At once, Lieutenant Wagstaff and No. 13 Platoon took over the railway station, which also doubled as Battalion HQ, with Captain Edwards and Lieutenant Pope taking No. 15 Platoon to hold the line around a slag heap further north. Captain Monteith and Lieutenant Davenport were initially held back to provide the battalion support with Nos 14 and 16 Platoons, but soon found themselves on the left flank of C Company, with the Dorsets to their left and shells falling all around them as they dug their rifle pits.

Higher up, the situation was becoming painfully clearer with every new report that filtered its way to the Staff HQ. Orders for a south-westerly retirement on the 24th were issued with all knowing that it would not be an easy task given that both flanks were reported to be swarming with columns of German infantry and cavalry. Added to which was the obvious and expected frontal assault that would be thrown at the thin British rearguard, doubtless supported by a considerable superiority in German artillery. Divisional transport was ordered to leave immediately, thus giving them and the rearguard troops a chance of getting away without falling over one another.

All in all, the following day promised to be difficult.

Dawn was breaking through on 24 August when the West Ridings appeared to relieve A and B Companies north of Wasmes, and bullets were starting to buzz around the men in their rifle pits. No time was wasted as the Bedfordshires hurriedly ushered the Yorkshiremen into position, then headed off at the double before the Germans could see them and inflict heavy casualties as they retired. Shells fell around them as they marched away around 5 a.m., having just completed the relief in time. A brisk 3km march to Pâturages was rewarded with a rest in the square before presenting themselves to HQ for further orders.

On the Bedfords' front, the shelling started as dawn broke on the 24th and the German assault began soon after daybreak but was halted time and time again by the accurate long-range rifle fire from the British troops positioned along the line of slag heaps, buildings and ditches. Major Onslow told how the "'battalion shot", lying down at junction of roads, seeing Germans crossing the street 300 yards lower down, put 10 rounds in his magazine and got 10 Germans consecutively as they ran across the road'.

The battalion's right flank was repositioned to face almost due east when it was realised the neighbouring 5th Brigade had moved and lined itself up further back. This proved invaluable, as once the German assault against their neighbours started, Sergeants Percival Hunt,[14] and Leonard Godfrey,[15] and their platoon from C Company, took up position in the houses facing their open flank and enfiladed the attacking columns, causing dreadful casualties with their accurate rapid fire. The attack was stalled and German gunners turned their attention to the houses, levelling them with shell after shell and forcing the platoon to seek cover in the open ground, in front of the houses. Undeterred by the concentrated enemy shelling, they continued pouring fire into the attacking troops.

Private Percy Green[16] and his section[17] held the advancing infantry away from the railway bridge for seven hours before German artillery eventually blew it in and forced the shrinking band to seek shelter in a nearby house. From their second-storey windows 'they had a good time shooting Germans until the guns found them again. They were upstairs and a shell came through the roof and blew the floor out and they all went downstairs without using the stairs.' The section escaped with only cuts and bruises and were fortunately none the worse for their impromptu flying lesson.

In a letter home,[18] Leonard Godfrey recalled the time they spent on the open flank:

At Mons we had a very funny experience. I had to take my platoon over to the right flank of the position which the regiment was holding and we got into five houses. We caught the German infantry a treat as they came over a corn field; but for a long time they had us on a string. This field was in the open between a wood and over a crest line. Well, how they got over that field! For a start the field was covered in stooks of corn and the Germans must have got some sheaves of corn from the other side of the wood and then got it in bunches of five, holding these sheaves in front and then slowly walked over the field, the distance being about 700 yards from us. But once we found out their little game they soon dropped it. There must have been hundreds of dead in that field before we retired. We lost about a dozen there. Our retirement in this case was not as per the book, because after about five hours the Germans spotted where we were firing from and soon had a battery of artillery at us, but we got away with the exception of five. The Germans brought those five houses down. The houses I and five more were in were hit in the centre and we had the pleasant experience of coming from top to bottom in one step, but the bed clothes saved us from serious injury. We came out looking like Millers – we were all dust.

However, as the morning wore on, the British cover was gradually worn away by enemy shellfire, leaving them exposed, and both flanks of the brigade started to fold inwards. The left section of the Bedfordshires and their neighbours in the Dorsets had been digging in the hot morning sun when a major assault against them had stopped their labours and a flanking movement from the east had driven them back. As a result, many men retired with no packs or greatcoats, having removed them to dig and being unable to reach them once the retirement started in earnest. Although the immediate result of having less to carry was appreciated, the lack of spare socks and the like later on would make life uncomfortable.

Around this time Major Weatherby from Brigade HQ rode up with orders to retire, causing disbelief among the officers and men as they were handed their instructions. With no time to lose, orders were issued and the battalion started to withdraw. Given the precarious situation, the decision was also taken to find a safe haven for one of the battalion's treasured drums. An inhabitant called Madame Chanoine was pleased to take the drum, understanding the importance the men placed on its survival, and promised to keep it safe until they returned.

The bulk of the battalion moved off south leaving just a small rearguard. Those platoons from the Bedfordshires, King's Own Yorkshire Light Infantry, West Kents and the Duke of Wellington's Regiment who were assigned to hold the advancing Germans and give their comrades time to get away, retired deep into the interior of Wasmes, letting the German columns come on unhindered.

Once again Sergeant Hunt and his platoon from C Company found themselves in the firing line, and upon the German infantry arriving in the market square, every rifle that could be brought to bear opened up and literally decimated the columns. Again and again the brave German infantry charged and the result was the same each time. Scenes of unchecked slaughter filled the market and a human barricade started forming from the dead and dying.

Lance Corporal Spencer was among the rearguard, writing:

Then the street fighting began. The Germans as fighters were no fools and much bigger than we. We blockaded the streets, took up the curbstones to put across the roads for head cover. The German artillery didn't give us much rest; on our left chimney pots fell; then a house would come down; still we stuck to it. … Men were posted in every window. … Being English, our troops had no such thought as retiring so we cleared the Germans opposite, leaving behind a good many dead.

House-to-house fighting developed throughout Wasmes as the German troops tried to make their way around the square, meeting fierce resistance from the outnumbered Tommies with each new room they came across.

After two hours of ferocious fighting the attacks halted, allowing the British troops to retire, their job of delaying the enemy having been well done. However, their brave defence had left them deep inside enemy-held territory and the job of returning to the British column was to prove as difficult as the fighting that had caused the situation.

These events not only left the Bedfordshires and their colleagues in an increasingly precarious position, but also saw the entire 5th Division in danger of being enveloped while they made their stubborn rearguard defence that allowed the bulk of the other British divisions to retire. In response to the threat, British cavalry held the left flank and gave the rearguard remnants of the 5th Division time to retire.

As the mixed group moved quickly through Wasmes, Colour Sergeant Major Charles Hall from Croxton[19] was among those beating a hasty withdrawal. The fifteen-year veteran was fighting in his second war, having fought against the Boers as a private in the regiment. He found himself running through the cobbled streets when a Jack Johnson rumbled overhead, the displaced air making its presence felt as it did so, before exploding just a few metres in front of him. The force of the blast physically stopped all his momentum but, incredibly, he and those close to him survived unscathed. His good fortune would continue through the battles to come despite his repeatedly brave and unflinching leadership that would see him winning the Distinguished Conduct Medal and promotion to the rank of a commissioned officer.

At 1 p.m., the divisional reserve (being the Cheshires and Norfolks from the 15th Brigade) were ordered forward to provide the flank guard on the left, as the cavalry were also in danger of being overwhelmed by the sheer size and force of the unceasing German attacks. As the main columns of the British army retired south unmolested, a scattering of battalions continued their determined rearguard actions. The Norfolks and Cheshires were rushed into the line at Elouges to hold the left flank and found themselves engaging the entire German IV Corps. Although outnumbered more than six to one, they showed unwavering discipline and bravery by fighting the German corps to a standstill. The orders to disengage reached the Norfolks but not the men of Cheshire, who fought on, hand to hand with rifles, fists and bayonets, despite being overwhelmed. The survivors withdrew in small groups when the position was lost, just 200 of the 891 Cheshires reporting for roll call that night.

To their east, half of the Bedfordshires had made it back to the main column of the brigade, but the other half retired in the direction of Wasmes under growing pressure from large groups of Germans trying to penetrate their lines. Communication became less reliable and the battle turned into a series of localised actions involving hugely outnumbered groups of British soldiers fending off massed German infantry assaults, before retiring in any way they could. Having already lost so many men from the 15th Brigade, their commander, Count Gleichen, grew increasingly concerned as time passed that the missing half of the Bedfordshires (including their CO, Lieutenant Colonel Griffith) had been overwhelmed at Wasmes. However, he was unaware that orders had temporarily waylaid them.

Lieutenant Colonel Griffith and his half of the battalion, being portions of men from A, B and D Companies, had been ordered to rush south-east to a village called Montignies-sur-Roc, just inside the Belgian border and some 12km away to support a British artillery unit. The order to retire from Pâturages had confused the men enough, but this strange new order bemused them even further. Having started the day facing north, then being moved to face east, they passed through the village and took up defensive positions facing west among the cornfields. In every direction black columns of smoke could be seen, yet no German units came within firing range. Several officers stood watching a curious sight unfolding that afternoon as British cavalry to their west were outflanked by a troop of Germans, who in turn were outflanked by another troop of British cavalrymen. Minutes later they saw the distant figures of more Germans outmanoeuvring the British, who in turn moved a fresh unit west and into a flanking position. After twenty minutes, German cavalry reached as far west as their eyes could see, forcing the badly outnumbered British troops to retire or face the very real threat of being surrounded. With the cavalry, the Horse Artillery also limbered up and charged off southwards, leaving the Germans commanding the entire flank. Short moments passed before one of the officers, who had been watching the spectacle unfold, realised that not only had their reason for being there disappeared south at speed, but that they were the only British troops left as far as was visible. With the German cavalry crossing rivers some distance off, but definitely headed in their direction, orders were issued to move to rejoin the main body of the battalion.

Just to the south was the village of Onnezies, where Lieutenant Colonel Griffith halted, realising that A and B Companies had not stopped for breakfast or lunch that day. The men were fed by the villagers before moving south again along the back roads running parallel with the road to Bavay. On the way they were joined by dozens of stragglers from various units in the 5th Division, all of whom had become lost during the retirement. Passing through Gussignies, 7km later, they reached Bellignies and headed for Houdain to the south-east. Incredibly, and considering all that was happening around them, their small group had managed to march the entire afternoon without being noticed by any interested German units.

The 'missing' half of the battalion, buoyed by their afternoon's adventures and swelled by stragglers, joined the rest of the main column at Houdain from a side road, much to the relief of both their comrades and the Brigade Headquarters staff.

By dusk on the 24th, the column that was the remnant of the 15th Brigade camped around Saint-Waast, 2km west of Bavay, having simply spread out among the fields in whatever formation they happened to be in. Considering the scale of casualties suffered elsewhere, the Bedfordshires did extremely well to come out of the day's rearguard action having lost less than seventy men, including Captain John McMaster Milling and Lieutenant Charles Shearman wounded. One of Shearman's platoon, Private Arthur Chandler from Spaldwick,[20] wrote home[21] that Shearman 'was as cool an officer as you could find. He was first wounded in the wrist. He bound it up and then went into the firing line again with a wounded fellow's rifle and had another go at them until he got wounded in the shoulder. He then had to come out of it and he said to us "I'm finished fighting boys; do your best and good luck to you. Rub it up the Germans well."' Lieutenant Shearman would recover quickly, serve in several other battalions within the regiment and eventually return in the final months of the war. He was mentioned in Sir John French's despatches in September and October and was later awarded the regiment's first Military Cross on its introduction in December 1914. By the end of his war, more awards would be added to his already impressive tally as well as many more wound scars and stripes.

That night the exhausted, foot-sore, thirsty and hungry men enjoyed a brief rest in the open fields. However, the constant movement and fighting, little sleep and the need to stay alert, would begin to have a serious effect the following day.

At 1.20 a.m. on 25 August, the march resumed as the seriousness of the British position was obvious. Any chances of saving themselves from being surrounded and wiped out rested on their capacity to put distance between themselves and their pursuing enemy. On another hot summer's day, II Corps and I Corps moved apart to pass each side of the thick Forêt de Mormal. The Bedfordshires were part of the column that marched along the straight Roman road between Bavay and Le Cateau, with no food or water other than what could be gathered along the way. Only days before, they had tramped along that very road headed towards Mons. Accounts from veterans who survived highlight the condition of the men, 'stumbling along more like ghosts than living soldiers, unconscious of everything around them yet still moving under the magical impulse of discipline and regimental pride. Marching, they were hardly awake; halted, whether sitting or standing, they were instantly asleep.'

As well as the arduous feat of keeping on the move, rearguard actions were fought at Pont-sur-Sambre, Landrecies and Maroilles by exhausted troops, none of whom involved the Bedfordshires.

Having marched 29km through the hottest of days, with no supplies and a determined enemy pursuing them, the men finally got orders to stop at Troisvilles, 2km south-west of Le Cateau, around 3.30 p.m. To their joy Regimental Quarter Master Sergeant William Bartlett[22] had already found the spot and magically led his transport section there ahead of the battalion despite the organised chaos all around. Therefore, once the forward trenches were inspected and sentries were posted, the men enjoyed a well-earned rest and a meal. After a horrific day things improved a little, as the brigade commander explained: 'We got a good deal more food – bully beef and biscuits – here, besides a cart load of very smelly cheeses and some hams and vegetables and fresh bread, and the men got their stomachs fairly full by sundown.'

Small groups joined the resting men as the afternoon wore on, including Sergeant Percival Hunt and his platoon. During their dogged rearguard action at Wasmes, Sergeant Hunt and his men had found themselves without an officer, cut off and surrounded almost a mile inside the German lines. Surrendering was not on their minds so Hunt led the platoon through their difficult day as they crept and fought their way through German-held territory, managing to rejoin the battalion against the odds. His leadership and bravery ensured that he was mentioned in Sir John French's despatches in September and October, also winning him the regiment's first Distinguished Conduct Medal of the war, in addition to the French Médaille Militaire for his behaviour at Mons. Sergeant Hunt would survive the war, going on to become Regimental Sergeant Major and serving well into the 1930s.

Late that afternoon as the men rested in their field they were distracted by the sight of six divisions of French cavalry under General Sordet cantering past, heading to the open western flank and taking a full three hours to do so. Shortly after they had passed, another move to positions around 2km west was ordered and, on arrival, B Company was sent into the night to form the outpost line 500m south of the road to Cambrai, facing north. Around 9 p.m., D Company replaced B Company, with Captain Edwards and Lieutenant Montieth in command of the left section, Lieutenant Davenport in the centre and Lieutenant Wagstaff on the right. Sergeant William Nolias[23] commanded No. 16 Platoon on the extreme left of the line. Other than a scare around midnight, when a picket from No. 16 Platoon fired on an unmanned Royal Engineers' cart as its horses trotted down the road looking for their owners, nothing disturbed the line that night.

By nightfall on 25 August, II Corps was in a bad way and intelligence warned that the Germans were hot on its heels. As the battle-worn soldiers of British II Corps rested gratefully and waited for what they knew would be another testing day, the heavens opened up and a massive thunderstorm erupted. But other than a wet dinner and the occasional disturbance of sentries firing at imaginary enemies in the torrential rain, an uneventful night passed.

British casualties amounted to just over 2,600 of all ranks, killed, wounded and missing, a quarter being from the valiant Cheshires, who held off the entire German advance in that sector by themselves. German casualties were undisclosed but are estimated at around 8,000 for the two days. One captured German prisoner summed up the imbalance between the casualty figures from the opening battle well, remarking that 'the Russians can't shoot at all, the French are good shots but the British shoot and kill'.

Chapter 3

The Battle of Le Cateau and the Retreat to Paris

25 August – 6 September 1914

'Hold them to the last ... the Corps was to be sacrificed to save the other Corps.'

By nightfall of 25 August 1914, the retreating II Corps, including the Bedfordshires, was being closely pursued by the German First Army; I Corps was many miles away to the east and therefore unable to help in the following day's events. Although the newly arrived 4th Division was moving up alongside II Corps it was clear that the disorganised and extremely tired units faced a disaster the next day if the withdrawal was continued. Early in the morning of the 26th, corps commander Horace Smith-Dorrien issued orders for II Corps to stand and fight. Three exhausted and battle-worn British divisions were lined up to face the frontal assault of seven German divisions. There was also the added problem of both flanks being wide open and many other German units known to be moving down past them, presumably to cut them off.

After a night's rest in fields north of Troisvilles, the Bedfordshires resumed their march southwards at 9 a.m. as per their orders, but after just 150m a staff officer arrived with hurried orders to take up positions in the half-dug trenches. Reading the orders, Major Onslow's gaze was drawn to the instruction to 'hold them to the last' and, while riding away, the staff officer was overheard to have said that 'the Corps was to be sacrificed to save the other Corps', which the battalion adjutant Captain Macready remarked was 'unpleasant' news. So the Bedfords' II Corps was arranged in the open downs to the west of the small village of Le Cateau, with some of the British commanders doubting whether any of them could be extricated at all.

In an unusual twist, 568 years ago to the day, a small English army of longbowmen had faced and beaten a much larger army of Frenchmen at Crécy. Today the modern descendants of those longbowmen would fight in a similar battle against superior odds, but with the added irony of the French being their allies this time.

The 5th Division held the right of the line from a point halfway between Le Cateau and Reumont, to Troisvilles, with the 15th Brigade covering the left half of the line, just east of Troisvilles. Then came the three brigades of the 3rd Division, the 9th Brigade being north of Troisvilles, the 8th Brigade on the left of it north of Audencourt, with the 7th Brigade curled round the northern side of Caudry in the shape of a horseshoe. Beyond was the newly arrived 4th Division at Hautcourt. The whole frontage covered some 11km, about half of which ran along north of the Cambrai to St Quentin railway.

The Bedfordshires held the left section of the brigade line with the Dorsets on the right and the Norfolks and Cheshires in the supporting second line. The battalion lined up with D Company under Captain Montieth on the far left, C Company under Major Allason next to them, followed by B Company under Major Thorpe and A Company under Major Onslow on the extreme right. A single platoon from A Company was pulled off to act as the meagre battalion reserve and held near the headquarters section. Curiously, over half of the battalion lines were in a hidden natural dip and only the flanks could readily see events unfolding on either side, while the balance relied on messages and chit-chat being passed along the lines.

The trenches were poorly dug, due to the lack of spades, and the ground was wet and waterlogged, while a heavy morning mist lingered over the field. Their line faced north just behind the Cambrai–Cambrésis road and was positioned a long way down the reverse slopes of a hill that allowed the Bedfords and their neighbours a clear field of fire against anyone who appeared along the crest, while being hidden from the enemy troops, batteries and observers beyond it.

As they waited for the inevitable onslaught, the men tried to deepen their trenches, all the while listening to the artillery duels on either side of their lines. While the companies worked on their trenches, the Machine Gun Officer, Lieutenant Joseph Mayne, spied some civilians near a road junction but was told not to open fire on them despite his misgivings. Soon afterwards it was found that a German machine gun

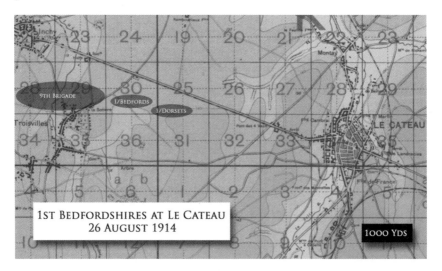

1ST BEDFORDSHIRES AT LE CATEAU
26 AUGUST 1914

1000 YDS

was being set up there and that the German troops had deliberately worn civilian clothes to avoid being shot at. Two British artillery batteries assembled a few hundred metres behind the Bedfords and although they attracted the unwelcomed attentions of German gunners, the men in their trenches were content to see shell after shell passing well overhead and not worrying them in the slightest.

The mist started clearing mid-morning and the first German guns opened up on the British positions. Although it started slowly, the bombardment gradually picked up in pace and determination until the sheer scale of it almost overwhelmed the thin British lines. The weight of the German attack fell on the right and centre of the 5th Division's lines, to the right of the Bedfordshires, which was II Corps' most vulnerable flank with the least support. As the afternoon wore on, rifle and machine-gun fire increased in intensity, especially on the right flank, and column after column of German infantry assaulted the British positions. In a replay of events at Mons, intense and accurate British rifle fire and field guns firing over open sights from positions alongside the infantry held the Germans back. During the assault, the Bedfords themselves were spared the attentions of the German infantry and contented themselves with providing supporting fire to the units to their right when the opportunity arose.

The far left of the Bedfords' line was held by No. 14 Platoon under Lieutenant Davenport, who watched the massed German attacks thrown against the 4th Division to his left around Troisvilles. They were out of range so his men could not help in any way and sat on the edges of their rifle pits watching events unfolding, enjoying the curious sensation of being a spectator in a battle they could be called upon to join at any moment. On the one hand the men were impressed by the concentration and accuracy of British fire as they watched them wreak havoc in the advancing lines. Yet on the other hand, they had nothing but respect for the advancing German waves, who filled the gaps in their ranks and advanced time and time again regardless of their losses. On the far left of their vision hundreds of German artillery pieces appeared on the crest of the hill, out of range of their rifles. The gunners calmly set themselves up for the bloody business of the day, while a local woman in a field to the front of the Bedfords was equally calm as she milked her cow, determined that her routine would not be disrupted by the carnage and danger all around her. With death and destruction in every direction, life still went on as normal.

By mid-afternoon the massed German guns had all but wiped out the 4th Division's artillery, had pounded the 5th Division's artillery that was in range, and were working on the left flank of the Bedfords' line too. D Company now had ample targets as the infantry assault had developed to its front, but had to keep low as its lines were being swept by both concentrated machine-gun fire and German shrapnel.

The tornado of German artillery had all but destroyed the shallow British trenches on both flanks of the line by mid-afternoon and the situation became increasingly obvious to the corps commanders. The Commander-in-Chief's despatch recorded: 'It became apparent, if complete annihilation was to be avoided, that a retirement must be attempted, and the order was given to commence it about 3 p.m.'

By 4 p.m. the bulk of the 5th Division was already retiring and orders reached the Bedfordshires to 'retire by bounds' if possible. They were to make their rearguard action deliberately slow and ensure the advancing enemy paid dearly, thereby allowing the main body to get away as unmolested as possible. To their right, the King's Own Scottish Borderers retired and A, B and C Companies followed suit in small groups. D Company on the extreme left was pinned down by intense machine-gun fire but got away eventually, Captain William Wagstaff from D Company being wounded in the thigh during the withdrawal. Corporal Frederick Holloway[24] passed the news on to Lieutenant Davenport after he himself had only narrowly escaped, but attempts to recover the captain failed, leaving him to be cared for by the Germans, who took him prisoner when they advanced after the rearguard. The ground across which the battalion retired was flat and open but luckily the German fire was noted as being 'wild', causing very few casualties among the exposed bodies of men.

One such casualty was Private Frank Cousins from Eaton Socon[25] who was in the Machine Gun Section.[26] After orders to retire came, Frank rose from the shallow trench and turned to move but a bullet smashed through his right arm, shattering the bone. The two unscathed members were unable to carry the gun by themselves so dismantled it and retired, helping their wounded comrade along. Miraculously, the three-man team got away despite the air around them being alive with bullets and shrapnel, and Frank would recover to return to the battalion.

Private Bob Pigg of D Company was among those pinned down and later wrote home about the battle,[27] remarking that: 'On Wednesday we were fighting from dawn until 4 p.m., when we had to leave the trenches under a hail of bullets, crossing open country. It was God's mercy we were not all killed and since then a good many of us have said that someone in England must have been praying for us.'

For long hours during the morning of the 26th, the British, notably the field artillery, had held overwhelming numbers of the enemy at bay and inflicted severe losses. Against expectations, the corps then disengaged and withdrew towards the south during the afternoon. Many of the Bedfords passed piles of dead artillerymen who had fallen around the guns they had deliberately positioned close to the front lines, having been told there would be no retirement from the battle.

On the vulnerable flank at the extreme right of the line, two battalions east of the Bedfordshires, of the King's Own Yorkshire Light Infantry, had been given the written order that morning: 'There will be NO retirement for the fighting troops. Fill your trenches as far as possible with water, food and ammunition.' A further verbal order that afternoon confirmed it so the faithful Yorkshiremen obeyed their orders to the letter. As the afternoon wore on they were slowly and deliberately surrounded on three sides as their positions were pounded by artillery and swept by concentrated rifle and machine-gun fire. Even once their own ammunition was exhausted 'the battalion stayed to its death, faithful to the order'. They lay in their trenches and soaked the punishment up until Major Yate, the acting CO, saw the final German assault coming. Unable to fire, he ordered his men to meet the assault with their own charge, and with bayonets fixed they threw themselves at the massed German waves rather than surrender. Some 320 of the battalion were captured, with the rest falling during the desperate day's fighting that saw the battalion all but wiped from the army list for the time being.

An hour after starting their withdrawal, the rearguard platoons of the Bedfordshires' A and B Companies turned to face the pursuing Germans again at La Satiere crossroads and provided protection for those British troops still passing through before moving south-westerly at around 6 p.m. Nothing had been seen of either C or D Companies, who were still somewhere further north. Seeing Lieutenant Colonel Stephenson of the King's Own Scottish Borderers lying wounded in an untended ambulance cart, a group of Bedfords dragged the cart with them rather than leave him there, and the withdrawal continued. Similar occurrences were reported from all along the retreat, with men commandeering any wheeled transport they could find to carry the wounded back with them. Lieutenants Davenport and Lilley (from the Machine Gun Section of the Dorsets) had been among the last to leave the British line after their unsuccessful scout for the wounded Captain Wagstaff. On their withdrawal they had collected a large group of stragglers who stayed together as a makeshift platoon as they crossed the fields, ditches and hedges, all the while staying off the roads. A farmer's wagon had been found in a barn and was manhandled across the fields, loaded with the growing numbers of wounded troops they came across. On arrival at a village where a field ambulance was set up, they warned the doctors of the Germans' imminent arrival but the doctors simply could not leave, given the numbers of wounded men in their care. Reluctantly, but with little choice, the large platoon set off south again, meeting up with the brigade less than an hour later.

As the Bedfords' rearguard (the incomplete platoons of A and B Companies) rejoined the straight Roman road between Cambrésis and St Quentin they were greeted by the exhausted rabble that was the 5th Division. No semblance of order was apparent so the two companies just merged into the procession. Yet despite their exhaustion, the men of the worn division found themselves straightening up and trying to march more crisply when they came across their divisional commander directing the flow of troops at a crossroads.

Marching ever southwards, Captain Macready passed a battalion of Cameron Highlanders providing a protecting screen around Maretz, and by nightfall his procession plodded further south, his men following their base instincts that told them to keep moving or face certain capture. The column would 'shuffle ten yards, halt, walk half a mile, ten yards, halt, three yards, halt … and so it went on. One dare not sit down. To do so would have meant sleep and capture. One's knees were simply breaking. Weariness quite outmatched hunger and thirst.'

In an unusual sign of gratitude, groups of infantrymen, despite their exhaustion, were spotted frequently detouring off the road to silently pat the parked guns that lined the roads. The gunners in their turn openly appreciated the infantry who had covered their own withdrawal time and time again, and both arms had in turn been protected by often suicidal cavalry charges that relieved pressure where it was needed the most.

Around 2.30 a.m. on the dark, damp morning of 27 August the few hundred Bedfords in the column reached Oestres, 2km south-west of St Quentin centre, with no billets, food, water or orders beyond being ready to march again by 4 a.m. Other groups joined them over the next hour and by daylight the bedraggled corps was as ready to move off as it could be, given the experiences of the last week.

By the end of the day's fighting British casualties amounted to 7,812, and 38 guns were lost. Of those, the Bedfordshires got off incredibly lightly, suffering less than 40 casualties including Captain Wagstaff. German casualties were estimated at between 10,000 and 14,000, but unconfirmed

The retreat to Paris: 27 August – 6 September 1914

During the morning's march towards St Quentin gunfire was heard from the rear, but the men in the column were far too tired to pay much attention. About midday the main body of the Bedfordshires arrived at St Quentin and having reached the bottom of a hill saw the typically British Quartermaster General himself (Sir William Robertson) sitting at a table in the middle of the road, directing men to their respective divisions. Their amusement at this sight was soon replaced by relief when they came across the rest of their brigade in a field, which included most of the missing two companies that had not been seen since the retirement from Le Cateau. Unfortunately, no rest was possible as they had arrived just in time to join the brigade as it moved off again, the destination being Eaucourt, 18km further south-west.

Private Bob Pigg from Royston had been with D Company during the stand at Le Cateau and was one of the hundreds to become separated from the main body of his battalion during the retirement. He wrote: 'When we retired all the regiments got mixed up and three of us roamed about and eventually got with our transport, which took us to St Quentin where we had a good feed and got in with the Lancers who took us to our regiment after three days.'

Amazingly, not a single Bedford had dropped out during their arduous retreat and the men forgot their exhaustion and faced the next stage of the march, their moods having lifted at being reunited with their comrades again. On their arrival at Eaucourt at around 5 p.m. on the 27th, 5km south-east of Ham, they were greeted by the welcomed and reliable sight of RQMS William Bartlett again with the battalion transport. Billets and a meal were enjoyed by all and orders to resume the march at 4 a.m. gave the men what could be considered as their first decent rest for a week.

Another long, hot, tiring day of marching followed but the battalion was in the thick of the column so was spared any rearguard duties or fighting. Around midday on the 28th, Sir John French, the British Commander-in-Chief, waited by the side of the road and saluted the passing men. Having called II Corps' battalion commanders together he told them that their actions had not only saved the British army from destruction but that the French Commander-in-Chief, General Joffre, had wanted to pass on his personal thanks too. The stand of II Corps at Le Cateau had saved the entire left flank of the Allied army from a difficult time and delayed the German advance on to Paris. The men marched with an extra spring in their step on hearing the news and were very vocal about preferring to be able to turn and fight again.

Several more days of marching followed, the battalion skirting the east of Noyon and Compiégne during the moves. Overnight rests at Pontoise-lés-Noyon on 28 August, the high street in Carlepont the following night and Croutoy on the 30th, left the Bedfords passing the eastern edge of the Forêt de Compiégne on the 31st. That night the footsore men rested in fields south-west of Crépy-en-Valois, with A and B Companies providing outposts.

To be retreating was bad enough in the eyes of the Tommies but other than the occasional individual who was soon shaken out of it, their morale was certainly not flagging. When called upon to about-face and stand against any threatening enemy movements they did not bat an eyelid and followed orders without question. Long, exhausting days, short rest periods and meagre food supplies may have caused the odd grumble here and there but the filthy, battle-weary soldiers marched mile after mile without complaint. In the age-old tradition of soldiers on campaign, their own discomfort was not of great concern and the miles melted away as long as they had good company around them. Yet seeing civilians in distress played on their minds more than their own hardships could have ever done. In one of his letters home, Private Bob Pigg remarked on one such sight: 'The worst thing of all is to see the poor people leaving their homes and crying to come with us. One place we came to I saw a poor little girl about four or five get shot going across the road. I shall never forget the look on her mother's face.' Yet, in the next line of his letter, he is once again focused on the day-to-day concerns of soldiers on campaign: 'We shall be glad when it is all over and we all look forward to being home at Christmas. The only thing that is worrying us just now is that we don't get much to smoke.'

While preparing to move off the next morning C and D Companies were hurriedly assembled to help repel an attack that had developed to their left. Setting off at 6.30 a.m. in the fog, they moved through a ravine and took up positions on the right flank of the West Kents, north of Crépy, where the companies extended and adopted another defensive posture. It was not long before figures dressed in field grey appeared, including jaegers and cavalry. Although desperately outnumbered in his area, Major Allason ordered the adjutant to counter-attack with a single platoon and he followed up in support with another. The audacious counter-stroke halted the surprised Germans and undoubtedly saved the battalion from a hard day's fighting. Unbeknown to the Bedfords, the attack to their left developed into the fogbound Battle of Nery, and the Bedfords themselves faced and repulsed elements of Von Marwitz's cavalry.

Other than that action, the Bedfordshires continued along their route relatively unmolested, resting overnight in a field outside Nanteuil-le-Haudouin on 1 September and in an empty farmhouse in Vinantes near Juilly on the night of the 2nd. The long march south-west continued at 8.30 a.m. on the 3rd and took them due south towards the River Marne. After crossing it at Lagny-sur-Marne the bridge was blown as they were the last of the 5th Division to cross. Unexpectedly the battalion was marched east instead of towards Paris once on the main Meaux to Paris road, through Esbly and into Couilly, where D Company provided outposts.

Captain Basil John Orlebar arrived from the 3rd Bedfordshires with the 1st Bedfordshires' first draft of ninety men on the 4th as they held their positions and kept a watchful eye on the surrounding countryside from every vantage point available. Major Onslow recorded how they caught a spy that day 'wearing French peasant's clothes, but under them a British A.S.C. uniform, under that a French uniform and under all that a German one!'

During the day an American lady made herself known to the men who were guarding the ridge that ran just outside her home. She was incredibly helpful and friendly, with nothing being too much trouble. It transpired that she was called Mildred Aldrich and later wrote a book titled *A Hilltop on the Marne*. The second half of Chapter VII relates the day she met the 1st Bedfordshires:

> It was not much after nine when two English officers strolled down the road – Captain [Francis] Edwards and Major Ellison [Allason] of the Bedfordshire Light Infantry. They came into the garden, and the scene with Captain Simpson of the day before was practically repeated. They examined the plain, located the towns, looked long at it with their glasses; and that being over I put the usual question, 'Can I do anything for you?' and got the usual answer, 'Eggs.'
>
> I asked how many officers there were in the mess, and he replied 'Five'; so I promised to forage, and away they went.
>
> As soon as they were out of sight the picket set up a bowl for baths. These Bedfordshire boys were not hungry, but they had retreated from their last battle leaving their kits in the trenches, and were without soap or towels, or combs or razors. But that was easily remedied. They washed up in relays in the court at Amelie's – it was a little more retired. As Amelie had put all her towels, etc. down underground, I ran back and forward between my house and hers for all sorts of things, and, as they slopped until the road ran tiny rivulets, I had to change shoes and stockings twice. I was not conscious till afterward how funny it all was. I must have been a good deal like an excited duck and Amelie like a hen with a duckling. When she was not twitching my sash straight, she was running about after me with dry shoes and stockings, and a chair, for fear 'Madame was getting too tired'; and when she was not doing that she was clapping my big garden hat on my head, for fear 'Madame would get a sunstroke.' The joke was that I did not know it was hot. I did not even know it was funny until afterward, when the whole scene seemed to have been by a sort of dual process photographed unconsciously on my memory.
>
> When the boys were all washed and shaved and combed – and they were so larky over it – we were like old friends. I did not know one of

them by name, but I did know who was married, and who had children; and how one man's first child had been born since he left
England, and no news from home because they had seen their mail
wagon burn on the battlefield; and how one of them was only twenty,
and had been six years in the army – lied when he enlisted; how none
of them had ever seen war before; how they had always wanted to,
and 'Now,' said the twenty-year-older, 'I've seen it – good Lord – and
all I want is to get home', and he drew out of his breast pocket a
photograph of a young girl in all her best clothes, sitting up very
straight.

When I said, 'Best girl?' he said proudly, 'Only one and we were to
have been married in January if this hadn't happened. Perhaps we
may yet, if we get home at Christmas, as they tell us we may.' I
wondered who he meant by 'they'. The officers did not give any such
impression.

While I was gathering up towels and things before returning to the
house, this youngster advanced toward me, and said with a half-shy
smile, 'I take it you're a lady.'

I said I was glad he had noticed it – I did make such an effort.

'No, no,' he said, 'I'm not joking. I may not say it very well, but I
am quite serious. We all want to say to you that if it is war that makes
you and the women you live amongst so different from English women,
then all we can say is that the sooner England is invaded and knows
what it means to have a fighting army on her soil, and see her fields
devastated and her homes destroyed, the better it will be for the race.
You take my word for it, they have no notion of what war is like; and
there ain't no English woman of your class could have, or would have,
done for us what you have done this morning. Why, in England the
common soldier is the dirt under the feet of women like you.'

I had to laugh, as I told him to wait and see how they treated them
when war was there; that they probably had not done the thing simply
because they never had had the chance.

'Well,' he answered, 'they'll have to change mightily. Why, our own
women would have been uncomfortable and ashamed to see a lot of
dirty men stripping and washing down like we have done. You haven't
looked as if you minded it a bit, or thought of anything but getting us
cleaned up as quick and comfortable as possible.'

I started to say that I felt terribly flattered that I had played the role
so well, but I knew he would not understand. Besides, I was wondering

if it were true. I never knew the English except as individuals, never as a race. So I only laughed, picked up my towels, and went home to rest. Not long before noon a bicycle scout came over with a message from Captain Edwards, and I sent by him a basket of eggs, a cold chicken, and a bottle of wine as a contribution to the breakfast at the officers' mess; and by the time I had eaten my breakfast, the picket had been changed, and I saw no more of those boys.

During the afternoon the booming off at the east became more distinct. It surely was cannon. I went out to the gate where the corporal of the guard was standing, and asked him, 'Do I hear cannon?' 'Sure,' he replied. 'Do you know where it is?' I asked. He said he hadn't an idea – about twenty-five or thirty miles away. And on he marched, up and down the road, perfectly indifferent to it.

Just after the boys had finished their tea, Captain Edwards came down the road, swinging my empty basket on his arm, to say 'Thanks' for his breakfast. He looked at the table at the gate.

'So the men have been having tea – lucky men – and bottled water! What extravagance!'

'Come in and have some, too,' I said.

'Love to,' he answered, and in he came.

While I was making the tea he walked about the house, looked at the pictures, examined the books. Just as the table was ready there was a tremendous explosion. He went to the door, looked off, and re-marked, as if it were the most natural thing in the world, 'Another division across. That should be the last.'

'Are all the bridges down?' I asked.

'All, I think, except the big railroad bridge behind you – Chalifert. That will not go until the last minute.'

I wanted to ask, 'When will it be the "last minute" – and what does the "last minute" mean?' – but where was the good? So we went into the dining-room. As he threw his hat on to a chair and sat down with a sigh, he said, 'You see before you a very humiliated man. About half an hour ago eight of the Uhlans we are looking for rode right into the street below you, in Voisins. We saw them, but they got away. It is absolutely our own stupidity.'

'Well,' I explained to him, 'I fancy I can tell you where they are hiding. I told Captain Simpson so last night.' And I explained to him that horses had been heard in the woods at the foot of the hill since Tuesday; that there was a cart road, rough and winding, running in toward Conde for over two miles; that it was absolutely screened by trees, had plenty of water, and not a house in it – a shelter for a regiment of cavalry. And I had the impertinence to suggest that if the picket had been extended to the road below it would have been impossible for the Germans to have got into Voisins.

'Not enough of us,' he replied. 'We are guarding a wide territory, and cannot put our pickets out of sight of one another.' Then he explained that, as far as he knew from his aeroplane men, the detachment had broken up since it was first discovered on this side of the Marne. It was reported that there were only about twenty-four in this vicinity; that they were believed to be without ammunition; and then he dropped the subject, and I did not bother him with questions that were bristling in my mind.

He told me how sad it was to see the ruin of the beautiful country through which they had passed, and what a mistake it had been from his point of view not to have foreseen the methods of Germans and drummed out all the towns through which the armies had passed. He told me one or two touching and interesting stories. One was of the day before a battle, I think it was Saint-Quentin. The officers had been invited to dine at a pretty chateau near which they had bivouacked. The French family could not do too much for them, and the daughters of the house waited on the table. Almost before the meal was finished the alerts sounded, and the battle was on them. When they retreated by the house where they had been so prettily entertained such a few hours before, there was not one stone standing on another, and what became of the family he had no idea.

The other that I remember was of the way the Germans passed the river at Saint-Quentin and forced the battle at La Fere on them. The bridge was mined, and the Captain was standing beside the engineer waiting to give the order to touch off the mine. It was a nasty night – a Sunday (only last Sunday, think of that!) – and the rain was coming down in torrents. Just before the Germans reached the bridge he ordered it blown up. The engineer touched the button. The fuse did not act. He was in despair, but the Captain said to him, 'Brace up, my lad – give her another chance.' The second effort failed like the first. Then, before anyone could stop him, the engineer made a dash for the end of the bridge, drawing his revolver as he ran, and fired six shots into the mine, knowing that, if he succeeded, he would go up with the bridge. No good, and he was literally dragged off the spot weeping with rage at his failure – and the Germans came across.

All the time we had been talking I had heard the cannonade in the distance – now at the north and now in the east. This seemed a proper moment, inspired by the fact that he was talking war, of his own initiative, to put a question or two, so I risked it.

'That cannonading seems much nearer than it did this morning,' I ventured.

'Possibly,' he replied.

'What does that mean?' I persisted.

'Sorry I can't tell you. We men know absolutely nothing. Only three men in this war know anything of its plans – Kitchener, Joffre, and French. The rest of us obey orders, and know only what we see. Not even a Brigade Commander is any wiser. Once in a while the Colonel makes a remark, but he is never illuminating.'

'How much risk am I running by remaining here?'

He looked at me a moment before he asked, 'You want to know the truth?'

'Yes,' I replied.

'Well, this is the situation as near as I can work it out. We infer from the work we were given to do – destroying bridges, railroads, telegraphic communications – that an effort is to be made here to stop the march on Paris; in fact, that the Germans are not to be allowed to cross the Marne at Meaux, and march on the city by the main road from Rheims to the capital. The communications are all cut. That does not mean that it will be impossible for them to pass; they've got clever engineers. It means that we have impeded them and may stop them. I don't know. Just now your risk is nothing. It will be nothing unless we are ordered to hold this hill, which is the line of march from Meaux to Paris. We have had no such order yet. But if the Germans succeed in taking Meaux and attempt to put their bridges across the Marne, our artillery, behind you there on the top of the hill, must open fire on them over your head. In that case the Germans will surely reply by bombarding this hill.' And he drank his tea without looking to see how I took it.

I remember that I was standing opposite him, and I involuntarily leaned against the wall behind me, but suddenly thought, 'Be careful. You'll break the glass in the picture of Whistler's Mother, and you'll be sorry.' It brought me up standing, and he didn't notice. Isn't the mind a queer thing?

He finished his tea, and rose to go. As he picked up his cap he showed me a hole right through his sleeve – in one side, out the other – and a similar one in his puttee, where the ball had been turned aside by the leather lacing of his boot. He laughed as he said, 'Odd how near a chap comes to going out, and yet lives to drink tea with you. Well, good-bye and good luck if I don't see you again.'

And off he marched, and I went into the library and sat down and sat very still.

It was not more than half an hour after Captain Edwards left that the Corporal came in to ask me if I had a window in the roof. I told him that there was, and he asked if he might go up. I led the way, picking up my glasses as I went. He explained, as we climbed the two flights of stairs, that the aeroplane had reported a part of the Germans they were hunting 'not a thousand feet from this house'. I opened the skylight. He scanned in every direction. I knew he would not see anything, and he did not. But he seemed to like the view, could command the roads that his posse was guarding, so he sat on the window ledge and talked. The common soldier is far fonder of talking than his officer and apparently he knows more. If he doesn't, he thinks he does. So he explained to me the situation as the 'men saw it'. I remembered what Captain Edwards had told me, but I listened all the same. He told me that the Germans were advancing in two columns about ten miles apart, flanked in the west by a French division pushing them east, and led by the English drawing them toward the Marne. 'You know,' he said, 'that we are the sacrificed Corps, and we have known it from the first – went into the campaign knowing it. We have been fighting a force ten times superior in numbers, and retreating, doing rear-guard action, whether we were really outfought or not – to draw the Germans where Joffre wants them. I reckon we've got them there. It is a great strategy – Kitchener's, you know.'

Whether any of the Corporal's ideas had any relation to facts I shall never know until history tells me, but I can assure you that, as I followed the Corporal downstairs, I looked about my house – and, well, I don't deny it, it seemed to me a doomed thing, and I was sorry for it. However, as I let him out into the road again, I pounded into myself lots of things like 'It hasn't happened yet'; 'Sufficient unto the day'; and, 'What isn't to be, won't be'; and found I was quite calm. Luckily I did not have much time to myself, for I had hardly sat down quietly when there was another tap at the door and I opened to find an officer of the bicycle corps standing there.

'Captain Edwards's compliments,' he said, 'and will you be so kind as to explain to me exactly where you think the Uhlans are hidden?' I told him that if he would come down the road a little way with me I would show him.

'Wait a moment,' he said, holding the door. 'You are not afraid?' I told him that I was not.

'My orders are not to expose you uselessly. Wait there a minute.'

He stepped back into the garden, gave a quick look overhead – I don't know what for, unless for a Taube. Then he said, 'Now, you will please come out into the road and keep close to the bank at the left, in the shadow. I shall walk at the extreme right. As soon as I get where I can see the roads ahead, at the foot of the hill, I shall ask you to stop, and please stop at once. I don't want you to be seen from the road below, in case anyone is there. Do you understand?'

I said I did. So we went into the road and walked silently down the hill. Just before we got to the turn, he motioned me to stop and stood with his map in hand while I explained that he was to cross the road that led into Voisins, take the cart track down the hill past the washhouse on his left, and turn into the wood road on that side. At each indication he said, 'I have it.' When I had explained, he simply said, 'Rough road?'

I said it was, very, and wet in the driest weather.

'Wooded all the way?' he asked.

I told him that it was, and, what was more, so winding that you could not see ten feet ahead anywhere between here and Conde.

'Humph,' he said. 'Perfectly clear, thank you very much. Please wait right there a moment.'

He looked up the hill behind him, and made a gesture in the air with his hand above his head. I turned to look up the hill also. I saw the corporal at the gate repeat the gesture; then a big bicycle corps, four abreast, guns on their backs, slid round the corner and came gliding down the hill. There was not a sound, not the rattle of a chain or a pedal.

'Thank you very much,' said the Captain. 'Be so kind as to keep close to the bank.'

When I reached my gate I found some of the men of the guard dragging a big, long log down the road, and I watched them while they attached it to a tree at my gate, and swung it across to the opposite side of the road, making in that way a barrier about five feet high. I asked what that was for? 'Captain's orders,' was the laconic reply. But when it was done the Corporal took the trouble to explain that it was a barricade to prevent the Germans from making a dash up the hill.

'However,' he added, 'don't you get nervous. If we chase them out it will only be a little rifle practice, and I doubt if they even have any ammunition.'

As I turned to go into the house, he called after me, 'See here, I notice that you've got doors on all sides of your house. Better lock all those but this front one.'

As all the windows were barred and so could be left open, I didn't mind; so I went in and locked up. The thing was getting to be funny to me – always doing something, and nothing happening. I suppose courage is a cumulative thing, if only one has time to accumulate, and these boys in khaki treated even the cannonading as if it were all 'in the day's work'.

It was just dusk when the bicycle corps returned up the hill. They had to dismount and wheel their machines under the barricade, and they did it so prettily, dismounting and remounting with a precision that was neat.

'Nothing,' reported the Captain. 'We could not go in far – road too rough and too dangerous. It is a cavalry job.'

'All the same, I am sure the Uhlans are there.'

With that, duty called, the soldiers excused themselves and dusk fell so the men left her to enjoy her evening. When the author awoke the following morning, the battalion had already moved off on a 20km march that would take them south-west, through the Villeneuve forest to Tournan. Overnight on 5/6 September the men billeted between Tournan and Presles, where they were promised a rest in reserve.

The first phase of the war was over. Whether either side could realistically claim a victory was a matter for debate. The Germans had forced their way to the outskirts of Paris, yet had lost heavily in doing so.

Despite losing relatively few men in the Battles of Mons, Le Cateau and the rearguard actions, the Bedfords had held their lines without flinching, kept the enemy at bay, maintained an extraordinarily high morale and earned a superb marching record with just eighty men falling out despite being subjected to atrocious conditions.

Chapter 4

The Battles of the Marne
and the Aisne

7 September – 10 October 1914

*'It made me hold my breath when the order came to fix bayonets
ready to charge the German trenches.'*

Unbeknown to the British infantry at the time, the newly raised French
Sixth Army had attacked the open German flank as they had moved on
to Paris and that, coupled with an increasing supply problem, had caused
the retreat of Von Kluck's hitherto victorious forces. In conjunction with
the French Sixth Army, the British troops were issued new orders while
the Bedfords rested at Presles.

The adjutant, Captain Macready, summed up the battalion's condition
well:

*I remember looking at the men and thinking what a dirty, scraggy lot we looked. Some
with their boots cut open owing to blisters, others with puttees tied around their feet.
Then an Orderly arrived from Brigade HQ and I took an envelope from him. It read
'the British Army will advance tomorrow'. I went over and told the men. There was
a terrific cheer from all. Whatever we may have looked like, our spirit was the same
as ever.*

The worn and weary British troops finally turned, along with the larger
French army, to attack the retreating German army. Some 49 Allied
divisions attacked 46 German divisions along a 300-mile front and
gained around 16km of territory on 6 September alone. Once the
German army recovered from the initial blow and reorganised itself, it
retreated in an orderly manner and fought several determined rearguard

actions. Although the British army was a small part of the overall battle, it managed to strike a major blow in a sensitive part of the German line and caused them to abandon the field in favour of re-forming behind the River Aisne.

The morning of 6 September amused the watching officers and generals. The ragtag bunch that was the British army had endured the worst of times and conditions. Some of their reserves from England had arrived to swell the thinning ranks and they were finally doing what they had expected to do – advance. Generals watching the marching columns from their horses saw their battered but far from beaten army whistling and laughing as they passed with a noticeable spring in their step.

The Bedfordshires formed the advanced guard on the 6th and marched back through Tournan and Villeneuve, where they turned east and moved on to Mortcerf in the Forêt-de-Crécy. On the hot first day of their advance several German cavalry units were spotted but all bolted at the sight of the advancing British Tommies, and other than what Major Onslow described as 'a little scrapping' around Montcerf, the battalion was untroubled. That night was spent around La Celle-sur-Morin and the 7th saw them advance a further 15km eastwards, in the brigade's reserve position. Before resting overnight at Boissy-le-Châtel, just east of Coulommiers, the British troops had seen signs of the German occupation as houses were stripped and anything not of use or value was broken and left in the streets. Local inhabitants, seeing that the approaching army were not German, threw themselves at the Bedfords in gratitude as they searched their ransacked houses. At first the Germans were thought to be far ahead, but as the day wore on the Tommies found that they were closing in on them, as hurriedly discarded, half-eaten meals could be seen amid the looted houses.

Lieutenant Sheldon Gledstanes from C Company received some dreadful news on the evening of the 7th, which would make the following morning one of the worst in his already difficult war. A section of his platoon was ordered to provide the firing party at the execution of a British deserter at 7 a.m. and Gledstanes was to command them. Whether the young soldier was a straggler or trying to desert is a matter for debate elsewhere, but Lieutenant Davenport wrote that 'poor little Gledstanes loathed the job and was assisted by Monteith who was then acting as APM of the Division'. Killing the enemy was one thing but killing of one of your own at close quarters was, perhaps, one of the worst jobs a soldier could be involved in. Private L/10061 Thomas James

Highgate of the Royal West Kents was the British army's first soldier to be shot at dawn. Senior officers made the execution as public as possible, lining the Cheshires and Dorsets up to witness the event. Private Highgate was just 19 years old and his name can be seen on the La Ferte-Sous-Jouarre Memorial to the missing.

Once Lieutenant Gledstanes's section rejoined the battalion they moved off and started another march north, their mood more sombre than on previous days. As the morning went on, their commanders saw fit to pass messages up and down the marching columns to raise their spirits. Lieutenant Davenport wrote that in reality the men were fine anyway and 'utterly bored with the messages'. However, Davenport described one of the more amusing ones:

One of these messages came down on this march, reached us as follows – '2,000 Germans were drowned in seven gallons of beer'. One bright staff officer heard the message going down, did not know what it was although he knew what it should be. He was annoyed that the troops did not cheer and were only laughing and came and asked me the reason. I told him the message as it had reached us and he was very fed up and said it should have been '2,000 Germans were surrounded seven miles from here'!

Within days, official messages spread throughout the columns telling of how 'the whole German army had been surrounded, captured and otherwise destroyed', most of which the infantry paid little heed to.

Later in the day the Bedfordshires were forced to deploy in open formation under long-range German artillery fire as they moved northwards on the flank of the 13th Brigade, who attacked German positions south of the River Marne. Although fighting could be heard to the front and on either flank, the 15th Brigade was not involved directly. The 4th Division was out on the left and the 3rd on the right but the 5th Division in the centre met no serious resistance. They made so much headway that a temporary halt was called once it was realised they were 3km in front of the flanking divisions.

The Bedfords passed through St Ouen and crossed the River Petit Morin at St Cyr behind the two other brigades from their division who were brushing aside the little German resistance they met as they went. Meanwhile, D Company had moved further west, cleared the woods around Courcelles, and taken up positions on high ground overlooking the Marne, near La Ferté. Their orders told them to capture or otherwise stop any Germans seen retreating over the river, but none presented themselves that afternoon having already headed north some hours earlier. Late that afternoon they met Captain Alfred Corah with his company of divisional cyclists just off the La Ferté to Montmirail road. He had disappeared off to division for duty before Mons so the officers were pleased to see him again. His company were moving 200 or so prisoners back to the main British lines, but with all the fighting going on around them British artillery apparently saw them, identified the large group of German uniforms, thought they were a good target, and opened fire. In the resulting confusion many escaped only to be gathered up later, and casualties were inflicted on both the British and German troops. Earlier that afternoon the same group of cyclists and prisoners had already been fired on by a company of Surreys so were less than pleased. No. 14 Platoon took over the sixty-five or so remaining prisoners and guarded them overnight as the rest of the battalion bedded down in a farmhouse. That night the Bedfords rested around Saâcy-sur-Morin on the southern banks of the river before continuing the advance again on 9 September.

After crossing the River Marne at Saâcy on the morning of the 9th, with the sounds of battle coming from their left flank, the battalion moved through the wooded countryside under sporadic fire and was occasionally engaged by hidden clusters of German infantry and supporting artillery. At one stage the main body of the brigade was held up by a well-organised German barrage from the wooded Hill 189, but elements of the Norfolks and Dorsets were ordered to deploy and silence it. With the added firepower of other batteries out of sight of the advancing British column, the area became an unhealthy place to linger so the battalions sought cover as they waited. General Fergusson arrived to find out what the situation was and gave orders for the men to push on through the curtain of shrapnel being laid across the road in small groups and continue the advance. Although a few men were wounded during the rushes through the barrage, the Bedfords regrouped an hour later in a hollow 1km further north, where the general's orders were relayed. They pressed on northwards, bypassing a German strongpoint to their left, which the Lincolns were busily engaging, and followed a barbed-wire fence to the village of Bézu. Positions were taken up along the ridges north of the village and localised rifle duels broke out with German units to their front.

As the British divisions on either side were still moving up, the brigade advanced more carefully and deliberately, assaulting the prepared defences as they came across them. North of Bézu, Major Thorpe and his B Company had eliminated two German machine-gun posts, but knots of enemy infantry backed up by unseen artillery made an unsupported advance so late in the day a dangerous idea. Having secured the area to a relatively safe degree, the Bedfords eventually dug in around Bézu for the night, with A and B Companies on outpost duty. Overnight orders were issued for a dawn assault on the wooded hills to the north that hid the German batteries, so the brigade prepared itself for what would be a bloody start to the following morning.

The date of 10 September saw the 15th Brigade lead the division forward towards the Aisne valley. Major Onslow described how he 'was sent to ride out alone (!) to see if enemies' battery had been taken away over night. Glad to say I only found dead Germans and the abandoned guns'. By 4 a.m. the advance had started but the assault came to nothing as the Germans had evacuated overnight. The battalion soon passed the derelict German battery atop Hill 189, surrounded by twenty or so dead German gunners who had fought for their position to the bitter end. By 6 a.m. they had entered Montreuil and found a group of Germans who had decided to surrender.

Although the entire German rearguard had withdrawn overnight, one of their transport columns was spotted later that morning and the artillery was called forward to shell it. Some time later the Bedfordshires' advanced guard came across the shattered remains of part of the column and the men were allowed to help themselves to the unexpected array of items available from the wreckage. Captain Macready wrote of his surprise at the contents of the smashed wagons: 'Besides the usual articles of war there was, of course, loot, but what surprised me in a military nation was to find a General's cart, with scent, full dress uniform, a picture of the fall of Paris (1870), scented soap and hair wash.'

By nightfall the hot sun had been replaced by rain, which followed them doggedly during their advance north. The next two days would be spent moving through a similarly desolate countryside and passing the litter left by the retreating German army. Looted items that could no longer be carried were blatantly destroyed and discarded all along the route, with dead animals and occasionally dead men mixed in with the filth. Broken wagons and masses of personal equipment gave the distinct impression of an army retreating in haste, and knots of smashed carts strewn with destroyed supplies and dead soldiers showed where British artillery had been effective.

Private Basham, in a letter to his wife in Loughton, Essex,[29] wrote of the spectacle: 'Where we have followed up the Germans we have seen a trail of wine and spirit bottles, chicken, duck and pigeon feathers, cow and bullock carcases stripped of flesh and dead horses besides, motor wagons, guns, rifles, uniforms and equipment. We often see the filled in trenches where the enemy have hurriedly buried their numerous dead.'

After a fifteen-hour movement forward, much of which was spent as the advanced guard of the 5th Division, they stopped. By 6.30 p.m. on the 10th a further 15km had been covered and the battalion rested in fields next to a hamlet called St Quentin, 3km south of La-Ferté-Milon. A draft of ninety men under Lieutenants James Reginald Shippey and Edwin Allen James Edwards joined them as they rested, bringing them up to almost full strength again.

Over the next two days the Bedfordshires were placed in the column of march so had a quieter time. By the evening of the 11th, which marked the anniversary of the Battle of Malplaquet in which their military forebears had fought, the Bedfords were soaked through to the skin having progressed a further 16km north in heavy rain, after which they stayed near St-Rémy-Blanzy overnight. The area was a mass of small fires with men huddled around them trying to dry themselves off. The sight was generally brightened up by a sprinkling of soldiers who were dressed in a peculiar array of uniforms they had picked up along the way while their own saturated clothing steamed over a fire. A further 15km move through heavy rain and muddied roads on Saturday 12 September left them resting in a farm called La Ferme de L'Epitaphe, near Nampteuil, 10km south-east of Soissons.

En route, they halted at Hartennes where the prisoners they had been looking after were handed to the Military Police. There was a further halt that afternoon around Nampteuil as the British advanced guard clashed with a German rearguard unit less than 1km from their positions. The British army were within striking distance of the River Aisne, where their progress would be halted.

British casualties from their 100km northerly advance from Paris to the Aisne amounted to 1,701 of all ranks, killed, wounded and missing between 6 and 10 September. Several thousand German casualties were known of as well as many prisoners being taken, but the exact figure was not recorded. Of these, and despite being in the advanced guard of the British army during several phases, the Bedfordshires lost only three killed and around twenty wounded.

Over and above those already mentioned, Sir John French's despatches of September and October 1914, which covered the periods between the Battles of Mons and the Aisne, mentioned the following for their gallantry during operations: Lieutenant Alfred Geoffrey Corah (Cyclist Company) of Scraptoft Hall, Leicestershire, whose father became the High Sheriff of Leicestershire in 1916; Corporal Ernest Albert Higdon[30] who survived the war, rising to the rank of Warrant Officer Class II; Private Samuel Seaman[31] who was medically discharged in January 1918; and Private William Jackson of Middlesex,[32] who was killed during the advance on the Marne, 9 September 1914.

The Battle of the Aisne: 12–15 September 1914

Despite forcing the Germans to retreat from the River Marne in disarray, the Allies failed to engage the German army in the open fields and were forced to attack them in the Aisne valley. The terrain suited the Germans well and the weather had turned to being cold, wet and miserable. The southerly approaches to the valley were wooded and littered with spurs running steeply down to the river. On the northern banks the German army were dug in along a plateau that commanded all the approaches, with a road called the Chemin des Dames giving them easy access to all sections of their line. General von Kluck's First Army positioned itself on the western end of the line and General von Bülow's Second Army was to the east. However, Allied generals ordered the advance as no one was certain whether the waiting German units were set up for a delaying rearguard action or a major defensive stand.

The battalion's overnight stay at La Ferme de L'Epitaphe on the night of 12 September was cramped and wet, as both the Cheshires and Brigade HQ were already there when they reached it. The Bedfordshires were drenched on their arrival; they had marched through incessant rain all day and many of them still had no greatcoats, having lost them at Mons. Despite the building already being full, the Cheshires made room for them and around 1,000 men spent an overcrowded night in the modestly sized farmhouse. Fortunately, Lieutenant Mayne found another empty barn later that evening, which relieved the cramped conditions once half of the Bedfords had moved into it. This night was to mark the start of a similarly uncomfortable spell, with autumn rains and cold weather setting in just as they were about to become bogged down in a sodden river valley.

On 13 September the 3rd Division forded the river on the right around

Vailly and the 4th made it across on the left at Venizel. This left just the British centre on the southern side of the river and it had to be crossed to enable the advance to continue. Only one bridge remained intact, which was opposite the village of Missy and fell within the 5th Division's operational area.

At 3.30 a.m. the Bedfordshires left their billets and marched 2km north to Serches. The 15th Brigade then turned west and waited in a field from 6 a.m. for further orders. Being 400m behind a battery of field artillery, the Bedfords had a superb view of the artillery battle and watched them as they duelled with their German counterparts across the river. Although outranged, in a worse defensive position and severely outgunned, the British batteries gave a good account of themselves as the Bedfords looked on. Casualties and the hopelessness of their position eventually caused their retirement, but the heavier British guns could not move so stayed in position and slogged it out with the superior German batteries.

With the German barrage creeping closer once the field artillery had moved away, orders came to withdraw almost 1km further back and out of range, the move being completed around midday. Here, some of D Company had the welcomed distraction of a 'Pom Pom' anti-aircraft battery arriving and setting up for business next to them. Being an unusual and new weapon, the curious men struck up a conversation with the lone officer, who complained of the disinterest that had been shown towards his gun since arriving in France. He had initially been told to report to II Corps, who had shrugged and sent him to the 5th Division. The divisional staff had no idea what to do with him so told him to set up wherever he liked. Shortly after his arrival their curiosity was satisfied on seeing him in action for the first time, albeit ineffectively and against a French aircraft his spotter had mistaken for a German one.

All day the brigade waited in fields and amused themselves while the West Kents cleared the Missy bridge and surrounds of enemy and built rafts ready for the crossing. After an evening meal, the Bedfordshires were sent into the dark night around 9.30 p.m. to ford the river.

They completed the crossing in the pitch black on two rafts by 3.30 a.m. on 14 September and waited in the freezing cold, many still without any greatcoats. A long pause lingering in sodden fields followed, until orders moved them up the ridge to Sainte Marguerite. As dawn approached, the men of the battalion were delayed in the village under fire while an assault by the 13th Brigade unfolded to their left, but no orders arrived for the Bedfordshires until 11 a.m. When they did, they sent them back to Missy, which was not an easy task given that both villages and the entire approach were being swept with machine-gun and shrapnel fire. However, they followed orders and returned to Missy under heavy fire in small groups by heading for the light railway line, crossing it and retiring behind its limited cover.

Early that afternoon Major Allason and C Company fixed bayonets and advanced on to the Chivres Ridge itself alongside a company from the East Surreys, but the Surreys were withdrawn by orders early evening, forcing the isolated Bedfords to follow suit, much to Allason's annoyance. With hindsight, holding on to that small piece of ground and developing the Allied position from there may have made a difference to the war as a whole as it commanded access to the Chemin des Dames, which would prove important in the major battles to follow.

Among Allason's men was Private Frederick 'Stubb' Wagstaff,[33] a footballer from the Sandy team who wrote home about the advance: 'I got hit around 3 o'clock and had to lay like a little frog from that time until it got dark … it was pouring with rain all the time … it made me hold my breath when the order came to fix bayonets ready to charge the German trenches.'[34] Stubb's wound was to lead to the end of his war as he was medically discharged nine months later.

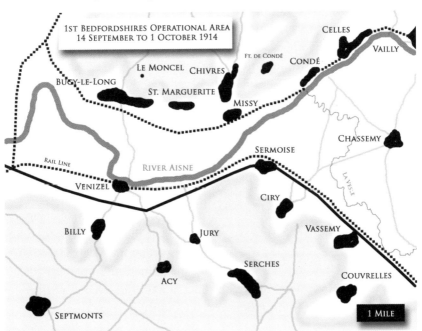

1ST BEDFORDSHIRES OPERATIONAL AREA
14 SEPTEMBER TO 1 OCTOBER 1914

CELLES
VAILLY
FT. DE CONDÉ
CONDÉ
LE MONCEL CHIVRES
BUCY-LE-LONG
ST. MARGUERITE
MISSY
CHASSEMY
SERMOISE
LA VESLE
RAIL LINE
RIVER AISNE
VENIZEL
CIRY
BILLY
JURY
VASSEMY
SERCHES
COUVRELLES
ACY
SEPTMONTS
1 MILE

Throughout 14 September, the battalion was waiting for specific orders while the battle raged all around. Despite the foothold gained on the ridge, by nightfall the British infantry were still pinned down in the sodden valley.

Following a night spent in Missy, a further attack on the very ridge Allason had evacuated against his will and better judgement was launched on the morning of the 15th. With the Bedfordshires in support halfway up the hill, the Norfolks could not make their gains stick against a blistering concentration of machine-gun and artillery fire. To add to their woes, some of the shells came from British guns, who could not see there were British troops on the ridge. With the British barrage falling to the front of the pinned Norfolks, and the German shells falling to their rear, directions became confused and the Norfolks bayonet-charged some of their own men who had taken up positions in the wood.

After several difficult hours, both battalions were ordered back early that evening and sheltered among the houses of Missy, where they endured an unending barrage of shells designed to stop them coming up the hill again. When darkness fell they retired in groups to the southern side of the river once more and rested briefly before returning to what there was of the front lines.

Captain Robert McCloughin of D Company was hit by a machine gun during the retreat from the ridge and, although he was carried to a house in Missy by Sergeant Leonard Godfrey, he died there from his wounds. McCloughin was mentioned in despatches in September and October for his leadership and bravery from the initial fighting at Mons, to his death on the Aisne. Captain Francis Edwards, who had been treated to eggs and tea by Mildred Aldrich ten days earlier, Machine Gun Officer Lieutenant Joseph Mayne and around forty men were also wounded during the day's fighting.

Private Bob Pigg was involved in the charge up the hill, writing: 'In a village near the river I had my first experience of a bayonet charge. ... The three regiments were ordered to take a hill in front of us. That was where I saw Sergeant Godfrey, of Royston, bring out a wounded Captain under heavy fire. It was a brave deed and had the Captain lived, Sergeant Godfrey would have probably been awarded the Victoria Cross.'[35]

In fact Godfrey was not so much as mentioned in despatches for his bravery and was more matter of fact about the event, as may be expected. He wrote to his parents on 6 October:

I have had many lucky escapes and hope to keep on dodging them. ... I shall be able to tell you tales forever if I ever get home safe again, but I don't think that will be before Christmas. You will no doubt think that I am lucky but on the 17th [sic] my Company was fighting in a wood ... when the Germans tried to rush us and the Captain on my left was shot through the stomach and had his leg broken and the Private on my right had his head blown off. I never got a scratch. Considering there was only four yards between us I think I was lucky. Don't you? The Captain's name was McCloughin. I took him on my back out of the firing line down to the field hospital about a mile and it nearly creased me. The poor chap died that night.

Although the left and right flanks of the river had been successfully secured, that day had seen the British centre conduct a difficult frontal assault against well-sited German positions with limited artillery support. British casualties for the battle ran to around 12,000, including 10 senior British officers. Of these, the Bedfords lost 10 men killed and around 90 wounded.

Further to the west the French Sixth Army had tried to find the extreme flank of the German position around Compiègne but were stopped by a dogged resistance. On the eastern end of the British line the French Fifth Army came across a gap between the two German armies and advanced as far as Berry-au-Bac before being brought to a bloody halt by the newly arrived German Seventh Army. The failure to break the German lines and the realisation that a heavily entrenched defensive position was difficult to overcome effectively marked the beginning of four years of trench warfare.

After their aborted assault against the ridge the battalion held their positions around Missy on the 15th, lining the light railway line to the edge of the village, and a day of sniping and heavy shelling developed. Although the main path of resistance was along the railway line, forward posts north of Missy itself were established, but many of their occupants were unable to move during daylight due to the active and plentiful snipers above them on the ridge.

Lieutenant Davenport had made his way to talk to his friend Lieutenant 'Johnnie' Ker, who was sitting on a bank. Telling Davenport how tired he was, Ker stood up, stretched, yawned and was shot by a sniper through the head. His death was instantaneous but Lieutenant Hugh Courtenay, who was hit in the left temple at the same time, perhaps even with the same bullet, survived. Courtenay would return later and, despite being almost blind in his left eye, win the Military

Cross and the Distinguished Service Order, leading the battalion until his death in action less than three months before the end of hostilities.

The battalion's second in command, Major Cranley Onslow, a veteran officer whose service included the Isazia and Chitral expeditions of the 1890s, was also wounded that day, caught by a German sniper as he was checking on his men around 6 a.m. Thirty-five men were also hit, which was a remarkably light casualty list considering the time spent under fire.

Around 9 p.m. the battalion's first two officers to lose their lives – Johnnie Ker and Robert McCloughin – were laid to rest in the orchard near the light railway line, just south of the village, in a simple ceremony. Shortly afterwards, orders came through to retire for a rest, having been relieved by the West Surreys.

On the journey back to the concentration area near the river the men retired in small groups, being under the watchful eye of German snipers and artillery observers. Captain Macready wrote about his journey, being accompanied by the CO and a wounded private along the way:

The path was nothing more than liquid mud and required very careful walking. I led and the C.O. was just behind. I heard a squelch and turned round to find Colonel Griffith on his back in the mud. This seemed very funny to me but I did not laugh. One does not laugh at C.O.s! Eventually he pulled himself out of the morass and stood upright. He then took a step forward, and slipped completely face down at full length into the mire. This was too much for me. I roared with laughter and, quite rightly, got it in the neck from him.

Once assembled in the darkness the soldiers of the battalion prepared to move across the river when a star shell illuminated their positions. Being in a large marching column as they were, it took the tiniest moment to realise what a tempting target they made and not many more moments to bellow orders to take cover. Immediately bullets started raining down on them, followed soon after by the inevitable shrapnel. Lieutenant Davenport commented that 'I was pushed into a ditch with about 50 fellows on top of me!' Luckily, for a change the reactions of 800 men and their need to find cover was quicker than the reactions of the enemy gunners and the battalion suffered hardly any casualties, other than the occasional dent to someone's pride upon finding themselves in an unfortunate or undignified position. Between the star shells they made for a wood and re-formed out of sight, before marching southwards and crossing the River Aisne.

Linking up with the Cheshires, the battalion moved to Montgard Mill near the villages of Jury and Acy, arriving around 5 a.m. on 16 September. Initially the building was very cramped until the Cheshires were moved to another location. The morning was spent resting, cleaning up and generally reorganising themselves despite an artillery battery setting up next to the mill and attracting the attention of German gunners in reply. In the afternoon A and B Companies were sent to dig a reserve trench line about 250m behind the river, on the southerly ridge parallel to the Sermoise to Soissons road. They were relieved by C and D Companies early in the evening who took over their fatigues. More digging followed the next day with the battalion working on the same line, and early on the 18th the brigade took up position in the trenches, which were sheltered by trees along much of the line. The brigade locked the area down with road blocks and patrols, ensuring no surprises were developing and that none of the rumoured spies were among their number.

The Dorsets took over at 8 p.m. and the Bedfordshires returned to their mill, having also seen the arrival of several men who were returning after being treated for wounds. Another day of rest on the 19th in and around the mill was broken up by orders to evacuate at 5 p.m., as they expected a German barrage to hit the area. In the event it came to nothing and the battalion was again split in half to carry out two-hour digging fatigues in shifts before retiring for the night.

Lance Corporal Richard Wheeler from Ampthill,[36] known as Dick, had already spent almost seven years with the battalion but like nearly all of his comrades had not been in combat before August. Having survived the rigours of life in A Company since landing with the battalion from Dublin, Dick was among those who composed a letter to his parents while the break in operations allowed. He wrote on the 18th how he was safe and well, although he was having a dreadful time adjusting to the experience of intense warfare:

I have only God to thank. It's a miracle I am alive to tell the tale. We have been in the hottest corners in our lifetime and did not know which way to look or go; the shells have been bursting all over our heads and around us ... we have been short of food and lay out every night in hay or straw and several nights in trenches with nothing but what we stand up in – wet through several times. We have seen terrible sights both with the Germans and ourselves. It's cruel – I never saw what war was like until this turned out.[37]

The brigade was held on the southern side of the river until the 24th, the men spending their days preparing the defensive trenches and their nights between holding them and resting in the mill. The nights in the trenches were getting colder and therefore more uncomfortable as many of the men still did not have any greatcoats.

On the afternoon of the 24th orders arrived for them to move back to the front lines so the battalion packed itself up and was moving by around 6 p.m. The soldiers crossed the Aisne using the same pontoon bridge around 9 p.m., and were in Sainte Marguerite by 11 p.m. After a very careful search through the woods under constant threat from German searchlights, D Company took the forward trenches over from the Duke of Cornwall's Light Infantry, which were just 30m from the German lines. Their first night was much like those that would follow, being spent in shallow, cold ditches, edgily waiting for an enemy attack that never came.

During a week in the marshy wood north of Sainte Marguerite the battalion suffered from sniper fire and lost a few men in the process. One such example was Drummer Herbert Chequer from Croydon[38] who was talking to Lieutenant Davenport as they lay in their trench on 25 September. A sniper caught them unawares, the bullet passing through Drummer Chequer's shin and leaving a 6in hole. He simply shrugged it off until he could be evacuated after dark, not having complained once during the entire day. Sadly he lost his leg and died on 28 September in No. 4 General Hospital in Versailles, earning a mention for gallantry in the Commander-in-Chief's despatch that October.

The battalion's time in the front line was spent improving the positions and burying the dead who had fallen during the early fighting in the wood. After 'standing to' every morning before dawn, the men would trickle back in groups to get hot tea and warm up a little, in a barn away from German snipers. They also engaged in the deadly sniping duel when the opportunity allowed and claimed to have enjoyed more success than their German counterparts.

During their game of cat and mouse on the Aisne, both sides settled into some peculiar routines, often preferring to warn their counterparts not to try and use particular vantage points instead of killing them outright. Sergeant Leonard Godfrey gave one example of this in an interview with a reporter from the *Royston Crow* newspaper:

We had a fine piece of sport whilst waiting there. One night two Germans had climbed into a big bushy tree near their trenches with the idea of sniping us in the morning. We spotted them a bit before they were ready and thinking it would be a pity to give them a chance to come down in the usual way I sent for my chum, the machine gun instructor. He gave that tree a belt of ammunition from top to bottom in a zig-zag fashion. Those two Germans came down like a sack of spuds and no-one else tried getting up that tree again.

Various ploys to improve the men's view of the German lines were tried, including making an angled mirror, which was an early version of the trench periscope. Now and again a sniper would see it being held above the parapet and fire at the reflection. On 26 September Sergeant George Garrett[39] lost a finger when a sniper saw him using it and was back in the 4th Northern General Hospital within days. Having recovered, he returned as Company Sergeant Major, winning the Distinguished Conduct Medal for gallantry shown throughout the early battles, and was commissioned as an officer.

Shells from both sides often troubled the Bedfords' positions, especially from the 'Pom Pom' on the southern side of the river. It would shoot at the German aircraft circling overhead, invariably miss, and the shells would fall in the wood, scattering the Bedfords each time. Although no harm was done, the men learned to identify the telltale sound of it being used and found themselves instinctively seeking cover more often than not.

As is often the case in warfare, this period also saw some examples of the duality of soldiers. On the one hand soldiers from both sides were vocal in their scorn for one another, yet on the other hand they shared, almost amiably, in their mutual positions and discomfort. One moment they could be giving their all in an effort to kill those opposite them, and within hours, sometimes even minutes, the victors could be seen sharing cigarettes and chatting comfortably with the vanquished.

Lieutenant Davenport – whose excerpts from his diary on just one day, below, demonstrate this paradox – delighted in catching groups of the enemy with machine-gun bursts and felling snipers from their tree-shrouded hideouts. That day they spotted a 'great fat German come out of a gap in the wall and waddle down to a hollow' and fired on him at close to 1,000m. This brought a group of forty other soldiers right into the sights of Sergeant Cooper's machine gun and led to Davenport's remarks: 'The machine gun then got busy and as we had the range to a nicety did some great execution. It was a most thrilling sight.' His amusement at annoying their opponents or upsetting their daily routines is apparent when he shares a story from the battalion to his left. They 'worried' a German sentry who was almost outside their machine-gunner's range, but panicked nonetheless when fired upon. He called his platoon out from a building and gave the British gunner a superb, if extremely long-ranged target. In turn a group of officers also rushed from the building and waved their arms about until the situation settled down and they all returned to the safety of a house. Amused at the reaction they had created, the British waited until the lone guard was half asleep again before repeating the process over and over again, with the same results.

Yet, a British Guards battalion, who represented the cream of the infantry, got an almost friendly game going with the Germans opposite them. Davenport reported that 'the Germans stuck up a dummy figure in their trenches and when the Guards potted at it the Germans signalled in our fashion; bull, inner, magpie, outer, etc., with a shovel while the Guards cheered each bull!'

However, while the stalemate and resulting trench warfare along that section of the River Aisne would remain for years to come, it would not last long elsewhere. With the Germans on the high ridge above, and the British in their saturated, uncomfortable, shallow trenches below them, it was not long before the next phase of the war broke out – the 'Race to the Sea'. Although the Battle of the Aisne continued until the end of September, it became the place where both sides tried to pin their opponents' forces down while they probed ever northwards with their own reinforcements, always looking for the open flank of their enemy.

The 'Race to the Sea' – 2–11 October 1914

Around 7 p.m. on 1 October news arrived that the Bedfordshires were to be relieved, which was completed around 11 p.m. Having crossed the pontoon bridge once again and spent what seemed to be an almost luxurious night back in the mill near Jury, the men woke to very specific orders. Although they were unaware at battalion level, the 4th Division had relieved the soldiers of the entire 5th Division, who were to be moved north in secret with their entire corps. Therefore the order was short and direct: keep out of sight of anything moving above or on the ground. To that end, lookouts were arranged wherever the battalion worked or relaxed outside, and at the first sign of an aircraft the men all bolted for cover, often laughing heartily at the game of hide and seek they felt they were playing. However, the marches that followed were long and exhausting with D Company's Bob Pigg of Royston recalling that 'at each halt the men would be asleep as soon as they got down'.

At 7 p.m. on 2 October, a series of overnight marches started so that, under cover of darkness, German aircraft could not spot them. Speculation about their destination was rife along the 10km, six-hour march south that took them through Nampteuil and on to Launoy. A day of hiding from any curious eyes followed until 6 p.m. on the 3rd, when they marched 16km east through Hartennes and Longpont, before billeting in and around the wood-shrouded village of Corcy. The officers stayed in a deserted chateau belonging to a countess while the men bedded down in a large barn.

While resting in the chateau that day one of the officers wrote home, remarking that they actually had 'a bed to sleep in, the first since leaving England; also a small piece of butter!' His opinions stretched as far as to say that 'the papers annoy me … the Germans are liars and awful rotters'.[40]

Another 6 p.m. start on the 4th took them 20km further east, passing through Villers-Cotterêts and arriving at Vattiers around 5 a.m. on the 5th. Along the route a huge convoy of around 2,000 French buses passed, headed east in a hurry. It turned out that they ferried a French army who were destined for Arras to help stop the German advance there. The men had no choice but to sit at the side of the road and watch as the army raced east, taking some three hours to pass despite their speed.

The battalion remained at Vattiers and enjoyed a peaceful rest until 2 p.m. on 6 October, at which time the men moved off again. After passing Gilocourt and covering a further 11km, they billeted at Béthisy-Saint-Pierre, 65km north-east of Paris. Along the route they crossed the line of their retreat from Le Cateau to Paris only a few weeks earlier and arrived at their destination by early evening. Although no clues were given yet as to their destination, the officers were warned that there may be a train journey in the near future, so prepared the battalion accordingly.

A 7 a.m. start on 7 October took them 12km further east, passing through Saintines and Verberie. Along the route they passed corps commander General Smith-Dorrien, who sat on the side of the road watching his men marching past, and not long afterwards the battalion halted for thirty minutes at Pontpoint. The final leg of their march away from the Aisne took them on to Pont-Sainte-Maxence by midday, where they briefly rested in fields near the railway station before entraining and leaving the area at 5 p.m. The entire train was crammed with the battalion, but C Company – now under Lieutenant Gledstanes – and one transport wagon had to follow up on the next one, as there was simply not enough room.

Passing through Creuil in their cattle trucks, the first train stopped for a half-hour break at 9 p.m., where cocoa was served and the men stretched their legs. Overnight, the train stopped regularly to take orders regarding its direction, as complete secrecy was still being maintained. By 5 a.m. on 8 October, the train came to a halt in Abbeville, 100km north, and the battalion detrained.

A gruelling 30km move north-east followed, as the battalion moved through the peaceful French countryside. Matters were not improved by the lack of directions, guides or maps, which led to the soldiers marching some 9km out of their way. Around 10 a.m. they paused for the day in the village of Millencourt-en-Ponthieu, but they were off again at 6 p.m. Their route took them through Agenvillers, Brailly-Cornehotte and Boufflers, before reaching their overnight billeting spot near Gennes-Ivergny around midnight.

C Company rejoined them at Gennes-Ivergny and the men of the battalion were paraded in readiness to resume their move towards the front lines at 2 p.m. on the 9th, but were left waiting in the village street. Around 4.30 p.m. they finally set off, and after a relatively short leg of 7km, stopped at Haravesnes. They arrived at around 7 p.m., expecting to be picked up by a fleet of French buses, but none could be found. It transpired that a series of confusing orders had left a good proportion of the brigade lying around in a field waiting for buses which did not arrive. Although the men rested in the surrounding fields, the brigade's transport sections continued moving north-east with the intention of meeting up again closer to the front lines.

During the morning of the 10th, the men were seen to drift to the hedgerows to watch one of the curious sights that soldiers on campaign stumble across. Lille to the east had almost fallen, with just a few French territorial battalions holding out at the time. As the town had been a major training area, the French recruits had to be evacuated quickly, and enormous columns were marching continuously past the Bedfords in their field. Tens of thousands of Frenchmen tramped past that day leaving both 'sides' of the hedgerow to marvel at their respective views. The veteran British Tommies saw the massed ranks of untrained and enthusiastic men moving west, while the recruits came face to face with veteran British soldiers who had not only earned a name for themselves but bore the look of battle-hardened soldiers.

At 10 a.m. on 11 October, the fleet of vehicles finally arrived to transport the battalion. They made their way north-east, towards Bethune; 25km later the fleet passed through Fillièvres and St Pol before arriving at La Thieuloye, some 7km north-east of St Pol. Not long after the buses had reached the village, the ever-reliable RQMS Bartlett and their transport section joined them.

The pause at St Pol saw another group of reinforcements join, led by Lieutenant Claude Charles Stafford, who had landed in France almost a month earlier and now escorted more of the reserves to restore the battalion to its full strength. In a letter home soon after his arrival, Lieutenant Stafford shared how he was met by two surprised and excited former Bedford Football Club teammates, namely Lieutenants Downes and Shippey, who had both been in the firing line since August. The trio were delighted to meet up again, blissfully unaware that the battalion's next engagement would see the end of their friendship.

The men knew they were close to the fighting now, as a continuous line of refugees from Lille trudged past them, although accurate military news was sparse at best. All anyone could say for sure was that battles were erupting to the north and south of their line of march, near the Forêt de Nieppe and around Arras respectively, and that they would soon be in contact with the Germans. With that as their only real indication of what to expect, at 6.30 a.m. the next day they set off again in a cold, thick mist. The Bedfordshires provided the advanced guard for the 5th Division and moved north-east through Diéval, Ourton and Bruay-la-Buissière before arriving at Bethune some 17km later. The French army were in position at Bethune so the decision was made to move further east. Crossing the Canal D'aire, they moved to Essars, only to find a unit of French territorials there. After discussions, the French troops gladly vacated the positions and the battalion spent the cold, frosty night in the village. Overnight and despite the noise created by a group of drunken French cavalrymen to their front, the men could hear gunfire and see sporadic flashes from artillery fire to the east, although no one knew for certain what was happening.

Chapter 5

The Battle of La Bassée

12 October – 2 November 1914

'All the company's officers are either dead or wounded.'

The plan for the coming battle was for II Corps, including the Bedfordshires in the 5th Division, to attack through Aire and Bethune towards La Bassée; III Corps to attack further north towards Armentières; and IV Corps to position itself at the northernmost section of the line and not far from Ypres. Within the larger plan, the 15th Brigade was to push forward to Festubert and hold the line between there and the canal, effectively becoming the fixed hinge on the swinging door that saw the rest of the British and French armies attack further north.

On the left of the 15th Brigade were the men of the 14th, who were manning the line from Festubert to Richebourg, and as those of the 13th Brigade were required further south they were unavailable to the British frontage. The two brigades holding the 5th Division's sector were notably overstretched in manning the 6,500m-wide portion of the line, which left next to no reserves to be pulled off for the coming battle.

The morning of the 12th started in another thick fog that allowed for no more than 20m of visibility. Marching eastwards through Beuvry and on to Gorre, the 15th Brigade was greeted by groups of French colonial troops in their bright red, white and blue uniforms, including Moors, Sipahis and Algerians. Both sides were equally as curious to meet one another, as the Tommies had not seen such colourful uniforms up to that point and the Frenchmen had not yet come across the khaki of the British army.

Halfway along the road between Gorre and Festubert, the battalion was called to a halt. With German aircraft circling overhead and German shells raining down on Festubert itself less than 1km ahead, the men were ordered to take cover in the roadside ditches. After an hour orders came and the brigade advanced once more.

The Dorsets were sent to take the southernmost sector of the line and attacked along the Bethune to La Bassée canal road, from Gorre towards Cuinchy, while the Bedfordshires moved to their left towards Givenchy-les-la-Bassée. To the left of the Bedfords were the Norfolks, who advanced on Festubert, with the 14th Brigade extending the line north from the Norfolks. The Cheshires were held in brigade support ready to move to any part of the brigade lines under threat.

Advancing on to Givenchy from the north-west, D Company was sent to take the village early that afternoon, with the rest of the battalion extended northwards. No. 16 Platoon made it across the road from Le Plantin to Givenchy unscathed but as soon as the other three platoons followed up, fire opened up on them from La Bassée to the east and Festubert further north. Catching them in the open caused casualties immediately but the men sprinted on in bursts, making it into the houses along the western and southern edges of the village before starting to move towards the centre. Luckily, many of the bullets were spent by the time they hit the Bedfords so, although dozens of men found themselves spattered with bruises that night, their casualties were remarkably light.

Rumour had it that the Germans held Givenchy, but upon their arrival the village was found to be empty, other than a group of French

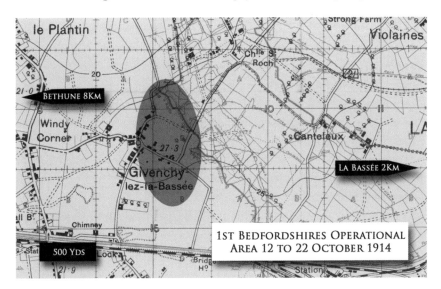

1ST BEDFORDSHIRES OPERATIONAL AREA 12 TO 22 OCTOBER 1914

territorials sharing a bottle of local wine with a few of the Dorsets who had been temporarily waylaid as they contentedly propped up a haystack. A defensive line was established around the village as the battalions to the north and south of them aligned themselves similarly.

German shells started raining onto the village as the battalion dug in, destroying and setting fire to house after house, but fortunately causing only a few minor wounds from falling masonry as the men dug in.

That afternoon saw the Dorsets launch an assault along the canal to the south and Nos 13 and 14 Platoons from D Company were ordered to support their open northern flank. Lieutenant Davenport extended his platoons out into the open fields and laid the men down, waiting for the advance to begin. As they waited, the German gunners spotted them and hit them from both the east and south simultaneously. Davenport's backpack was torn off, the shell bursting in the lap of Sergeant Thomas Haycroft[41] just a metre behind him. Although he crawled away in agony, Sergeant Haycroft was later discovered dead around 250m further back.

The two beleaguered platoons held position for a few more minutes before orders were issued to advance through the barrage alongside the Dorsets, whose own assault had begun. The din made the orders only audible to a small group and around a dozen men jumped to their feet and moved forward as the rest lay uncertainly among the crops. To the amazement of the rest of the group, a handful managed to return after dusk, having spent several uncomfortable hours being worn down by shrapnel and picked off by snipers.

Of the band of Bedfordshires who advanced into the madness, Corporal Ben Piggot of Guilden Morden[42] and Private Albert Bentley from Northampton[43] won the Distinguished Conduct Medal, both choosing to stay with three of their wounded comrades and tend their injuries, despite being under extremely heavy fire. In a letter home[44] Corporal Piggot described the event as a 'little job' but his pleasure was evident as he described how his medal was pinned to his tunic by the King on 3 December.

The Dorsets further south had advanced and met a much larger group of German troops who were intent on launching their own assault westwards. After a brief and one-sided firefight the Dorsets were pushed back to Pont Fixe, but the German assault was held, until a nasty trick cost the men from Dorset dearly. A group of twenty Germans walked along the canal to surrender and the Dorsets came out to accept their submission. Once enough of them were in the open, the Germans fell flat and a hail of fire mowed the unsuspecting Dorsets down. The men of the battalion were badly mauled and shaken yet retired back to Pont Fixe again and held all further attempts to push them back. Their CO, Colonel Bols, had been seriously wounded and taken prisoner during the fighting, yet, having been stripped of his clothes, managed to escape. He recovered from his wounds and later became the Chief of Staff for General Allenby in Palestine. Some 13 Officers and 396 men of the Dorsets were killed or wounded in the day's fighting, many from the 'dirty trick' along the canal bank.

The French to the south of the Dorsets lost Vermelles, leaving the 15th Brigade with an exposed flank, which would tell heavily on the British defensive line in the coming days. However, for the time being, the Bedfordshires and their comrades spent a sleepless night digging lines of protective rifle pits, ready for the next day's fighting.

All in all, the Bedfords had an incredibly lucky day, courtesy of the spent machine-gun bullets. They lost just Sergeant Haycroft killed and thirteen wounded during their first day in the Battle of La Bassée.

The next day saw the assault further south halted at the infamous Railway Triangle that remained in German hands until 1918. The 14th Brigade on their northern flank made some progress but had to fight for every house in every hamlet, so the going was slow and costly. However, on the 15th Brigade's frontage the situation was perhaps the worst, when a heavy German bombardment fell on Givenchy at 6 a.m. and rained on it all day. The village was rendered untenable and movement was very limited, but Brigadier Gleichen reported that the Bedfords 'held out gallantly'.

D Company was moved into support positions west of the village and B Company took over the right end of the battalion line. A Company held the middle, which extended from the northern edge of the village, through an orchard and into the open countryside. C Company was dug in on the far northern end of the battalion's line, with the Cheshires having taken over on their left.

Around midday, in one of the houses in the village, Lieutenants Gledstanes and Shippey were sitting resting, enjoying a drink of milk and quietly chatting, when a shell caved the roof in and burst between them. Both emerged from the ruined building staggering and covered in dust, much to the amusement of their fellow officers, but it transpired that Shippey was carrying internal injuries. He was moved by stretcher back to the village school for treatment.

The barrage continued and, having suffered heavy casualties, with many being buried by the falling houses, it looked as though B Company would be forced back to trenches west of the village. Not long after midday, soldiers of A Company were assaulted around the orchard but no help could reach them as the intensity of the barrage prevented any movement. They just held the Germans, as did C Company to the north, but the Cheshires were in an impossible position and forced to retire.

About 3 p.m. Lieutenant Colonel Griffith and Captain Macready went to see the brigade commander – Count Gleichen – to explain their deteriorating situation. Their brigadier described them as ghosts, remarking that 'their clothes and faces [were] a mass of white dust and plaster' and gave the order to retire.

The village school, serving as the battalion's hospital, was evacuated first, the ambulances roaring off at their best speed. Lieutenant Shippey's wagon was hit as it retired and although he was moved back to the 15th Field Ambulance at Bethune, carrying even more injuries, he died from his many wounds early on 14 October.

While the hospital was being cleared the shelling increased to a fever pitch when the German gunners realised what was happening. To the south the Dorsets also retired, leaving the men in the village pinned down and acting as an unplanned rearguard. With both flanks having been overrun, the village was peppered by German artillery from the east and machine-gun fire from both the north and south. German infantry started pressing towards the village from all three sides and although the remaining men temporarily halted their advance, the need to retire was getting urgent.

The men of the battalion retired in small groups, taking their chances and sprinting in short bursts as the opportunities allowed. By 4 p.m. they had extricated themselves and a line was formed along the road running from Le Plantin to Festubert. The Dorsets continued the line to the south and had been supported by two companies from the 1st Devons of the 14th Brigade. The Norfolks had appeared to the north and although the brigade was battle worn and very mixed up, the line was intact. Major Thorpe, Lieutenant Goff and Second Lieutenant Downes were all wounded, with Thorpe and Goff being mentioned in despatches for their part in the fighting. Thorpe had been hit in the foot and limped back to get his wound dressed, but the last two were nowhere to be seen, although Goff would turn up at a casualty station and go on to lead a Liverpool battalion later in the war. Dozens of men and both machine guns had also been lost in the barrage, most being buried in falling masonry, their whereabouts unknown.

D Company had just eighty men and B Company was left with just one officer – Captain Edwards – so a hasty reorganisation was needed. By 7 p.m. the battalion had moved to the east of the Festubert to Givenchy road and spent until 3 a.m. digging in. The evening settled into a quieter time along the front line with just occasional, sporadic bursts of fire. Some 7 officers and 140 men from the Bedfordshires had become casualties that day, with another 100 being slightly wounded but choosing to stay on in the line. Among the fallen was Lieutenant Claude Stafford of Bedford, the former captain of the Bedford Rowing Club and keen Bedford Rugby Club back, who had only been with the battalion three days. However, all four battalions from the 15th Brigade had suffered throughout the last two days, and the southern end of the brigade line had to be strengthened with half of the Devons who had been pulled off into a reserve position.

Dawn broke on the 14th and the men stood to in the cold, wet morning after a few hours' rest. Lieutenants John Litchfield and Robert Harding, along with Second Lieutenant Walter Graves and a large draft of welcomed reinforcements, joined the battalion that morning, practically rebuilding D Company in the process. A day of sporadic shelling and sniping from Givenchy developed, with the Bedfords crammed into their shallow, inadequate trenches. Although a fresh attack was planned for 3 p.m. on the 14th, it came to nothing as the troops on the south of the canal could make no headway despite their gallant attempts and heavy casualties. All day the 15th Brigade listened to the distant sounds of fighting to the north and south but no orders followed for the men to take their bayonets forward and clear Givenchy out.

At dusk, intense rifle fire developed from the Norfolks' section, quickly spreading along the front lines to Givenchy and on to the Dorsets to the south. The air above the Bedfords' heads was suddenly alive with bullets and the line of sentries peered expectantly into the failing light. Within moments a message came from the Norfolks to the north to urgently evacuate the front trenches, and Captain Edwards ordered his men to retire quickly. As most of them were newly arrived replacements that had not been under fire before, they moved back double quick, the darkness adding to their uncertainty.

The men in the second line saw a horde of shapes rushing towards them in the dark with bayonets fixed and, with the heavy fire going on around them, thought they were being attacked. Although it did not take long to realise their mistake, shots were fired into the darkness and many of the second line retired with those from the front, leaving just a handful of stalwarts who were not happy at the thought of vacating their positions. Lieutenant Davenport and Company Sergeant Major William Sharpe[45] rushed along the second line and managed to maintain cohesion, despite many sections moving back before they reached them. Then came the uncertain period when the painfully thin line of remaining Bedfordshires heard the order to fix bayonets and hold. CSM Sharpe was sent back to retrieve the rest of the company as Lieutenant Davenport held the few who were left in position. After half an hour the firing stopped and no assault came, so Davenport ventured into the darkness, not knowing who or what he might find. Fortunately, Sergeant Alfred Mart[46] was waiting, instead of an enemy-held trench, having coolly held his platoon in position despite the urgent withdrawal half an hour earlier.

CSM Sharpe soon returned with the rest of the company and they learned that the Dorsets to the south, with A Company in support, had assaulted German positions to try to recover the lost machine guns and the Dorsets' wounded Lieutenant Colonel Bols. Although they achieved neither, the colonel managed to get away himself in spite of his wounds.

Later that evening C Company was moved in to relieve the nervous and now highly embarrassed men from D Company, but no rest was to be had by any of the men on either side. A noisy night followed, as rifle fire would suddenly erupt in the dark, rise in a deafening crescendo, then die down again after ten minutes or so. As a result of the Dorsets and A Company's raid, both sides now 'had the wind up' and were imagining new attacks coming at them in the darkness.

After their dawn 'stand to' on 15 October, the companies swapped positions again. Second Lieutenant Edwin Edwards was moving between trenches to check his men's positions when a sniper in Givenchy caught him, the bullet passing through his neck. Bandsman and stretcher-bearer Albert Hodgson[47] grabbed his stretcher and rushed out into the open to retrieve the wounded officer but was hit before reaching him. In the end the Medical Officer, Captain Patrick Hanafin, reached them and managed to get them both back to the trenches. Bandsman Hodgson died that night but the severely wounded 19-year-old Lieutenant Edwards was moved back to be treated in Fishmongers Hall Hospital near London Bridge, finally succumbing to his wounds on New Year's Eve.

Although 15 October was filled with sporadic shelling and sniping, the day's main assaults were unfolding elsewhere on the battlefield. The French were attacking Vermelles to the south as the British assaulted further north, and the 5th Division remained in position as ordered, waiting for the decision to move its own lines forward. During the welcomed lull, the Bedfords and their battle-weary colleagues to either side dug their defensive trenches deep and news reached them that afternoon that Givenchy had been evacuated.

The Norfolks were on the left of the Bedfordshires and overnight the depleted ranks of the Dorsets to the south were replaced by the Devons, whose two other companies had joined them, thus strengthening the brigade's lines again. At around 4 a.m. on Friday the 16th, the Norfolks unleashed a huge volley into the thick fog after an outpost saw an imagined attack and brought the entire line to a premature 'stand to'. Hours later, everyone relaxed and stood down, so the daily routines began once again until the brigade advanced later that day.

Lieutenant Leonard Rendell took a patrol forward through the cloying mist that morning to scout the rubble that had once been a village. No bodies of troops could be found but they cleared several snipers out, one of whom mortally wounded the officer. He was carried back to head-quarters and managed to report that the village was practically clear before dying of his wounds, being mentioned in despatches for his bravery and leadership. Having reported the information to brigade, orders came at midday that the Bedfordshires were to reclaim Givenchy. It was not until 4.30 p.m. that A and D Companies moved forward, with B in support and C in reserve, the idea being to secure the village before nightfall, thus avoiding enduring another full day of shelling. The small rearguard left behind by the Germans was quickly overcome with few casualties and the village was back in British hands.

Not fully grasping the situation, many of the inhabitants rushed back to the remains with the intention of trying to move back in. In the end, they had to be contented with gathering any valuables that were left behind by the Germans, before being hurriedly ushered out by the Englishmen who had taken up residence among the rubble.

Private Herbert Brazier,[48] one of the few original D Company men left, was among the soldiers who helplessly witnessed the inhabitants' plight, moving him enough to write home about it: 'It is awful to see the poor homeless people, especially the little children; they have nowhere to go because the Germans burn every village or town they come across. It is quite a common sight to see bedding or clothing from the poor people's houses in the German trenches.'[49]

To the north, the Norfolks moved up to a new line along the Rue d'Ouvert, and in the south the Devons pushed forward to the footbridge that led across the canal but were forced back towards Canteleux by an intense defensive action when they tried to close in on it.

While settling back into the village, the Bedfords also found and recovered many of their wounded comrades who had been lost during the retirement a few days earlier. Some were dead but many had been given basic first aid and left by the retiring Germans as they vacated Givenchy. In the same letter home, Private Brazier remarked: 'The Germans were very kind to the wounded; they dressed their wounds and gave them wine to drink. We had to leave these behind because they were down in the cellars in people's houses.'

Bob Pigg supported his opinion, writing: 'In the village we found many of our dead and wounded and here I should like to say that there are good Germans as well as bad. They had laid our killed out reverently side by side, covering them over with white sheets. … He [one of the wounded] told us the German officers made their men go and milk the cows for milk for our wounded men.'

Second Lieutenant Villiers Downes was among the wounded found in the village, but having been moved back to the No. 1 Clearing Hospital in St Omer, he died from his wounds on 18 October. He was the last to be killed of the trio of friends who had played together at the Bedford Football Club, all three having fallen within a matter of days of one another. Within a month his younger brother, Archer Downes, was also killed while helping a wounded man, leaving their parents in Aspley Guise with no surviving sons.

Around dusk, news arrived that the Devons were planning a night attack to take the village of La Bassée further to the east. A and D Companies were allocated to advance on their flank in support, with B Company acting as the Devons' support. Lieutenant Davenport led the advanced guard as the Bedfordshires moved out in the pitch black night. He quite literally bumped into the Devons on the way to the jumping-off lines and learned that a mixture of zero visibility and lack of reconnaissance had led to the attack being called off. By this time, the two battalions were hopelessly mixed up, but after some time were re-organised and returned to their own positions around 9 p.m.

The morning of 17 October was spent improving their positions around Givenchy and trenches were dug close to the piles of rubble, so they could be moved into once the shelling started again. The advance was renewed in the afternoon, as the French again attacked positions further south. The Cheshires took Violaines and extended their line north to meet the 14th Brigade, and the Norfolks made it into Canteleux. To the south of the Bedfordshires, the Devons, although advancing to the bridge once more, were forced back by enfilade fire from south of the canal, as the French could not clear German positions there. In between the Norfolks and Devons, the Bedfords advanced their outposts towards the northern fringes of La Bassée but could not go further until the Devons were able to advance along the canal again. Most of the battalion was kept in and around Givenchy, acting as support if required. Shelling also played a large part in their occupation of what remained of the village, with falling masonry claiming more casualties than direct fire. Sergeant Leonard Godfrey's birthday became a day he would remember as he explained in a letter home:

It was at La Bassée that we had been fighting in our trenches for about 12 days without a stop and with the rain and shells it was not very pleasant. All the time we had been drawing our rations of tea, sugar, bacon, etc., but we had a very hard job to get anything cooked. To try to do this, small parties cooked for the lot of us in the trenches.

Behind our trenches was a nice little house (minus the roof) where five of us went one morning to 'drum up'. We were getting on first rate when suddenly one of the German's best 'coal boxes' hit our cottage. The result was that all the lot came down in a cloud of dust on the top of us, but what became of my comrades I hardly know. One of them was a Baldock chap named Ginger Denton. I think they must have had a nasty smack. I think I was the lucky one to crawl out as I did, with a piece of shrapnel through my left knee and another bit in my right shoulder blade and with other minor scratches from brickbats.

Sergeant Godfrey would later mount the piece of shell fragment that went into his knee on his watch chain to remind him of what he called 'a novel birthday gift from the Kaiser'. After some months, he recovered from his wounds and returned to his battalion in the summer of 1915. Leonard was promoted to Quartermaster Sergeant in September 1915 and commissioned into the 10th Royal Welsh Fusiliers in April 1916 as their Scouting Officer. Having survived numerous intensive battles in the thick of the fighting, his luck was to run out on the Somme. Len was killed there on 20 July 1916 and although buried in Delville Wood where he fell, is now remembered on the Thiepval Memorial to the missing. Writing to his next of kin after his death, Second Lieutenant Godfrey's CO remarked that 'he was quite fearless'.

Sunday 18 October passed in the same dispositions, mainly due to the French army's continued assaults against the formidable Railway Triangle to the south of the canal. As long as it was still in German hands, the Devons were cruelly exposed to enfilading machine-gun fire, in turn holding the Bedfords up from advancing further. There was nothing more to be done than dig in east of Givenchy and wait for events elsewhere to unfold.

Private Arthur Basham, the source of so much humour during the battalion's final peacetime parade, was among those waiting for orders. Writing home to his parents in a style almost literary, he remarked:

Still in the land of the living and a little war wearied for after a week of horrible and heavy fighting we fellows all feel the necessity to get away from the boom of the guns and the crack of the rifles. In the midst of a shell shattered village with pigs, cows and a dog or two all wandering disconsolately about streets heaped with the debris of cottage homes, here and there houses afire, we are sitting on the edge of bomb proof trenches. All the company's officers are either dead or wounded. If there is a man in England skulking to preserve himself a few years of life, let him imagine us burying our dead and setting our teeth as we face Maxim fire galore, rifles innumerable and shells by the hundred. And we still stick on unrelieved.[50]

The 29-year-old Sergeant Robert Burnage from Shefford,[51] a veteran of over ten years in the regiment, also took the opportunity to write home to his parents during the reprieve, his thoughts happy to stray on to matters more pressing than the constant fighting: 'I suppose you have read a lot about this war. Well, we don't get much time to read the papers and we cannot get them very often … you at home know more about it than we do. I have not had a beer since we arrived here on 15th August.'[52] Sadly, Sergeant Burnage's yearning for a beer would not be satisfied as, within a few weeks, he was killed in action during a lull in the ferocious fighting around Ypres, despite having survived the entire campaign without a scratch.

On the morning of the 19th, an attack was planned for 7 a.m., but was delayed. The 6th Battalion of the 295th Regiment from the French army eventually charged the footbridge from the northern side of the canal around midday. No support could be given to the men, due to the angle they chose to advance towards the bridge, and they lost heavily despite a courageous attempt. That afternoon Generals Morland and Franklin visited the 15th Brigade commander, Count Gleichen, to see why his brigade had not taken La Bassée. Although events were happening on either side, the section in the centre simply had nothing to attack. La Bassée was still almost 2km away and the German gunners to the south had a clear line of sight across every inch of the ground they would have to advance over. After the situation was explained, orders came simply to dig in but, late that day, the Cheshires advanced a further 500m at the northern end of the brigade line. They, along with elements from the brigade to their north, had almost got back into Violaines but were held up by a sugar factory that housed multiple German machine guns. Their advance overstretched them badly so B Company from the Bedfordshires was moved to support them around Violaines at 7 p.m.

That day, following a failed French attack further north, the remnants of the 2nd Royal Irish Regiment became surrounded. After a determined stand, around 300 men, mostly wounded, had to surrender at Le Pilly on Aubers Ridge, forcing the handful of survivors from the battalion to be withdrawn from the line so that yet another British battalion could be rebuilt.

Overnight the brigade line ran from the canal to Violaines, passing through Canteleux to the east of Givenchy. Other than B Company at Violaines, the rest of the Bedfords were effectively in brigade reserve, where they remained over the 20th and 21st.

The men found that despite choosing their routes around the village carefully they were still being picked off by accurate German artillery fire. It took several days to understand why, as Private Brazier described: 'The Germans are very cunning; we caught a number of them in civilian clothes in a village behind our positions with a telephone laid on to communicate with the German positions and every time we moved, we were fired at by shrapnel. We have a fine lot of lads in the regiment and when they hear the shells coming, they start to sing.'

Up to now, the badly battle-worn 5th Division had fought at Mons, withstood the brunt of the Le Cateau fighting, had been heavily involved in the Marne and Aisne battles, and had been pushed to their limits around La Bassée. Now began the next phase, as the Germans launched their massive series of assaults between Arras and the North Sea. There had been no opportunity for a rest since arriving in the area, and the next week was to push the division even further as several fresh German corps were arriving in the area and ready to make their lives even more strenuous.

At 8.30 a.m. on 20 October, B Company were still in Violaines with the Cheshires. The village started buzzing with bullets and shells, one shell killing the 20-year-old Private Ernest Taylor[53] as he waited in the church with his platoon. They moved forward to the eastern edges of the village to wait for an assault, but by 11 a.m. the firing stopped and shelling continued intermittently during the afternoon.

A sleepless night in Violaines was followed by a German dawn assault against the village on the 21st, which was repulsed with heavy losses. Although their day was quiet, at 7 p.m. the Germans tried a night attack, striking a section of the Norfolks' lines too. The company was split into sections and formed guards across every road in the village as the situation was unclear and any more surprises would have caused serious problems. Around midnight information came that the brigade to the north had been pushed back, leaving Violaines as a salient in the lines. Given their condition, lack of officers and shrinking numbers, it became apparent that the garrison holding the village would need to retire the following day, so the Cheshires and Bedfordshires set up for a hard day's defence.

At 4 a.m. on the 22nd, the company moved out quietly, to dig a defensive supporting position north of the village, south of a hamlet called Rue du Marais. Lieutenants Litchfield and Coventry took a platoon each and worked on separate sections of the trench, the other two platoons being held around the barn on the fringe of the group of houses. In a thick mist and with visibility at a mere 20m, some 600 Cheshires and Bedfordshires were digging trenches in readiness for the anticipated assault. Unexpectedly, at 6 a.m. a huge group of German infantry burst from the fog and charged the digging men, having swept through the village with hardly a shot being fired. They attacked from two sides and their impetus and sheer force of numbers carried the position. The British had no time to drop their spades and pick up rifles, so fought with their shovels, pickaxes and fists in a brutal hand-to-hand brawl. Some 200 of the 600 men became casualties and the line was thrown back towards Rue du Marais, where it held.

Initially, the line around Rue du Marais was a jumbled collection of Cheshires and Bedfordshires, Royal Engineers and artillerymen, with elements from a few other unexpected units thrown in for good measure. Establishing a firmer line of resistance was their first priority, with folding into their line the stragglers who appeared coming a close second. Around forty of the company could be found, although more turned up as the day went on. However, Lieutenant William St John Coventry, who would be mentioned in despatches in January 1915, and Second Lieutenant John Litchfield had both been killed leading their platoons during the vicious brawl and almost fifty more were killed or reported missing.

Around 8.30 a.m. the rest of the Bedfordshires were ordered to move to the east of Violaines, but made slow headway as the German artillery-men were saturating the reserve areas to stop any supporting troops moving up.

Several attempts to retake the village were made by the remnants of the Violaines garrison, reinforced with units from the 13th and 14th Brigades. At every attempt, they met with heavy rifle fire and the idea was soon given up, the last attacking men being forced to lie flat in front of the village for hours until they could creep back to their own lines. Among the final assault was Colour Sergeant Major Charles Hall and what remained of his platoon, who were forced to dig in hurriedly under heavy fire. During the exchange, CSM Hall was hit in the arm by a bullet, which physically spun him round and rendered him incapable of wielding his rifle as well as giving him a ticket to a Newcastle hospital for a break from the fighting.

When the Manchesters and Worcesters relieved the remnants of the Cheshires and B Company that afternoon, Lieutenant Davenport took his exhausted men back to their battalion, arriving around 7 p.m. The rest of the battalion had spent their spell in reserve enjoying a relatively quiet time, so orders arrived to take them back into the front line, despite B Company's condition. By midnight the Bedfordshires were moving again and established a new line in the open fields around 1,500m east of Festubert, a job which kept them busy all night and throughout 23 October. Although an attack was expected, there were a few false alarms during the day but nothing developed to their front. That period also saw the battalions so mixed up that none of the brigades were in their original format, with the 15th Brigade's commander, Count Gleichen, even having a battalion of French infantry temporarily under his command.

The next few days were difficult as no divisional or brigade level reserves were left to support any section of the British line, so orders were issued to hold at all costs. The Bedfords had a long line to hold and not enough troops, so no battalion reserves could be kept back ready to move into a hard-pressed section, or to counter-attack with if required. The Germans dug several saps from their own trenches towards the British lines, many ending a matter of 15m from their main defensive positions. The threat of attack, the lack of sleep and the men being kept on a constant state of alert started to tell by the 25th.

The 'dirty tricks' did not stop either, with groups of Germans holding their hands up to surrender before falling to the floor and their comrades behind firing on whoever came out to accept their submission. However, with their tolerance for that behaviour wearing thin, on the 25th C Company caught a German patrol, their badly wounded officer being the only survivor.

Second Lieutenant St John Alan Charlton, who had been with the battalion a matter of days, was wounded in the front line that day. On the way to the dressing station, his cart took a direct hit from a shell and he was killed instantly. Around 9 p.m. Captain Frederick Horace Gale arrived with around ninety reservists, having been in France for five weeks beforehand, gathering the trickle of regimental reserves as they made their way to France.

On 26 October, the dawn chorus was accompanied by the shriek of German shells. Lieutenant Walter Walker was moving between trenches to check on his men's positions when shrapnel caught him in the stomach and he was moved back to the casualty clearing station at Gorre, where he died on the 30th.

Further north that day, a massed German formation stormed and took Neuve Chapelle and pierced the centre of the 7th Brigade's lines. The West Kents to the south of the village immortalised themselves that day as they withstood shelling, atrocious weather and constant attacks from several sides, yet would not flinch or retire. When they were finally relieved, just 2 officers and less than 200 men remained.

That evening saw some relief from the difficult conditions when the Lahore Division moved in to replace the 5th Division. The 1st Manchesters, who took over from the Bedfords, were freshly in from India, looked out of place with their suntans and did not fully grasp the situation. A mixture of confidence and not believing how close the Germans were led to them chatting merrily as they went into the trenches, causing arguments as the Bedfords told them to keep quiet! Relief was completed around 10.30 p.m. and by 1 a.m. the Bedfords had moved to around 3km behind the front lines, into barns in a village called Rue de

Bethune, along the Bethune to Festubert road. They were held in brigade reserve in case of an attack, but were ordered to retire further west around 5 a.m., ending up in Gorre. A welcomed day away from the front lines saw them clean up, replace lost kit, send and receive letters home and generally relax a little. However, orders took B and D Companies back to the Rue de Bethune again at 5 p.m., in support of the 15th Brigade and A and C Companies under Major Walter Allason were moved to support the 14th Brigade further north.

Major Allason's detachment was to counter-attack Neuve Chapelle after the 3rd Division had been prised from the village. On the way he collected stragglers from various regiments but the attack was postponed on their arrival. The British assault on the 28th almost retook Neuve Chapelle but was unable to hold on long enough before German counter-attacks drove them back to their jumping-off positions.

During the retirement from Neuve Chapelle, a garrisoned house on the road junction south of the village was causing British troops considerable trouble. Seeing this, one platoon of Bedfords surrounded the house and engaged the occupants in a ferocious firefight while Corporal Joseph Goodman of Rickmansworth[54] and Private William Medlock from Great Gransden[55] advanced under heavy fire and assaulted the position. Despite housing around fifty Germans, the two men set fire to it, forcing the garrison to vacate the position. Both men were awarded the Distinguished Conduct Medal for their gallantry.

Further south B and D Companies were stood down at 5 a.m. on the 28th and returned to Gorre, where they spent another welcomed day in reserve, preparing themselves for their next spell in the line. That day also saw them supplying the Royal Engineers with working parties of 100 men to dig second-line trenches in front of Gorre, the parties being rotated after around two hours. Although three men from D Company were wounded when a rifle went off during an inspection and the bullet 'bounced around' the room, they were spared any attention from German artillery.

Second Lieutenant Alfred Garrod arrived from the 3rd Leicesters on the evening of the 28th and was posted to D Company.

After another quiet night in Gorre and an uneventful 'stand to' the following morning, the battalion received orders to move back to Rue de Bethune at 10.30 a.m. and, on arrival, heard a tremendous fight going on to the east. It transpired that the 2nd Manchesters, who had also just arrived and were attached to the 14th Brigade, were being hard pressed and just after midday the Bedfordshires were ordered to move in and support them.

They advanced in open artillery formation as the ground was being peppered with a mixture of stray bullets from the fighting to the east and German artillery fire intended to suppress any movement behind the front lines. Passing through Festubert, the Bedfords continued moving east until they met the Manchesters' transport section, who warned them of a dangerous junction ahead. Finding a way past the danger zone using ditches, the battalion hurried further east, towards the sound of the guns.

Finally, at 4.30 p.m. they reached the 2nd Manchesters. On arriving, they heard a loud cheering from the front, which turned out to be a small group retaking a lost trench. Second Lieutenant James Leach, Sergeant John Hogan and their small band of Manchesters launched a bayonet charge against the German occupants, killing or capturing the entire section. Leach and Hogan both won the Victoria Cross in the process.

The Bedfordshires moved into the Manchesters' trenches alongside them and D Company took possession of the trench that had just been so bloodily retaken, along with all its former inhabitants, making clearing the trench a priority. The bodies were used to rebuild the parapet but the entire section was described as being 'a beastly place'. Around midnight the 8th Gurkhas from the newly arrived Meerut division came to relieve the Bedfordshires, making as much noise as the Manchesters had on their arrival. In an unexpected twist, the trenches turned out to be too deep for them so they had to set about building fire steps to allow them to see over the parapet. This, coupled with the continuing and vigorous attacks against them, would lead to the Bedfordshires being called back within hours.

Despite the shells and bullets flying from the German lines in response to the noise created by the Gurkhas, the Bedfords vacated the line and moved back to the Rue de Bethune. After standing to at dawn on 30 October, they spent five hours organising themselves and were warned to move several times, all of which came to nothing. However, at 10.30 a.m. orders came to advance urgently.

Following the failure of two attacks the previous day, the Germans dug saps forward towards the British lines and managed to drive the Gurkhas from their trenches by shellfire. It turned out that the Gurkhas had lost all of their officers to shellfire and no one had realised they were physically too short to see over the trench parapets. As they were without orders, being heavily shelled and unable to repel the assaults with rifle fire, they calmly retired.

The half battalion of Bedfords at Gorre were recalled from their brief spell away from the front lines to retake the Gurkha trenches and did so late that day with a bayonet charge. The Devons, who were to the south of the road leading out of Festubert, also had their own problems. Thick, cloying mud had clogged up their rifles and those who could still fire could only reload painfully slowly, which was only just enough to keep the German troops at bay. At around 5 p.m., Lieutenant Davenport took half of B Company to support the Devons while they cleared their rifles, with the rest of the battalion attacking positions north of the road. Along with remnants from a further four battalions, the thrown-together unit advanced with Lieutenant Colonel Griffith at their head, but had trouble identifying the line of trenches in question in the growing darkness. German troops calling out 'We are Gurkhas' further added to the confusion, but a line was taken up that evening, with very few casualties.

Captain Frederick Gale, who had only been on the front lines for a few days, was wounded leading half of B Company as they attacked the former Gurkha trenches north of the road. He approached two Gurkhas, not knowing they were German troops dressed in Indian uniforms as their backs were to him. They turned and wounded him badly in the left arm before running back to their own lines, a story that was repeated many times along the section of the lines that evening.

Sergeant Allen Cooper[56] had already had a busy war. Landing in France with the battalion in August as a private, his courage had by this time been noted both by the men in his platoon and the officers around him on several previous occasions. He was also wounded while carrying a message across the fire-swept battlefield during the fighting, having already led his section towards the Manchesters' trenches, arriving just after the actions that led to the Victoria Crosses had finished. Despite being wounded then, and again the following day, he continued tirelessly organising the defence and would be awarded the DCM for his gallantry and leadership, with promotion to a commissioned officer following. Other than their leader, only a handful of Bedfordshires were wounded during the attack itself, although a difficult night saw the casualty levels rise.

The front line was in a dreadful condition, with shallow trenches being threatened by German saps all along the front, some less than 20m away. Sporadic salvos of stick grenades sailed over the parapets throughout the night, although most were either caught and thrown back, or failed to explode. No one was allowed to rest even for a moment given the precarious nature of their lines and intelligence that warned of superior German forces facing them.

It was about this time that A and C Companies under Major Allason were rushed north to Ypres where reinforcements were desperately required, and Captain Francis Edwards rejoined them, bringing 113 men in a badly needed reinforcement draft. The First Battle of Ypres was now in full flow further to the north, which would see both of the Bedfordshire Regiment's battalions who were on the Western Front at that time heavily engaged.

As dawn broke on the 31st, it became clear that the Germans had moved their saps forward all along the line and a lethal mixture of snipers and occasional shells ensured none of the British or Commonwealth troops could put their heads over the parapet for more than the tiniest of moments. Corporal Jeffrey Tearle[57] was one of those who bravely tried to catch a sniper, only to be killed instantly with a shot through the head as soon as he peered over the edge of the trench.

The telltale sounds of mining could also be heard beneath them, increasing the worries of the defenders even further. They were pinned below the ground and unable to move, effectively making them surrounded, as there was simply nowhere to go. However, as darkness fell the 107th Dogras crawled forward and took over from the half company from south of the road, much to their relief. Although the vacating troops warned of a mine being built, the Indian troops were not convinced – until it went off the next morning, taking hundreds of their number with it.

The half battalion around Festubert spent the next few days moving between the front lines and Gorre in reserve, fetching and carrying when they were away from the fire-swept trenches east of Festubert. The Indian Corps had taken the place of the now exhausted II Corps and the heavier German artillery had moved north to Ypres, bringing a close to the Battle of La Bassée. Although no significant attacks developed in the Festubert sector for the remainder of their time there, B and D Companies continued losing men to sniper and shellfire, until orders came to move off at 5 p.m. on 5 November.

By the end of the Battle of La Bassée, the structure of the original British Expeditionary Force has ceased to exist. As well as the high casualty rates suffered, divisions, brigades and battalions had been fragmented and separated as the circumstances demanded. British casualties had risen to around 60,000 since the war had started, of which II Corps had lost a staggering 14,000 men during October alone. However, the survivors had little time for rest or reflection as they were marched north towards a little-known Belgian city.

Chapter 6

The Battles of Ypres, 1914
First Battle of Ypres 30 October – 22 November 1914

'If anyone speaks to me about the "Glory of War"
when I get home I shall be damned rude to them.'

Early in October 1914 the British 7th Division, including the 2nd Bedfordshires, had landed at Zeebrugge and moved south to join the British Expeditionary Force. Within two weeks they were heavily engaged, having run into a large German force that was trying to find the open flank of the Allied armies. The final battle of 1914 started east of the ancient city of Ypres, a place that would be the scene of a stubborn defence by British and Commonwealth troops for the next four years.

On 30 October A and C Companies under Major Allason had moved north by a series of marches recorded in a personal diary kept by Corporal William Newbound.[58] Overnight rests on the 30th in a mill at Calonne sur-le-Lys and at a farm near Pradelle the following night took the half battalion to billets in a farm north-east of Bailleul by the evening of 1 November. On the 2nd the two companies were called out to support a cavalry attack near Wulvergem, where they remained overnight, the next day being spent under artillery fire sheltering in a house in Wulvergem itself. A day's rest followed on the 4th, but orders arrived to take them into the line east of Ypres at 6.30 a.m. on the 5th. By 7 p.m. C Company were in the firing line and A Company were in dugouts in support, neither knowing where the rest of the battalion was.

By the time B and D Companies under Lieutenant Colonel Griffith started moving away from the Festubert area to join their comrades, British units had been trickling north for some time to support the hard-pressed troops who were holding off a series of massive assaults around

Ypres. The arrival of the Indian Corps to the Bethune front released more troops and now it was the turn of the remaining Bedfordshires to head away from the mud around Givenchy and Festubert.

A 4km march north-west got them to Locon, where they rested for a few hours, and at 6 a.m. on 6 November, the two companies marched to the town square, ready for the next leg of their journey. They were greeted by the welcomed sight of a fleet of London buses, complete with their own London drivers; 500 of them had volunteered to go to France two days earlier to help ferry the troops around and, despite being painted grey, the London signs and advertising could still be seen underneath the neutral paint.

Although the men had no clue where they were going, many could guess once they had worked out they were heading north. The huge convoy moved slowly along the badly worn roads, passing through Lestrem, Le Douilieu, Bailleul, Loker and Dikkebus.

On the road between Bailleul and Loker, the half battalion of men were surprised to see familiar faces resting by the side of the road and stopped to explore. To their amazement the small group were the remnants of the 2nd Bedfordshires; many of the 1st Bedfordshires' men did not even realise they had landed in France. This was a historic meeting, as the last time the two battalions had been together was in Ireland in 1870. The 2nd Bedfordshires had arrived bronzed from South Africa exactly a month earlier, over 1,100 strong. Now they presented a dreadful sight as they rested, filthy and exhausted, having been through the early phase of the First Battle of Ypres in the 7th Division. The division had earned itself the nickname the 'Immortal Seventh'. Just Captain Charles Foss, Transport Officer Lieutenant Stephen Mills, a handful of NCOs and around 200 men remained. After a brief ex-change of greetings and stories of their battles, as well as the fate of shared acquaintances, the 1st Bedfordshires were ushered further north, their destination now becoming clearer.

The convoy stopped just west of Ypres and the men were moved to a field and told to lie down as German artillery had the entire sector well mapped. The move to Ypres had taken them almost 50km north and they rested for a few hours, around 600m west of the city centre, as the heavy-calibre German shells pounded away incessantly at the city that was being reduced to piles of rubble.

At 5 p.m. the half battalion moved off, apparently headed for what was left of the 1st Division, now in positions somewhere east of the city.

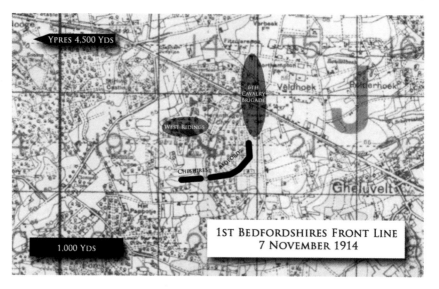

Passing the intact cathedral and Cloth Hall, the men managed to free themselves of the packed streets and left the city along the eastbound Menen (Menin) Road, headed for Hooge. A short rest in Hooge followed before moving on towards Geluveld (Gheluvelt), but just before the village they left the road and headed south, into the pitch black Klein Zillebeke wood.

The battalion halted in the foul-smelling, battle-littered forest around midnight, not knowing where they were, where the Germans were, or with any firm orders. The men had arrived in the West Ridings section of the line, and were given instructions not to smoke or light any fires of any kind, which was their only real clue as to how close to the front they were. Unsettling news of the French retiring to the south, battalions surrendering to the north and the British lines being only very thinly held greeted them, making their arrival even more uncomfortable.

Soon after, the men realised that the other two companies under Major Allason were to their front, having arrived earlier in the day. It transpired that they had relieved the 2nd Bedfordshires' positions and, on closer inspection, they further became aware they were among many of the graves of their regimental brothers who had held the ground at such a high price. Completely disoriented, the battalion settled down to a short night's rest.

As dawn broke on Saturday 7 November, the mist in the wood was thick and damp, muffling most of the sounds around them. Attempts to familiarise themselves with the area proved futile as no visibility, and lack of information concerning the dispositions of the units around them, made their efforts complete guesswork. Overnight they had understood that not only were their trenches far too shallow but that the water table was so high in the wood that any attempts to deepen them made the trenches uninhabitable.

By this time, the 15th Brigade was temporarily made up from around 1,100 men of the 1st Bedfordshires, 550 from the 1st Cheshires and over 700 from the West Ridings, who were attached from another brigade but would be rushed to a different part of the line that afternoon. As they got their bearings and information started trickling in, it turned out that the 15th Brigade had taken up positions on the eastern edge of the wood with the Cheshires to the south, the Bedfords to the north and the West Ridings in support. The 6th Cavalry Brigade were north of the Bedfords and the 7th Infantry Brigade linked up to the southern flank of the Cheshires.

The fog cleared in the late morning but the men had to lie low once it had, as bullets and shells started peppering their positions. All men who could be spared were set to digging a track through the wood, but as shelling increased steadily it became clear that another German attack was unfolding somewhere out of sight of the battalion.

About 3.30 p.m. the woods became alive with whipping bullets coming from the rear of the left flank of the battalion. Officers from several battalions tried to establish what was happening without success as the situation was confused. Groups of Germans could be seen within 15m of the Bedfords' positions but it was unclear whether they were armed or prisoners, so the men were unsure whether to engage them. News reached the front-line companies that the Germans had broken through the Northumberland Fusiliers about 200m to the left of the battalion line and were swarming through the wood. The left flank of the Bedford-shires also retired, having heard orders shouted from somewhere to their right, probably from a German officer in hindsight. Many of the men were half asleep, feeding or part dressed, but retired slowly and delib-erately, to the mixed horror and amusement of the brigade commander who looked on from his position further back. Lieutenant Walter Graves from Sandy was killed in the confusion, being shot while his platoon calmly retired. Lieutenant Graves had only arrived with the battalion a few weeks earlier and despite being just 29 years old, he had already served for many years in the regiment's militia, as well as having been a member of Cardiff City Council.

The West Ridings had hurriedly left the brigade, leaving just the 1,600 men of the Bedfordshires and Cheshires. With no support or reserves available it was down to them to regain control of the situation, so Captain Monteith's company fixed bayonets and eagerly moved to the left flank to retake the lost trenches.

After advancing back through the woods a loud cheer could be heard as the counter-attacking Bedfords made their final advance. A manic bayonet charge through the trees saw over twenty German prisoners taken and the trenches regained, but so few Bedfords survived that their resulting defensive line was too short to get in touch with the 5th Royal Fusiliers, who were expected to be on their left somewhere. It turned out that the Germans had taken the Fusiliers' positions too and broken through towards the Herentage Chateau. Lieutenant Davenport gathered a selection of fifty men from various units together and another counter-attack was launched immediately, which saw the Germans driven back and further advances stemmed. Quartermaster Sergeant Thomas Byford[59] and Private William Falla[60] both won the DCM for their bravery in the counter-attack. QMS Byford from Leighton Buzzard later became CQMS and survived the war, but Private Falla from Ipswich, who rose to the rank of sergeant, was killed at Oppy Wood in June 1917.

Bob Pigg of Royston found himself mixed up in the charge. He reported:

It was terrible work there; 120 of our chaps were killed in 20 minutes and I cannot tell you how many were wounded. Captain Monteith was wounded and when he fell Comp. Qr. Master Sergeant Bidford [sic] said 'Come on boys, over the top.' I cannot tell you how I felt but over we went and drove the Germans from their trenches. … Our Comp. Qr. Master Sergeant, who led us after Capt. Monteith was wounded, got the D.C.M. and it was presented to him by the King in France.

Arthur Chandler of Spaldwick was also present in the hand-to-hand brawl, writing:

The Colonel said 'we will charge them' and our boys gave a 'view hollos' like fox hunting and we went for them. One of our fellows was scrapping a German officer with his fists but he soon had him bottled up and another of ours got round the back of the German trenches and took six prisoners. One other said 'I'm going to have a German', so he went to a trench and found four Germans in it, he killed two, wounded one and took the other prisoner. When he brought him back, he said 'I have got a whole German this time, he has not got a bullet in him anywhere.'[61]

Of the fallen from the assault was special reservist and Lloyd's of London employee Lieutenant Robert Harding. Captain Monteith, himself wounded in the fighting that day, described Harding as falling as they advanced up a lightly wooded slope in a letter to his next of kin.[62] He added, 'I did not see him fall but missed him when we got to the ridge and on going back found him quite dead.'

Lieutenant Davenport was badly wounded in the left arm leading the final counter-attack and as he crawled back to find a doctor, paused to rest. From his vantage point he described the scene in the wood as being filled with groups of men engaged in their own bayonet duels, adding that 'Frenchmen were in some places hanging out of the chateaux cheering and the whole scene was indescribable.' Once back at Herentage Chateau his wound was crudely dressed, and Major Allason arrived, slightly wounded in his shoulder. After insisting on returning to the battalion he was wounded almost immediately in the thigh, but Davenport explained that 'even then he wanted to go on and find out how things were going on the left but was, I believe, forcibly restrained'. Davenport, Allason and Macready were to meet later that evening in a horse ambulance behind Herentage Chateau, with Macready suffering from a bad stomach wound. All three would also be decorated for gallantry shown during the fighting, with Allason and Macready winning the Distinguished Service Order and Davenport a Military Cross.

Company Sergeant Major William Sharpe was mentioned in despatches and also won a Military Cross during the dogged defence, being wounded in the process. He would recover and become a second lieutenant in the 2nd Bedfordshires the following May, later serving in the 4th Bedfordshires and as an acting captain while employed as a brigade musketry instructor.

A Company under Captain John Milling made three bayonet charges in all that afternoon and retook three of the lost Northumberland Fusilier trenches, but could not regain part of one of their own or recover two machine guns lost when the section was wiped out. Captain Milling was awarded one of the newly introduced Military Crosses for his leadership and gallantry. During the fighting a strong attack was also launched against the right of the battalion. When a gap in their defensive line was discovered, Company Sergeant Major Ernest Watson[63] and around twenty men charged forward with bayonets and, having cleared the trenches, fired for all they were worth to repel a further assault, thus saving the right flank. CSM Watson was mentioned in the

Commander-in-Chief's despatches of January 1915 and awarded the Distinguished Service Medal for his gallantry and leadership, but after twenty years of service in the regiment, he fell to a sniper's bullet in March 1915 just six days before his 39th birthday.

The battalion lost around 150 officers and men killed or wounded that day, with scores more being lightly wounded but remaining at duty, yet they held their position despite being hard pressed. The already thinned ranks of the Cheshires lost a further 35 killed or wounded. As the brigade was at just one-third strength now, but could not retire as there were simply no reserves left, they strengthened their lines as best they could, fully expecting a further attack to come their way the next day.

With the heavy casualties suffered between the two Bedfordshire battalions at Ypres, the terrible news of the fate of relatives began circulating at home. Losing a son, brother, husband or friend was bad enough, but the Cogan family, who ran the Fox Inn at Albury in Hertfordshire, paid a higher price than many. They had already received news that one of their four sons serving on the front with the Bedfordshire Regiment had been wounded in the fighting at Ypres; Charles, a private in the 2nd Bedfordshires had been shot in the spine. Within days came the shocking news that their sons, Sergeants Alfred Cogan[64], aged 29 and William Cogan[65], aged 33, had both been killed on 7 November, fighting in the 1st Bedfordshires. The country's debt to this family was to be increased yet further when a third son, Phillip, was killed at Neuve Chapelle in the 2nd Bedfordshires the following March. Incredibly, Phillip's wife also lost her brother, Sergeant Thomas Hutchins, the day before her husband, also killed in the 2nd Bedfordshires alongside Phillip. Of the four brothers, just Charles survived, although he was invalided out of the army in June 1916, courtesy of the bullet wound from Ypres that did not properly heal.

Around 250 mounted reinforcements from the 3rd and 5th Divisions arrived in the brigade area at 7 a.m. on 8 November, thus providing a brigade reserve, and the Bedfords spent the day in a heavy, wet mist, improving their lines, recovering their wounded from the wood and burying their dead. Fighting could be heard from the south as the French attacked around Zillebeke but, other than shelling and several fusillades of rifle fire from the jumpy Germans to their front, no infantry assaults came their way.

That day Sergeant Alfred Mart[66] and Corporal Philip Cyster[67] crept to the German lines, to the point where two of their machine guns had been lost the previous day. They found one of the guns, killed the Germans in the position and recovered the gun along with a wounded Bedford, dragging both back to their own lines. Lieutenant Alfred Garrod helped Mart by taking it in turns to keep the Germans' heads down as they slowly retired, and although Sergeant Mart was shot through the neck during the raid, they all returned to their own lines. The brigade commander, Count Gleichen, wanted to propose Mart for a Victoria Cross, but not enough men were present to witness Mart's actions and support the claim, so a DCM was settled for. Alfred Mart was one of five incredible brothers in the regiment, with two of the others winning their own DCMs during the same battle, but in the 2nd Bedfordshires, and the fourth falling in action while earning a mention in despatches from General Haig in 1917.

Although the fighting had died down in their sector for the time being, the deadly games of cat and mouse between the opposing troops continued, and Private Alfred Hall[68] was sent on a hunt with a corporal to flush out a German sniper who was reported as being on a small island in a lake to the south of their perimeter, just east of Dumbarton Wood:

We found a boat and pushed off in it, but the bottom gave way and the boat sank. We hung onto the side of a bridge which we managed to reach and in time, we got into the chateau. After making a thorough search we were unable to find a living soul inside. There were a number of ducks and we shot four of them … we returned to the bridge, thinking what a fine feed the duck would provide when we got back. But we were sadly disappointed for we were forbidden to light a fire … and in the end had to bury the ducks.[69]

Lieutenant Garrod was wounded on 10 November and mentioned in Sir John French's despatches of January 1915. He recovered from his wounds, later returning to active service and becoming a squadron leader in the newly raised Royal Flying Corps. Otherwise, the men spent another day improving their lines throughout intermittent shelling but without having to hold against any form of attack.

The date of 11 November saw the Prussian Guards attack on both flanks but, although they broke the British and French lines for a while, order was restored in the heavy rain that fell late that afternoon. The battalion was warned to expect a large assault and stood in readiness all day but nothing developed along its front. German patrols probed the Bedfords' lines but all were scattered and no infantry assaults followed.

The 12th and 13th were relatively quiet days, yet the battalion had lost a further eighty men to shelling, sniping and skirmishing by the time the morning of the 14th opened and had been moved back a further 150m to conform with the ground lost on either flank over the previous day's fighting.

At 8 a.m. on 14 November the Prussian Guards launched another massive assault on the Allied lines, determined to break them once and for all and push the British into the sea. For the first two hours all the Bedfords could do was crouch in their trenches as a barrage on the scale the men had not experienced before smothered their area. Around midday the infantry assaulted in wave after wave but were shot down by the concentrated aimed fire of the shaken, deafened but resolute Tommies. A massive, hour-long assault was launched at the British all along their lines, and fighting in the wood where the Bedfords were positioned was very confused. Trenches and posts were lost one minute, only to be retaken the next, and the men could see nothing beyond their immediate front due to the nature and layout of the ground around them. After a bitter struggle, the British line folded on both flanks, and the Cheshires and Bedfordshires were ordered to retire around 180m in mid-afternoon.

Private John Feary[70] was among the morning's wounded, being hit by shell fragments around midday. Unable to move, he was covered up, made comfortable and left in relative peace as events unfolded around him. As dusk fell digging noises close by caused him to glance over in their direction, only to find German troops in control of the trench. He wrote home: 'So I began to crawl towards the supports, when I found myself sinking up to my elbows in mud. I got up onto my feet but soon fell down again. Eventually I got to the wood and suddenly I could hear voices far different from Englishman's. So I began to crawl further into the wood. … When I lifted my head I found myself within five yards of the Germans but I lay down flat on my stomach until they were under cover.'[71] After hours of painful crawling and dodging German troops, Private Feary stumbled across his own lines and was stretchered back for treatment, surviving as a result of his determination.

Enfilade fire from a machine gun that had been worked forward onto the Cheshires' flank to the right of the Bedfordshires caused their retirement around 4 p.m. but they were unable to warn the Bedfords, which left their flank badly exposed again. Lieutenant Cyril Pope and ten men in an advanced trench in a hollow on the right flank of the battalion line were surrounded, rushed and captured in the confusion. As dusk fell the battalion received hurried orders to fall back a further 130m where the line was being re-formed and here they held firm against further German attempts to push them back.

Despite their incredible professionalism, the Old Contemptibles had dished out and soaked up so much punishment over extended periods that some individuals started to show signs of reaching the limits of their endurance. Even long-serving veterans struggled with the enormity of their actions, as Private Pigg explained: 'At daybreak we saw the famous Prussian Guard advancing across our front and we had a dust up with them for the first time. The machine gun Sergeant from the 1st Cheshires accounted for no less than 800 of them. When the Sergeant was taken to view his work his nerves gave way and he had to be sent to base.'

The bulk of the fighting that day fell on either flank of the quarter-strength 15th Brigade as battalion after battalion of Prussian Guards were thrown forward and bloodily repulsed. Yet despite this, of the 1,100 Bedfordshires and 550 Cheshires who had marched through the Menin Gate at Ypres on 5 November, just 540 Bedfordshires and 220 Cheshires remained.

Of the battalion's casualties were two brothers, Privates Will and Ted Medlock from Great Gransden,[72] who, by sheer coincidence, lay next to one another in hospital beds in England less than two weeks later. Ted had been through La Bassée but was caught by a German sniper at Ypres, whereas Will had survived every battle his battalion had been engaged in. Will had also assaulted a fortified farmhouse near Neuve Chapelle only weeks earlier and had come through unscathed, but a random Jack Johnson saw to it that he would spend some time away from the front recovering. Not knowing that he would later be awarded the Distinguished Conduct Medal for bravery at Neuve Chapelle, Will wrote in a letter home: 'I myself have seen enough to make the strongest man's nerves break and I am not ashamed to say have made me cry, but they are only everyday occurrences and one gets hardened to anything at the front. … Out of 17 in my section at Mons I was the only one remaining until I got my present which got me home.'[73]

Over the coming days sleet and snowstorms added to the overall discomfort in the trenches as the fighting drew to a close. The woods around the Bedfordshires were nothing more than a shambles of destroyed trees, impassable tangles of wire and debris, littered with mud and water-filled shell holes. Even those who had become familiar with the area still had trouble finding their way around, such was the overall condition of the forest, as Private Alfred Hall illustrated in an interview: 'A comrade and I wandered by accident into the German lines. The Germans opened fire on us, and I began to laugh. My pal said "I don't think it's a laughing matter." This took place in a wood where two lines of trenches had been cut and we lay there from 11 o'clock at night until six next morning. Then we made our minds up to find our own trenches … our comrades had given us up for lost and I can tell you they were very glad to see us both safe and sound.'[74]

Around 15 November the battalion could muster just a few officers so Second Lieutenants Thomas George Skeats and Arthur Digby Dampier joined it. Both men had initially enlisted into the Royal Fusiliers before being commissioned and had served with the 1st Cheshires for almost three weeks before transferring to the Bedfords' depleted officer corps. Thomas Skeates went home with a rupture within a few days of his arrival, but Arthur Dampier found himself made up to temporary captain and in charge of a company. He had already experienced many close shaves, including bullets through his water bottle and cap, a 5in scar across his boot from shrapnel, and a bullet hitting the trench wall 2in from his head. In a letter home on 24 November he remarked that 'everybody, including myself, will be glad when the whole thing is over. If anyone speaks to me about the "Glory of War" when I get home I shall be damned rude to them.'

Further attacks were expected so the brigade remained fully alert but the following days saw only localised, small-scale German actions, all of which were repulsed. Ten more Bedfords were lost between the 15th and 18th despite regular enemy shelling and the half-hearted German assaults. Agreements were made for the French to relieve British troops from around Ypres once it was clear the fighting had died down, and rumours of a relief on the 19th started circulating around the battalion but were dashed when it was learned the French troops could not get to them in time. However, the unexpected and welcomed sight of the Worcesters arriving to take over from the exhausted men at 8.30 p.m. on the 19th brought their intense fortnight of fighting to a close.

Private Bob Pigg wrote of the battle for Ypres: 'The fighting at Ypres was terrible. We had eighteen days in the trenches and I can tell you it put years on me. The first day we got there we had to do a charge, a thing I shall never forget. We lost 332. I saw as many as 12 buried in one grave.'[75]

In addition to the many gallantry medals already awarded to men from the battalion, the following were also mentioned in Sir John

French's despatches of December 1914 and January 1915 for their part in the fighting at La Bassée and Ypres: Sergeant Richard Allsopp from Yardley Hastings,[76] who had served in the regiment since April 1905 until his death at Givenchy on 22 October; Company Sergeant Major Michael McGinn from Co. Donegal,[77] a life-long soldier, whose father was also a sergeant major, who would be killed on the Somme in 1916; and Private Herbert Cattle (Kettle) from Peterborough,[78] who had enlisted into the regiment in 1905 and fought with the battalion from Mons. He survived but was medically discharged and worked at Rolls-Royce in Derby from February 1916.

The British had lost around 55,000 men during October and November but had managed to hold a larger, well-motivated force at bay despite their best efforts. These were to be the last actions to use the pre-war 'fire and movement' tactics, as the fighting settled into trench warfare from this point. By the end of November 1914, many battalions were so weak that careful planning was needed to allow them just to hold the trenches, and British casualties had risen to over 86,000 men in all. Almost 90 per cent of the Old Contemptibles had been killed or wounded in the first three months of the war and, although many would return to the front lines, having recovered, Britain's professional army was now a shadow of its former self.

Chapter 7

A Winter's Lull

November 1914 – April 1915

*'Although they are our deadly enemies we can behave as friends
on Christmas Day.'*

After two weeks in the line without rest and having been subjected to
severe fighting, bitterly cold conditions and waterlogged trenches, the
two battle-worn battalions that comprised the 15th Brigade were relieved
and moved 1km back from the front lines, arriving at reserve positions
around Stirling Castle at midnight on 19 November. Following an uneventful spell in reserve, at 2 a.m. on the 21st the Bedfordshires and
Cheshires marched back through Ypres and Vlamertinge, on to billets in
Loker (Locre), 11km south-west of Ypres.

Describing the condition of his brigade, their brigadier wrote that
'having arrived and their feet having swollen terribly during the long
march, any number of them could not get their boots on again, and they
went to hospital by twenties and thirties, hobbling along the road with
their feet tied up in rags or socks, for they were deformed with rheum-
atism and swollen joints (what would now be known as "trench feet"),
and would not fit any boot'.[79]

Then followed a relatively blissful spell in billets. Although described
as freezing and very limited, the battalion was reorganised and refitted,
with the men enjoying hot baths, warm food, spending time under cover,
being issued with fresh socks, and even parcels and post from home.
Many of the men were the recipients of gifts created by whip-rounds
from people in their local communities, including Private Herbert Hill of
Maulden,[80] known locally as Bert, who was handed a very welcomed
parcel from his local pub, the George, while at rest. The 20-year-old even

went as far as to remark in his letter home that 'I received the fags safely this morning and I shall have enough for a month as my mates had a lot sent too. I had 150 packets come. The trenches are all water and mud. You would laugh if you saw us, but one thing makes it better; we have coke fires on the firing line and those who are not on look out all sit round and spin yarns.'[81]

The breathing space also allowed the survivors to tell those at home they were still alive, creating a glut of letters in the process.

Private William Reed,[82] known as Bill to his mates, wrote home on 23 November while enjoying the rest. Considering what he had experienced, seen and endured, the last line of his letter speaks volumes about the mindset of the British troops on the front: 'The people at home must be thinking of us because we get any amount of fags and other things. We get a change of linen whenever opportunity offers, that is about once a month. So on the whole we are pretty well off.'[83]

The same day, Arthur Chandler from Spaldwick penned another letter to his parents to assure them that 'I am still knocking along alright. … I saw the 2nd Battalion on the 5th and they told me that Percy had got wounded about the end of last month. I was very disappointed at not seeing him. … We have been in the trenches just lately … and at night we had to get our coats over our heads down the bottom of the trench to get a smoke. … My section was 15 strong when we came out, now there are only 3 of the original 15 left.'[84] Percy was Arthur's brother who had arrived from South Africa with the 2nd Bedfordshires the previous month, only to find themselves instantly engaged in the ferocious fighting around Ypres.

During the rest Corporal Frederick Laird of Bedford[85] also wrote to his mother: 'I have been made Corporal for twice going in front of the firing line about 500 yards and fetching wounded men into safety and for digging out Sergeant Box who got buried with a shell at Ypres, under heavy fire, after being slightly wounded myself in the ankle. I have a lot to tell you when I get home which I hope will be soon.'[86] Sadly, Frederick's tales were never to be shared as he was killed two weeks later while the battalion held the lines during a quiet spell, despite having come through every battle since Mons.

Naturally, many letters were being heavily censored before reaching the recipients but it did not stop attempts to beat their ever-attentive gaze, as one of the battalion officers showed. The unnamed man wrote home of his experiences, adding the afterthought that 'If the censor cuts any of this, then he is a deplorable ass!'[87] The officer's parents were amused to read that once the censor had completed his task, he added at the end, 'Oh, he is!'

On the 25th the surviving 220 Cheshires were posted to II Corps' reserve as most of them were suffering from trench foot and, as such, the battalion was incapable of active duties. Thus, just the Bedfordshires remained in the brigade and were moved to new billets 4km south-west in Saint Jans-Cappel. While there, Major John Mackenzie, VC, a former sergeant in the Seaforth Highlanders who had won his Victoria Cross at Ashanti in 1900, Second Lieutenant Cyprian Francis Thurlow Baker and eleven men joined the bedraggled band of survivors.

Sir John French, Commander-in-Chief of the British forces, inspected the single-battalion brigade on the 27th. Brigadier Gleichen wrote of the inspection that 8 officers and 587 men were present, with just Lieutenant and Quartermaster Peirce being the only officer left from those who had sailed from Ireland with them three months earlier. Lieutenant Colonel Griffith and Lieutenant Gledstanes were both on leave and were the only other original officers remaining, all other officers having been killed, wounded or taken ill following their costly introduction to the war.

D Company's Private Bob Pigg of Royston remarked on the inspection in one of his letters home:

Our regiment had the honour of being inspected by General French and he said that those in England that had anyone in the Bedfordshire Regiment out here ought to be proud of them as they have always done what has been asked of them. That is nice to have praise like that and for what we have done for dear old England. If the people at home were to see some of the men praying in the trenches it would do them some good as this is the place to bring one to their senses. We are having a heavy thunder-storm as I write this but the old Bedford Mud-Larks[88] are not for the trenches tonight.[89]

The following day saw the battalion march 10km east, through Dranouter and back to the front lines again. By 8 p.m. they had relieved the Worcesters in the line north-west of Wulvergem, taking up residence in badly dug, incomplete and saturated trenches.

The area they were to spend around three months in had been productive farming country but was now simply a waterlogged quagmire and not a good defensive position to hold. Trenches varied from 5in to 5ft deep, depending on the part of the line, and making fascines or revetments attracted enemy artillery so the men were faced with freezing cold, uncomfortable conditions even without the attention of enemy artillery or snipers. Draining the trenches using buckets and shovels and rebuilding collapsed trenches formed the bulk of the men's day-to-day activities, but no sooner than one section of trench wall was firmed up, another would slide away, heavy with water. Opposite Mesen (Messines) the main trenches were 700m apart due to the low ground between, but in other sections of the line just 50m separated the British and German troops.

Periods in the front line around Wulvergem, support trenches further east, or reserves around Dranouter varied between three and eight days, according to the situation at the time.

Although the men spent the winter alert in case of attack, hindsight showed that the area was generally very quiet, which provided a welcomed break for the battle-worn division.

The battalion's first day in the line, 29 November, saw eight men lost to enemy action and, despite being at half strength, almost 300m more of the front was handed to them the following day. Conditions were far from ideal, with the new section of trench being full of dead French soldiers in badly dug and sited trenches that were just 20m from the German lines in places. A company from another battalion was attached as there were simply not enough Bedfordshires to hold the line, a scene that was being repeated all along the British-held section.

On 2 December Major Benjamin Robert Roche, Captain Charles Augustus Ogden, Lieutenant George Paterson Nunneley, Second Lieutenants Cecil William Bartram, A.H. Stratford, 2 further officers and 190 men arrived as a welcomed reinforcement draft.

For two weeks the men aggressively patrolled, sapped and disrupted the activities of their counterparts on the other side of No Man's Land, losing men daily. A two-day period in support, which saw the arrival of 140 NCOs and men, was unexpectedly cancelled on the 8th when the battalion was moved into the line near Wulvergem, taking over from the 1st Norfolks until relieved, and then sent 10km east into billets in Saint-Jans-Cappel two days later. Here they reorganised, refitted and took what rest they could in divisional reserve but were unable to clean up as orders moved them back to the front again late on the 13th.

While waiting for orders Lance Corporal Allan Brown's[90] thoughts turned inevitably to home and the approaching 1st birthday of his baby son. On the 11th he penned this letter, which doubtless summed up the feelings of numerous soldiers on both sides of No Man's Land:

My Darling Boy George

I now take the pleasure in writing to you and wishing you a happy birthday.

My Dear Son. When you are older and able to read you will be able to realise where your Daddy was when he wrote this letter to you. Well my Dear Boy I am out in France fighting for you and your Dear Mother and our homes and King and Country and when you are going to school you will learn how we fought the Germans. My Dear Boy if anything happens to your Daddy in this war I ask you to look after your Dear Mother and to love her always and to keep her from all harm as your Daddy has always looked after you and Mother and loved you both with a warm heart whilst he was with you. Dear Son I hope you will always be a good boy and grow up to be a man and also to pray and to thank God for his goodness to us as your Daddy trusts in him and thanks the Lord that he will return Daddy safely home to you both.

Now I think you will be able to read this some day and with my fondest love and kisses.

I remain, Your Ever Loving Daddy.

Allan, originally from Scotland, had served as a regular soldier in the regiment from January 1905 and was a postman in Aylesbury before being recalled from the reserves early in August. A signaller, Allan arrived in France with the battalion in August and he had come through the fighting from Mons to Ypres in one piece. His war was far from over and it would be some years before his wife and son saw 'Daddy' return to them. Sadly the war would take its toll on him psychologically too and it would be much longer before Allan's personality could recover from his experiences and enable him to return to them completely.

The date of 14 December was spent being held in readiness in a cold, muddy field near Dranouter as the 3rd Division assaulted Wijtschate (Wytschaete) and the Petit Bois in support of a larger French assault to their north. Although initially planned to roll the assault further south into the 5th Division's lines and beyond, the situation changed and the division was content with purely 'demonstrating'. The following day saw a move for the Bedfordshires into billets at Neuve-Église, Nieuwkerke, which allowed for a two-day rest from the front lines and even included baths for half of the men.

Private Arthur Perry[91] was a Royston Town footballer known locally as 'Kruger' and had served in the battalion transport since 1909. He had been among RQMS William Bartlett's determined, dedicated and ever reliable transport section since the battalion landed in August and had come through a challenging first few months without a scratch. In an open letter to his local paper[92] he showed how the men on the front were not completely preoccupied with survival and trench life when he wrote: 'If someone could send us out a football it would help us to keep the boys' limbs in working order. It is so very cold out here. When we come out of the trenches we want something to get the circulation up.' He got his wish, as Harry Stamford of Royston sent him one by return, and as he would in April 1915, when he was also sent a mouth organ he requested.

Headlined 'A "Jack Johnson" spoils Kruger's dinner', his letters also illustrated how time behind the lines was equally fraught with danger and subject to the ever-present element of chance: 'We are billeted in a school room in Dewar. It is a very hot shop. One day cooks were preparing dinner when a small "Jack Johnson" came and took the whole of our dinners away.'

Between 17 and 29 December the battalion was in the firing line close to Wulvergem, with the Royal West Kents and Dorsets on either side. The routine shelling, sniping, patrolling and raiding resumed, causing casualties daily. For the first two days only half of the battalion could physically fit into its section of the line, the balance being held in support in Neuve-Église. The men's first day saw a company of the recently arrived 1st/6th Cheshires attached to them for instruction in trench duties, and the following day saw an increase in shelling as the assault against Wijtschate (Wytschaete) to their left continued.

In December, Allied intelligence started seeing evidence of considerable movement of German divisions from the Western Front to the Eastern theatre. As a result, offensives were planned almost immediately, the brunt of which would fall on the much larger French armies. The First Battle of Champagne was launched on 20 December and would last until mid-March 1915, with British forces committed to diversionary, localised assaults in their own sector of the front, which now ran from St Eloi to the canal south of Givenchy.

A planned series of assaults all along the British lines were put on hold at the last minute after a strong German counter-attack to the north, and a fog-bound battlefield to the south around Arras made British attempts to advance in the middle potentially disastrous. As a result, orders were altered to encourage demonstrations all along the line and to take any reasonable opportunity available to capture enemy trenches without significant losses.

All along the II Corps frontage advancing was seen to be a high-risk option, given the overall lie of the land and the German defensive lines. In the Bedfordshires' sector of the front, on the 19th a reconnaissance of the German line to their front identified that an assault would bring down a heavy enfilade fire from both the north and south, thus dooming it to heavy casualties. So the following day, in support of the Indian Corps' assault on Givenchy to the south, a heavy bombardment fell on the German lines opposite II Corps instead of an infantry assault. When the German reprisals fell on the Bedfordshires' positions, fortunately their waterlogged trenches were only lightly occupied, leading to just a handful of casualties over the next few days.

From the 22nd until Christmas Eve, the men clung to their frosty, muddy trenches with little happening over and above the usual shelling and sniping. After the arrival of a further sixty-nine reinforcements they were moved slightly further south at 8 p.m. on Christmas Eve.

Any human noise generated while in the front lines invariably attracted hostile artillery fire so once the men had settled into their new positions later that evening, they were surprised at the level of noise emanating from the other side of No Man's Land. In an unexpected turn of events, the next twenty-four hours would see a series of impromptu truces spring up all along the Western Front, including one such event in a section of the battalion lines south of Wulvergem.

William Reed of Royston shared his curious Christmas in the trenches with his relatives in a letter home:

I am very pleased to tell you that we have got over Christmas better than we expected. We went into the trenches on the 23rd and spent 48 hours there. On Christmas Eve the Germans were singing and shouting nearly all night and asking us to go over and have a drink of Laager beer, cocoa, or anything we liked to ask for; but of course no-one went. On Christmas morning they gave us a nice reveille of 18 shells, but no-one got hurt. Then they did not trouble us anymore until mid-day, when they started to shout and ask us to go over. We gained permission from our officer to challenge them to come half way and we got out of our trenches. When they saw us they came to meet us and one or two shook hands. They sang us a carol and then we sang one. After that we all joined up and sang 'Tipperary' and gave three cheers for King and country. We exchanged fags and tobacco and when we returned to our trenches it was agreed not to fire until 12 next day. So you see that although they are our deadly enemies we can behave as friends on Christmas Day. They told us they were not there to fight as they were the Landsturm – what we call our last to call upon – and no doubt they were, for only one young man was amongst them and he was knock kneed and weary. The rest were old men with very long beards and appeared to be about 50 years of age.[93]

Sergeant William Blundell[94] had served in the regiment since 1894 and at 38 years old with twenty years' service in the regulars behind him, was certainly one of the battalion's veterans. In a letter to a Miss Whittington at Bedford barracks, William described how 'on Christmas Day we had a lot of firing over us, and shells too. All at once it ceased and I looked up and saw the Germans on top of their trenches shouting to us and asking us to meet them. All our Brigade went and we were talking to them about two hours. They asked us not to fire that day and they would not; and no firing was done until next day and then we were fighting for all we were worth.'[95]

Although in some sections of the front hostilities continued as usual, semaphore messages from the German lines opposite the Bedfordshires promised not to fire on them that day and the tired soldiers on both sides relaxed a little, enjoying the unofficial day's holiday. Another popular topic in letters home from the time was that all British soldiers on the front lines received a Christmas card from the King and Queen, with Princess Mary sending them all a pipe, tobacco and cigarettes.

With the arrival of dawn on Boxing Day the truce was over. Shelling resumed in both directions and when a party of Germans walked across No Man's Land to continue their friendships from the previous day, warning shots were fired to keep them away. Later that day Wulvergem was shelled, wounding one of the Bedfordshires, but other than a heavy fusillade of rifle fire from the Germans on 28 December, the next few days were relatively quiet despite the resumption of trench warfare.

Nevertheless, the arbitrary nature of life in the front lines continued, as shown in a letter home from Private Fred Ashwell of Letchworth:[96] 'One day a mate was jumping on his bag of sand to get it into the shape he wanted and in doing so his head must have showed just above the trench – he fell dead, shot through the head. The Germans are splendid shots. If you put your finger up out of the trench they could hit it.'

On 29 December the battalion was relieved and moved 9km south-west, into divisional reserve at Bailleul. Aside from route marches and drilling to maintain the battalion's fitness and cohesion, the entire week was spent in billets, resting, cleaning up, refitting and carrying fatigues.

The harsh realities of army life continued and Christmas 1914 was not all gifts from home and good cheer, as on 30 December a court martial was held after Private C.E.J. Martin was found asleep at his post. In what must have been a shock to the battalion and in spite of the trials he had already been through, Private Martin was sentenced to death, although this penalty was later reduced to two years' hard labour.[97] This was to be the first of two such sentences passed on men from the battalion, although not a single man from the entire regiment would face the ignominy of being shot at dawn.

Combat losses up to the end of 1914 were 15 officers and 246 men killed, 19 officers and 440 wounded.[98] In addition, many hundreds of men spent time away from the battalion suffering from trench foot and illness, with a further 162 Bedfords being listed as captured[99] during the 1914 battles.

January 1915 was a typical European winter month, with rain, sleet, snow and bitterly cold winds adding to the discomfort created by incessant shelling and sniping. While on the front line and in support, most of the men's time was spent repairing their inadequate trenches, which were often waterlogged courtesy of the low-lying land and clay subsoil. The River Lys rose by 7ft, with other streams and rivers following suit, and some sections of trench were entirely abandoned. Just isolated sections of infantry were left holding outposts in some areas, those small sectors of trench being dammed at both ends to make their hole in the ground habitable. Naturally, the conditions caused a long casualty list, with frozen feet being a serious cause for concern within the British army.

The British Expeditionary Force on the Western Front now comprised eleven infantry and five cavalry divisions, all of which were at around three-quarters of their strength following reinforcements throughout December and January. Early in January the British 27th Division arrived on the front and early February saw the arrival of the 28th Division, resulting in the British line being extended northwards to what would become known as Hill 60, or 'Murder Hill'.

On 4 January 1915 Canadian-born Captain John Jenkins Moyse arrived from England and the men of the battalion moved into support positions at Dranouter, where they supplied carrying and working parties for the front-line troops. The 7th saw them sent into the front lines near Wulvergem, losing around twenty men over the next few days.

Although uneventful in terms of the battalion's activities, Private Fred Senior of Biggleswade[100] wrote to a friend about an incident which typifies the numerous small, individual events not recorded officially. Fred had arrived a month earlier, as a replacement for the heavy losses during the Battle of Ypres, so was still bedding into trench warfare and finding his feet:

The Bedfordshires' regimental badge used between 1898 and 1919. (Steven Fuller, 2010)

The sergeants' mess in 1909; many of these NCOs would have led the battalion into battle at Mons. (Dermot Foley)

The battalion silverware circa 1900. (Sherry Jennings)

B Company acting as the enemy during manoeuvres in 1910. (Steven Fuller)

Attributed to being taken behind a Bedford pub before the BEF set sail in August 1914, this informal group of Bedfords is interspersed with friends and family from several other units. (Chris Barrett)

Taken in the same field as above, members of RQMS Bartlett's transport section exercise their horses. (Chris Barrett)

CAPTAIN
C. H. KER
BEDFORDSHIRE REGIMENT
15TH SEPTEMBER 1914 AGE 30

MY BELOVED HUSBAND
"O TRUE BRAVE HEART!
GOD BLESS THEE
HERESOE'ER IN HIS GREAT
IVERSE THOU ART TO-DAY!"

Lieutenant Cecil 'Johnnie' Ker, the first officer killed in action on 15 September 1914. He now lies in Vendresse British Cemetery in the Department of the Aisne. (Portrait: *London Illustrated News*, Headstone: Steve Fuller)

Private 10469 Fred 'Bruiser' Clifton seated front centre without his cap badge, enjoying time in the yard behind the Sun Inn, Markyate, surrounded by family and friends. (Mick Bonham 1915)

Captain Basil John Orlebar, killed in action on 15 January 1915 and subsequently buried at Dranouter churchyard, Belgium. (Steven Fuller)

Private 7602 Edward Warner who was awarded the Victoria Cross 'For most conspicuous bravery near "Hill 60" on 1st May, 1915.' Private Warner is now commemorated on the Ypres (Menin Gate) Memorial. (Steven Fuller)

A youthful-looking Lance Corporal 11011 Percy Craddock who, when the photograph was taken, had already been wounded and had served for several years, having enlisted aged just 15. (Dave Craddock)

RQMS 5710 William Bartlett (above left) in dress uniform and a slightly less formal Sergeant Bartlett larking around (above right). (Chris Barrett)

'Afford from Offord'; Sergeant 8939 Joe Afford, MC, DCM who survived an eventful war only to die in 1942, as an officer in the Royal Armoured Corps. (Phillip Afford)

RSM 7521 Cecil Walker, DCM, in the 1920s, who served from Mons onwards, was wounded twice, but survived, only to die in 1930, aged 45. (Barry Astle)

Lieutenant Colonel Cranley Onslow, who was commissioned in 1892, served in the 1914 battles and as the battalion CO during 1916. Seen here as a lieutenant colonel circa 1917 (inset), and as a Military Knight of Windsor in the 1930s (main image). (Steven Fuller: inset photo; Jane Dobner: main photo)

Company Sergeant Major 5362 John Stapleton, DCM, who served briefly as the battalion's RSM before taking up his post as the RQMS in 1916. (Chris Barrett)

Captain Sheldon Gledstanes, who died of his wounds on 9 May 1915, following his gallant stand on Hill 60. Sheldon's service dress jacket survives today in a private collection. (Steve Fuller: portrait; Bill Guzek: tunic)

F. W. FLIGHT
MILITARY OUTFITTER
WINCHESTER . ALDERSHOT
& LONDON . W.

Tuileries British Cemetery, 3 km east of Ypres, and the headstone marking the fact that 'Known to be Buried in this Cemetery' is Second Lieutenant Robert Fawcett, who lost his life on 26 April 1915. (Fighting High)

The grave of Second Lieutenant John Moxly who was killed on 12 March 1915 and is buried in the Ramparts Cemetery, Lille Gate, Ypres. (Fighting High)

The grave of Private F. Brimicombe, who lost his life on 9 March 1915 and is buried in the Ramparts Cemetery, Lille Gate, Ypres. (Fighting High)

(Clockwise from top left) Three 'Old Contemptibles' from the Royston area who served from Mons onwards and whose letters home told of their experiences: Private 8571 William Reed, Private 8059 Bob Pigg and Sergeant 8087 Leonard Godfrey. (Steven Fuller)

(Below) Private A. Rayner. (Steven Fuller)

The last three Bedfords killed while leaving the Somme on 27 September 1916: Private A. Rayner, Private J. Manning and Private J. Horne, who lie in Citadel New Military Cemetery, Fricourt. (Steven Fuller)

Sergeant 10027 William Newbound, taken while the RSM at a cadet school in the 1930s.
(Ron West)

These are the men who served with the regiment before war broke out in 1914 and who were still serving when the photograph was taken at the depot in Bedford, 25 May 1932.

Back row, left to right:
Private 8472 Arthur C. Fitzjohn; Private 9408 Sydney C. Dawks; Private J. Wren, MM (possibly 4/7113 James Wren or 10285 William Wrenn, MM): Private 8373 Arthur W. Clarke; Lance Sergeant P. Armstrong (number unknown); Private A. Ward (number unknown); Private 10354 Arthur W. Davies.

Front row, left to right:
Quarter Master Sergeant (Orderly Room Sergeant) 10242 Leonard J. Harper; Regimental Sergeant Major 9464 Percival J. Hunt, DCM; Captain James Charles Abbott Birch; Major Robert Bernard Lawson Hatch, MC; Captain Frederick Henry Osborne, MC; Regimental Quarter Master Sergeant 9009 Henry J. Maidment, MM; Sergeant 5944002 W. Tarbard. (Steven Fuller)

RSM Cecil Walker's medals, now in the care of a private collector. Left to right: Distinguished Conduct medal, 1914 Star medal, British War medal, Victory medal with oak leaf, Long Service and Good Conduct (Military) medal. (Luke Arnold)

I'll tell you what happened the other night. Two of us went to get some straw and when coming back we lost our way and got to some trenches which held some of our troops. They either directed us wrong or we misunderstood them, for we got within 50 yards of the German trench. They opened fire on us as soon as they saw us, but our luck was in. We were on the edge of another trench and rolled into it. It was full of water. We were crawling about for about an hour. Then they sent a star light up and we saw about 20 or 30 looking for us. We hadn't an arm of any description and we got up and ran for it. Well, we hit on the right direction and got back after dodging about for three hours. ... I should not like to take the same chance again, as bullets were all around us, and crawling about in water for an hour does one no good.[101]

At 6 p.m. on the 10th the battalion was relieved by the Dorsets and moved back into support at Dranouter, where the men again provided carrying parties for the front lines, and on the 13th they were sent back into the front lines until the 16th. Over twenty more men were lost to shelling and sniping during the tour, including Captain Basil John Orlebar, who was killed in action on 15 January 1915, aged 39.[102]

While in support Second Lieutenant Charles Kennedy, a veteran of the South African wars who had seventeen years in the regimental ranks already behind him, joined from the 1st Munsters.

Among those caught in the shelling was C Company's Private George Franklin of Sandy,[103] who wrote home of the occasion: 'I have stopped a bit of shell in my thigh, but am going on all right. Glad to say it was the last shell the Germans fired that afternoon, January 16th [sic]. The same shell killed the Captain and 2 men, so you see I have been lucky. It wounded 2 more besides me ... it seems a treat coming out of the trenches. I have not been out of bed yet. I don't mind this for a little time.' George's wound would heal and he would go on to win the Russian Order of St George for bravery on Hill 60, but his luck would run out when, in June 1915, he was killed by shellfire while on the same hill where he earned his gallantry award.

The battalion moved into divisional reserve at Bailleul between the 17th and 23rd. Daily route marches and exercise were organised to keep the battalion fit, in addition to being a way of fighting the cold weather. During their period in reserve Second Lieutenants Charles Sidney Kirch, Esmond Lawrence Kellie and Charles Cuthbert Aston joined.

On 24 January they were moved forward into brigade reserve at Dranouter as the First Action at Givenchy flared up 28km further south. Late on the 26th orders arrived to move the battalion into direct support of the firing line in case an assault was launched on the German Kaiser's birthday the following day. A Company moved into positions in support of the 1st Cheshires, B Company behind the 1st Dorsets, with C and D Companies being held in reserve alongside the Headquarters Company in farmhouses near Lindenhoek crossroads, 800m south of Kemmel. While in support a further draft of sixty other ranks arrived.

Private William Webb[104] was in D Company and had written home several times, sharing a string of lucky escapes. These included being hit in the head by shrapnel which tore his soft cap and knocked him over for a few moments rather than killing him, being grazed by a bullet across the back of his hand, and later being caught out by a sniper who hit his rifle butt less than an inch from his hand rather than the bullet hitting him in the head. In March he wrote home with further examples of how unpredictable trench life was:

One night I was told off with a party of other men to draw rations for the men in the trenches and the enemy opened a rapid fire on us but luckily no-one was hit, we all laid flat on the road and my goodness, the bullets did fly over our heads. They kept it up for about a quarter of an hour and after that we picked up our rations and walked on as if nothing had happened. One poor fellow who stood close to me in the trenches had a bullet through his head and he never murmured. A few minutes before he was shot he was making a place in the trench so that he could walk about without getting wet and he remarked he was going to lay down there to sleep and little did we think that he was preparing a place to die on; and another fellow who was a close friend of mine was killed on the very same spot a few days afterwards.[105]

On the morning of the 28th Second Lieutenant William Henry Fitzroy Landon joined, a former sergeant who had served in the South African wars. That afternoon the battalion moved back into the front line near Wulvergem, remaining there until the evening of 1 February. Other than heavy snow and two intense fusillades of rifle fire to their left on the 1st, the period was another relatively quite one, yet seven men were still lost to hostile fire while improving the trenches or out on patrol.

From among the inactivity, Private Frank Wright[106] described the conditions around him as he sat, alone and bored, in the front-line trench on 31 January:

It is snowing fast and my 2 comrades are fast asleep in the land of dreams. One of them knows how to snore, sitting over the empty fire bucket. We have run out of coke so must grin and bear it ... we know it has to be done and therefore it is done with a good heart. I have out a sack over our heads and the snow has melted and the water is dripping into our fire bucket, trying to put out the fire which is not there. It makes one laugh to sit here and watch it, although it is not very comfortable.[107]

The men were back in billets in Bailleul before midnight on the 1st where they would remain until the 9th. Marches, classes, carrying parties and inspections filled their time, with Belgian King Albert inspecting the battalion on 8 February. Major Walter Allason rejoined the battalion on the 4th and Captain Francis Edwards, along with a draft of sixty men, arrived with the battalion on the 8th, both officers having recovered from their earlier wounds. It was also around this time that the allotment of machine guns per battalion was increased from two to four, expanding their firepower in response to the new style of warfare the British army was engaged in.

Sir John French issued an operational memo on 5 February, drawing attention to the importance of raiding and harassing the enemy, as it was becoming apparent that the German army was 'showing considerable initiative'. Despite significantly less materiel being available to them, the Royal Engineers and infantry stepped up their activities, even gaining the upper hand over their opponents in the coming months.

Between 9 and 12 February, headquarters and two companies were held in Bus Farm near the Lindenhoek crossroads, the other two companies being posted to Cooker Farm and a farm near the local dressing station, in close support of the 1st Cheshires in the front line. They then spent between 13 and 20 February on the front lines, in D Sector. On the nights of the 14th and 15th the men listened to heavy artillery and rifle fire further north, but nothing developed in their part of the line.

An unidentified 1st Bedfordshire officer's diary spanning several days from this period, gives an interesting insight into the day-to-day conditions in the trenches:

What price chicken, pork, greens, pate de foie gras, grapes and plenty of tinned stuff for dinner, not two miles from the firing line? As our Job's comforter says 'It may be our last decent meal.' Every now and then bullets keep going through the roof of our barn but where we are quite safe. ... I've got the reserve trenches tonight. They are apparently quite dry, which makes up for any amount of shelling.

These trenches are the best I've had yet. I've got about 50 men, two to each dugout, for the trench consists of a series of bomb proofs with a layer of about six inches of dry straw to lie on in each. My hole is about five yards in the rear and has at its side a miniature coal cellar which, being quite full, will be useful as it's jolly cold.

There is nothing to do in these trenches except to sit tight on the off chance of the Germans breaking through, in which case it's 'fix bayonets' and do your best. Let's hope they don't break through, for their sakes, for we're in a strong position and bayonet fighting is so messy and looks unpleasant when it's all over. And I don't want another spell of taking the men out to make another German cemetery, of which there appear to be quite a lot round here.

Most of the dugouts have a pail used as a fireplace. The poker is usually a bayonet – usually French – as the men save the German ones for souvenirs. There are plenty of unopened bully beef tins round about, so we shan't go short of food.

We're up in the rottenest trench I've ever been into. It's full of thin mud and there is a spring running into it. This trench was originally German; no wonder they let us have it; it isn't the sort of place you'd invite your best friend to. The water in parts was over one's chest. Heaven help the bantom [sic] battalion holding this place! They'd be drowned before they got here.

In my platoon – we'll call it that, but it's the remnant of a company – there are two brothers who have been out since the beginning. They have always been together, and neither has been sick or wounded. When they think they've hit a German they scratch a mark on their rifle butt. One had thirty-nine and the other forty-two, and the rivalry is very keen.

The rifles in the trenches look more like chunks of mud than anything else. The sights get clogged up, but that isn't of much importance here for the firing is practically point blank, our trench being about, on an average, twenty yards from the German one; but we rarely see anything of them except their shovels. Their trench is evidently in the same condition as ours.

Today, while walking ('swimming' would describe it better) down the trench, I found two men cooking chickens by holding them on a French bayonet over a coal fire. They were thin, of course, and what little meat there was on them wasn't improved in flavour by the deposit of thick soot with which they were soon covered.

I'm having a chicken tomorrow; it will be an improvement on bully. Let's hope the rain and water don't put the fire out. That would be the greatest catastrophe I can imagine at the present time; we have a hard enough job to keep them alight as it is perching them up on old bully beef tins to keep them off the ground. Occasionally one falls over and then you see how hard a Tommy can work in his efforts to relight the fire from wet wood and burning fragments from other fires. Matches are no good here. There's not a dry one in the trench. There are wood tinder lighters, but they're no good for pipes. There are no cigarettes or cigarette papers so we have to light our pipes from the fires, which, owing to the lack of dry combustibles, is not easy.

Had an exciting night. We hopped over to their ration trenches by 10 o'clock and heard their ration party go for their rations. When they had gone, we broke through in two places. We got terribly cold waiting, for they didn't come back for about two hours. But when they did come we got them all for they were quite trapped. There were twenty altogether but, of course, we didn't stop to investigate the extent of the damage.

About six yards from our trenches there is a German lying face down with a bayonet through him. The rifle and bayonet are vertical and by the German's side is a Frenchman! One can guess what happened with those two.[108]

With the cold conditions, lack of shelter and often inadequate clothing, illness started to feature during February too, Captain John Moyse being one example when he was returned to England mid-month suffering from influenza.

The battalion lost another officer on 15 February when the 47-year-old Second Lieutenant (acting captain) William Henry Fitzroy Landon was killed in action. Lieutenant William Pottle, a former company sergeant major, arrived on the 19th with a draft of ninety men, which included returning veterans like Private Frank Cousins, who had recovered from his wound received at Le Cateau the previous August. Half the soldiers of the battalion were relieved and moved into close support and by the time full relief was complete on the 20th a further nineteen men had been lost to artillery and sniper fire.

Orders came on 18 February 1915 to move north and relieve the 28th Division around St Eloi but were cancelled, the battalion remaining in the same area until early March 1915. In the event the men were relieved from the front line on the 20th and sent into brigade reserve near Dranouter until the 23rd. A further draft of twenty men arrived on the 23rd before moving back into the firing line.

On the 24th the Bedfordshires and their neighbours in the Norfolks fired improvised trench mortars and rifle grenades at German positions on the Wijtschate road, opposite trench 13. In the exchange that followed several bombs landed in the German trenches and they replied with heavier bombs, wounding two Bedfords. The makeshift mortar in the Norfolks' trenches finally gave up and exploded, wounding a Royal Engineer and a soldier from the Norfolks as well as killing another. The exchange of fire continued the following day, Captain Richard Ratcliffe and three men being wounded in trench 13.

On the 27th a message was signalled from the German lines warning of an attack the next day. Although nonplussed by their games, the

British line stood to at midday in case but nothing happened and later that day the 84th Brigade from the 28th Division relieved the Bedfordshires in the line.

The British and Commonwealth forces continued to slowly build, with the first Canadian division arriving on the front in mid-February and the first complete Territorial Army Division (the 46th) joining the army at the end of the month. Both units were still largely untrained and completely untried, so needed to be introduced to the realities of trench life under the supervision of the veteran divisions. Two territorial battalions (9th Londons and 6th Cheshires) were assigned to the Bedfordshires' division for such training.

By the time of their arrival, all battalions in the 5th Division had been slowly brought up to around 850 men strong, other than the 1st Cheshires who still dwindled at around 300.

Brigadier General Edward Northey took over the brigade from Lord Edward Gleichen when he was promoted to major general and called on to command the newly raised 37th Division in England in February 1915. Brigadier Gleichen called Lieutenant Colonel Griffith the 'trustiest of COs who had been under heavier fire than almost anyone, yet never touched'. For his continually steady and reliable leadership over and above his personal bravery, Griffith was mentioned in Sir John French's despatches in September, October and November 1914, being granted the CMG to go with the DSO[109] in February 1915.

The battalion was rested in billets at Bailleul from 28 February until a move north took it to Ouderdom, 1km east of Reningelst on 3 March, twenty-five reinforcements having arrived while in billets. The 13th and 15th Brigades were temporarily posted to the 28th Division to help form a composite division after two of its brigades had an especially difficult first month in the line, having been heavily depleted by both fighting and sickness.

The men then took over in support on 4 March and two days later moved into the front lines with Hill 60 some 600m north-east. Their lines ran from the canal, past the Bluff and Ravine, including the International Trench, which was held by both British and German troops and disputed daily by shelling, bombing and rifle grenades.

By this time German troops had use of trench mortars, whereas British troops had none and were busily trying to improvise their own devices so they could at least return fire. While here an American trench mortar was trialled and Second Lieutenant Charles Kennedy literally had to sit on the breech just to enable the gun to fire properly.

Early on 8 March Captain Leonard Andrews and a fatigue party went back to fell a tree to make some steps for their trenches. By 5 a.m. the job was done and as the group were packing their tools away a German aeroplane flew over. Within minutes several German shells fell among them, killing one while wounding the captain, his sergeant and five others. Private Francis Brimicombe[110] was among the wounded but died later. A further eleven men were lost to such incidents before the battalion moved into support on the 9th. After a day in support the soldiers were sent back into the front line, which included trench 32(a) (International Trench) again. On the 11th the adjutant wrote in the battalion war diary, 'situation in 32(a) trench unpleasant'. With British and German troops still fighting for control of it, not an inch was safe. A trench ran parallel to the Bedfordshires' trench, from where their German counterparts could throw bombs into their positions. German snipers also dominated the ground, even stopping the Bedfords raising trench periscopes to survey the land around them, as whenever one rose above the parapet it was shot away within seconds. A German heavy trench howitzer also started firing into their positions, wounding Captain Charles Ogden and five men during the day.

On 12 March enemy focus remained fixed on their positions and the shells and bombs rained into their trenches throughout the day, the deadly mixture of shelling and snipers continuing to take their toll.

The 23-year-old Second Lieutenant John Hewitt Sutton Moxly had been with the battalion since early in January. Son of the late Reverend Joseph Moxly, principal chaplain to HM forces, he had enlisted as an officer on 15 August 1914 and was already well known and liked throughout the battalion. That day he was ordered to supervise the repair of a section of trench that had been blown in and while lifting a wire entanglement onto the parapet he was killed instantly by a sniper who 'shot him through the heart'.[111] His commanding officer wrote: 'It was the death of a brave and devoted gentleman. He was always the same; resourceful, alert, loved by officers and men, as good an officer as one could ever wish to meet.'

Lieutenant Robert Sterling, an old school friend of John Moxly's who was serving in the Royal Scots Fusiliers, wrote of his death:

To J.H.S.M., killed in action, March 13th 1915.
O Brother, I have sung no dirge for thee:

Nor for all time to come
Can song reveal my grief's infinity:
The menace of thy silence made me dumb.

Company Sergeant Major Ernest Watson of Carlton near Bedford,[112] who had been awarded the DSM and mentioned in despatches after the fighting on 7 November 1914, was also killed during the day's shelling and another man was wounded. A veteran with twenty years of service in the regiment, CSM Watson was killed six days before his 39th birthday, while crossing an exposed section of trench as he tried to arrange some water for his thirsty men. When told of his death, the CO could only remark with a sigh: 'Another good man gone.' CSM Thomas Byford,[113] a veteran of over two decades in the regiment, who had served alongside Ernest for many years, wrote to Ernest's widow about his death. Showing how much the sergeant major was respected by his comrades, his letter included an unusual list of each of the sergeant majors who especially wished to be remembered to Ernest's widow, including Regimental Sergeant Major Wombwell.

A draft of twenty men arrived during the day and at 8 p.m. the battalion was relieved into support positions again for two days. Its brief spell in support saw it lose one man killed and two officers, and nine men wounded by the continued heavy shelling.

On 14 March German artillery bombarded the lines between the canal and St Eloi and a mine exploded under a feature called the Mound. The 27th Division on the right of the 15th Brigade were forced to yield and St Eloi fell to the Germans. A British counter-attack that night retook the village but not the Mound. During the shelling that day, B Company lost two men wounded as the chateau they were billeted in was hit.

A draft of forty-five other ranks arrived on the 15th and a move back into the trenches that day resulted in a further five killed and fifteen wounded during their brief two-day tour in the front line, one of those killed being Arthur Chandler from Spaldwick who had written home about his adventures from Mons to Ypres the previous year. Sadly, his family would have more grief to contend with later in the war when his brother, Company Sergeant Major Percy Chandler[114] died from wounds sustained during a raid in June 1916, while serving in the 2nd Bedfordshires.

By the time the battalion was relieved on 16 March 1915, just four company officers remained, twenty others having been lost over the last six weeks to a mixture of enemy activity and illness.

After returning to Ypres by midnight on 16/17 March, the battalion
moved into brigade reserve south of Vlamertinge, where the men enjoyed
a four-day rest in newly built huts instead of the usual draughty, shell-
damaged buildings.

On the 21st the Bedfordshires were sent back into support positions,
returning to the front lines on 23 March, in front of Sanctuary Wood and
with the French 'Iron Corps' to their left. In no time at all men from both
armies were busily chatting away, exchanging food and swapping stories
despite the close proximity of their mutual foe. The trenches were
described as being 'very zig-zag and confusing, as they face in three
directions' but the men set to improving them and making them
defensible. The casualties continued, with the battalion losing one man
killed and a further seven wounded over the next three days. The final
day also saw Lieutenant Sidney Tabor, who had joined the men in
January, slightly wounded in the head and by 11 p.m. on 25 March they
were resting in support in Ypres. Waiting for them were Second
Lieutenants Dennis Harvey, William Bernard Knight, Richard Owen
Wynne and a Second Lieutenant Scott.

The following day, Second Lieutenants John Webb and Ronald
Marmaduke Dawnay Harvey joined from the 4th North Staffords and
one man was wounded while in a working party.

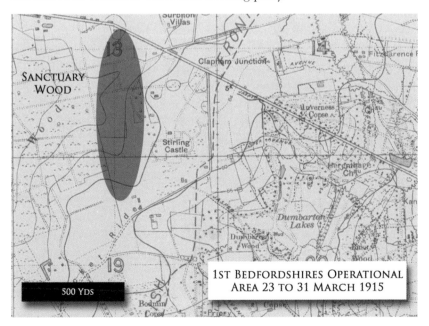

1ST BEDFORDSHIRES OPERATIONAL
AREA 23 TO 31 MARCH 1915

500 YDS

On 28 March Second Lieutenants Charles Alan Smith Morris and Hubert Henry Worsley Pulleine arrived with a further 119 reinforcements in time for the battalion's return to the trenches that night.

During the 29th news reached the battalion of an impending attack using gas. Initial reaction was surprise, followed closely by a belief that using gas to inflict casualties was 'absurd', so although the news was passed on, no real credence was given to the threat.

On the 30th the Bedfordshires in trench 50 were engaged in a long day of constant rifle grenade duels with their opposite numbers in the German lines. Although outgunned and lacking a constant supply of parts to make the grenades, the men stuck to the one-sided skirmish, losing many of their comrades in the process.

Bob Pigg wrote to his brother telling of the death of fellow townsman Private William Reed that day. Bob asked him to relay the news to Bill's mother, saying, 'I am writing to tell you that poor old Bill has gone. ... He died a true soldier's death. He did not suffer at all. It seemed hard to lose him and his last words were 'Mother and Jack'. I feel lost without him now as he used to come and see me about every day.'[115]

Sergeant Frederick Spicer[116] also wrote to Bill's mother, declaring: 'It is my painful duty to write and tell you that your dear son was killed in action on the afternoon of 30th March. He died a hero. He was a brave man and buried in a soldier's grave.'

Private Reed was a typical soldier who had served in the regiment since the summer of 1907, spending time in Gibraltar, Bermuda and South Africa. He transferred into the reserves not long before war was declared and was working at the Arlesey Asylum as an attendant when he received the call to mobilise. Bill had been on the front since the beginning and had survived all of the intense, early battles only to be killed in the duel that erupted that day. Sadly, as is the case with a high proportion of the early war deaths, Bill's grave was later lost and he is remembered on the Ypres (Menin Gate) Memorial to the missing. His family lived in Royston, next door to his cousin's family, the Smiths. Ironically, on the same day that Bill fell, his cousin, Sergeant John Smith,[117] was also killed while serving in the 2nd Bedfordshires.

Early in April the British took over a further 7km of front, thus taking on the defence of Ypres once again. After the reorganisation, the British and Commonwealth troops held over 40km of continuous front, running from the La Bassée canal south of Givenchy at the southernmost tip to 1km south-west of Poelkapelle (Poelcapelle), 9km north-east of Ypres.

The French method of defence relied heavily on their massed artillery supporting thinly held front-line trenches and, as a result, their trenches were lightly prepared and often behind breastworks above ground. As the British army had only meagre artillery in comparison, their own defensive plan was based on infantry holding sunken trenches below the ground, with stronger contingents of infantry being present in the front lines. So on arrival in the new sections of the line, British troops had an enormous job ahead of them to prepare the ground for a defensive stance that suited them.

Between the Belgian and British armies were two French divisions, creating further command difficulties in the vicinity and, with the removal of the French anti-aircraft batteries, German aerial activity increased considerably. All in all, it was an ideal area for a German assault and, with their customary efficiency, the German army would capitalise on the apparent weakness.

From 1 to 4 April the battalion was held in reserve, the men spending their time away from fatigues in hutments west of Ypres. The Bishop of London was among the stream of visitors who stopped by to address the troops, so although their time in reserve provided a welcomed break from the front-line trenches, it was full of speeches, as one of the battalion officers remarked:

We have been resting for the past four days in newly erected wood and canvas huts – very uncomfortable and crowded at first and in the middle of a mass of mud – but the fine weather of the past few days has made a wonderful difference and a bit of scraping and engineering has made the place a desirable residence. We have been overrun with Generals – first day, Brigadier, second day, Divisional and Corps Commanders, third day, Army Commander, Corps ditto, Divisional ditto, Brigade ditto. Our Army Commander was more than complimentary. He told us that we had more than fulfilled his expectations and that 'the Bedfords and Norfolks are considered two of the best battalions in the Army', which was gratifying.[118]

A small draft joined them while resting, consisting of returning 1st and 2nd Battalion men. This draft included Privates William Quinton,[119] known as 'Quint', and Albert Petchell,[120] known as 'Petch'. Both had been on the front since October 1914, serving in the 2nd Bedfordshires through the First Battle of Ypres and had struck up a friendship while in the coastal reserve areas recovering from illnesses before transferring to the 1st Bedfordshires.

As the rest of their brigade stayed in reserve, on the 5th the Bedford-shires were moved into support in Ypres itself and were subjected to the attentions of German artillery, which was systematically targeting the remaining structures in the city.

Following a long day of heavy shelling and equally heavy casualties on 7 April, the battalion was unexpectedly ordered back to join their brigade in reserve at Reningelst that evening, 9km west of Ypres. The rest of the 5th Division had arrived in the area the previous day and concentrated around Reningelst, ready to move into the line as a complete unit once again. Once the battalion was ordered back into the front lines overnight on 10 April 1915, the men found themselves manning the line between trenches 38 and 45, facing an unimpressive rise in the ground that would soon become infamous as Hill 60.

Chapter 8

'Murder Hill' and the Second Battle of Ypres

April – July 1915

'The gallantry and endurance displayed by all ranks throughout the operations were beyond all praise.'

In itself, Hill 60 was merely a mound of earth less than 6km south-east of Ypres's centre. Although just an innocuous-looking rise 150ft high, which had been created from the spoil from digging a railway cutting, it allowed for observation across the plain on which Ypres stood. Therefore, the Germans understood its value and were determined to hold it at all costs and in their turn the British recognised the urgent need to gain control of the slight rise that caused so much trouble and inconvenience in the surrounding countryside. By the time the Bedfordshires arrived in the area, British and German tunnellers were both working frantically to lay their mines under the hill and it was simply a case of who would finish first and win the grim race.

The British troops in the vicinity were given the monumental task of preparing their lines for what they guessed was to be a new offensive. Vast quantities of materials were brought from the ruined village of Zillebeke under cover of darkness and a series of shelters, trenches, posts and a dressing station were all hurriedly prepared. While going about their work, curious things started arriving in their trenches, thrown over from the opposing German lines: 'One day two letters were thrown in, addressed "Dear Honoured Comrade", stating that as the war had been going on nine months it was high time it came to an end. Cigarettes were also thrown over.'[121]

However, not all curiosities were welcomed and the soldiers' trusting nature and spirit of fair play still created problems from time to time: 'On another occasion in broad daylight two Germans jumped over their parapet (about 50 yards from ours) and began digging. Our men thought it was for a grave and withheld their fire; presently ropes were passed out to them, and after some hauling the wheels of a field gun appeared just above our parapet. A few moments later it opened fire and demolished our parapet at that point.'

Fresh reports reached British Headquarters on 15 April of an impending German attack using 'batteries of asphyxiating gas', which was expected against the French division on the northern flank of the British sector around Ypres. Coming a day after an unusual incident around St Eloi that saw a methodical German artillery barrage that was not followed up with an infantry assault, general awareness was heightened. As the reported attack did not materialise, it was written off as a ruse to distract the Allied forces and an attempt to create terror as a 'new form of frightfulness'. Sadly, information was also gleaned from German prisoners two weeks earlier but was largely ignored and no precautions were taken against what was to follow. Added to which, attention was also drawn away from the front lines by the renewed shelling of Ypres from German heavy howitzers that quickly reduced the reopened cafés and shops to rubble.

On 15 and 16 April 1915 the battalion was supported by men from the 14th Brigade in its work to prepare assembly trenches for the coming assault, which also served to confirm the men were about to go into action once again.

On the morning of the 17th, two companies were moved back almost 2km, to a position around the Reformatory, so the assaulting 13th Brigade could take to their jumping-off positions. The day itself was fine, dry and remarkably quiet, the veterans on both sides instinctively sensing this was very likely to prove to be the calm before a storm.

At 7 p.m. the waiting men around the hill inexplicably felt the ground shake and rumble around them. After some seconds had passed a huge, ugly, black cloud spewed into the sky from the centre of the hill and after a further ten-second pause that seemed like an eternity, a dirty yellow flame erupted into the darkening sky. Within a heartbeat the quiet day was broken and an inferno of artillery and rifle fire pounded the area from both sides, adding to the smoke and dirt already filling the early evening sky.

As the Royal West Kents from the 13th Brigade charged the shattered hill, the Bedfordshires held position, half being in direct support of the assault at the base of the hill and the other half being on a ten-minute warning to move further back.

The initial rush on the hill had gone well, as almost the entire enemy garrison had been obliterated by the first mine explosion and subsequent barrage, but by midnight German counter-attacks were in full swing. Sergeant William Newbound and his section were among those rushed forward to consolidate the hillside, arriving just as German heavy artillery focused in on their positions. Working frantically to prepare the new front line for a defensive action, the veteran of every battle since Mons recorded how they had 'just got barricade fixed up when 4 shells burst on top of us, everyone being wounded including myself'.

The size and ferocious nature of the German attack meant they re-gained most of the hill and the dispute continued throughout the 18th, with both sides losing heavily. The two companies of Bedfordshires on the hill lost 'considerable' casualties that day, and at 6 p.m. the two companies being held at the Reformatory were called forward to help retake the hill, supporting the West Ridings in their gallant and costly assault. Once secured, the 13th Brigade handed over control to Lieu-tenant Colonel Griffith and withdrew to regroup.

More warnings of a planned attack using gas surfaced when prisoners were taken, carrying strange masks covered with a slimy substance, leav-ing the British troops uncertain.

In the early hours of 19 April the 13th Brigade had completed their withdrawal and the already battle-worn Bedfordshires took over control of the hill, with the East Surreys in support. Both battalions at once set about preparing their positions before the expected counter-attack erupted, under the constant scrutiny of enemy snipers and artillery observers.

At 2 p.m. the hill once again became the focal point of the fighting as an intense bombardment fell onto the Bedfordshires and Surreys, follow-ed by a massive counter-attack. Just as the situation became dangerously unpredictable, Major Allason was suddenly rushed away to command the Surreys, their officers having been badly hit by the barrage and command temporarily lost. With hardly any of the Surreys left on the hill, the Bedfordshires were isolated and under extreme pressure, their superb leadership at platoon and section level, in addition to their stubborn individual resistance, being the only elements that held the hill in British hands. Without orders, the men left what shelter they had and moved immediately to whatever place was under the most pressure, regardless of the intensity of enemy artillery and rifle fire being brought to bear on them.

Among the men fighting for control for their own small section of Murder Hill was Herbert Spencer, now a sergeant in charge of a section of bombers: 'A counter-attack was formed. I, with 10 men, got the bombs to work and with the aid of our artillery the charge was formed; we were then able to retake our trenches but not the hill.'

The ferocious assaults and equally determined resistance continued relentlessly throughout the day, and darkness only reduced the intensity slightly until a hush finally fell on the hill late that night. Although the defenders took the chance to draw breath and reorganise their survivors as best they could, the German pause did not last long.

At 2 p.m. on 20 April, another massive bombardment once again pounded the hill's inhabitants. Enemy fire came from three sides as every available gun was turned onto the hill in a desperate attempt to regain the position. Despite the German bombardment continuing unabated, as one infantry attack after another was thrown at the shaken and shattered British positions, each was propelled back in their turn by the incredible determination of those who were still capable of wielding a rifle. The Germans employed bombs, bayonets, machine-gun and artillery fire against the exhausted Bedfordshires, even using flame-throwers for the first time in their desperate attempt to prise the stubborn defenders from their besieged posts. On the left flank the German infantry broke into the Bedfordshires' lines twice and were thrown out again both times.

By nightfall the hill was a dreadful place, littered with the debris of one of the bloodiest fights of the war to date. Ammunition was running dangerously short, as were the survivors who were still capable of resisting. A company from the territorial Queen Victoria's Rifles under Major Lees arrived with ammunition around 1.30 a.m. on the 21st. Being a carrying party, they were only lightly armed but still joined the Bedfordshires as they launched a localised counter-attack against a section of the line that had been lost on the right shoulder of the hill. As Lieutenant Charles Kennedy of the Bedfordshires had been put out of action with a shattered leg, Lieutenant Wooley of the QVR became the ranking officer on site and won the first Territorial Army Victoria Cross during the action.

At 3 a.m. on the 21st came the first hint of dawn and with it a fresh

German barrage. By this time, defensible trenches did not exist and the men held shell holes in small groups, often unable to move without attracting deadly machine-gun fire. Almost out of ammunition and with very few men left to sustain the fight, a group of Bedfords conducted a fighting retirement from their exposed positions, far to the front of the main line of resistance. Seeing their comrades in trouble, between twenty and thirty men behind them charged out to help and joined them in setting up a fresh line of resistance among the carnage.

Throughout the small hours of that morning the position was critical, the hill being held by the most fragile of grips and with command of what remained of the companies often falling to subalterns and NCOs. German field guns were brought to within 30m of the hill and blasted away at point-blank range; trench mortars rained down on the dwindling band of survivors and machine guns were even able to enfilade the reverse slope of the hill, ensuring that not an inch of the ground was safe. German bombers and supporting infantry tried once again to force the Bedfords from the hill, but without success. Although the infantry attack faded away after more heavy losses, German artillery pounded the position relentlessly, pinning the men down, and any movement above ground was reduced to a deadly game of chance. At 4.30 a.m. a company from the Devons arrived to strengthen the line, followed by fifty bombers from the Royal Fusiliers. No one on the hill had any bombs left so the Fusiliers could only be used as supporting infantry, but their arrival swelled the thin ranks of surviving Bedfordshires considerably.

With little ammunition and no bombs, the defenders took every opportunity to keep the heads of their enemies down and, during one such exchange, Private Frank Cousins was hit at 6.30 a.m. Drummer Charles Bellamy[122] was with Frank at the time of his death and wrote to Frank's mother that 'he was firing over the parapet at the Germans. He had just fired when they returned one. I was about two yards from him when he got hit and I did all I could for him but it was no good, no one could save him … he was one of my best chums I had ever since I left school.'[123]

Three hours later a further company from the Devons arrived and took over what remained of the Bedfordshires' lines completely, being visibly shocked at the condition of the survivors. Once the relief was complete the survivors assembled in support positions and the battalion was withdrawn 12km west to billets in Reningelst that evening to rest and refit.

Of the 630 Bedfordshires who went forward into the inferno on 17 April, around 200 marched and limped back on the 21st, many with no ammunition and most being slightly wounded but not considering themselves as needing treatment.

From the already under-strength company officers, the battalion lost a further five killed: Second Lieutenant Esmond Lawrence Kellie, a 20-year-old former insurance clerk who had enlisted into the Artist's Rifles the day after war was declared and was killed on 19 April; and Second Lieutenant Charles Sidney Kirch, a 19-year-old from Hong Kong who had enlisted into the Artists' Rifles the day after Esmond Kellie, been commissioned into the battalion on the same day, and had fallen on the same day. The other three officer casualties came from the group of young officers from the 4th Prince of Wales Regiment who had arrived only a month earlier, with all three being killed on the same day: William Bernard Knight, a 28-year-old former solicitor on 21 April; Ronald Marmaduke Harvey, another young subaltern, overnight on 20/21 April; and Lieutenant John Webb, a 20-year-old who had joined the battalion with William Knight and Ronald Harvey. Webb's last words to one of his sergeants when their position became desperate epitomised the determined, resolute attitude displayed throughout the battalion, when he remarked: 'Anyway, it will be a glorious death.' The battalion war diary records that eight officers were also wounded on the hill, with six of them being: Major Walter Allason, a veteran of the early engage-ments who had already been wounded in 1914, was injured again and mentioned in despatches for his gallantry on the hill; Captain John Moyse who was wounded by shrapnel in the jaw and shoulder on 21 April; Lieutenant Charles Kennedy,[124] whose leg was shattered on the 20th and was mentioned in despatches in June 1915; Lieutenant William Ernest Cannon, former sergeant major in the Bedfordshire Militia; Lieutenant James Thurston Dukinfield Derbishire, who had only joined the battalion a matter of days earlier; and Lieutenant Frederick Wolff Ogilvie who had been with the battalion for around one month before being wounded.

Four men from the battalion were awarded the Distinguished Conduct Medal, with other gallantry awards going unsatisfied as there were simply no survivors left to tell the tales of the individual heroism that ensured the hill remained in British hands throughout the savage fighting.

Sergeant Reginald Fearn[125] had spent the early part of his life in the children's home in Dunstable before joining the regiment at the end of 1905, aged 16. He had been fighting with the battalion since their arrival in August 1914 and won his DCM on 20 April. His citation reads: 'For conspicuous gallantry and ability throughout the campaign, especially at "Hill 60" on 20th April 1915, when he led his platoon and occupied a crater on the hill successfully under heavy bombardment until relieved.'

Sergeant Henry Trasler[126] won his DCM during the crater fighting on 20 April, being included on the King's birthday honours list.

Private George Whiting[127] had been with the battalion since September 1912 and arrived in France five days after the bulk of the battalion but had been present throughout all the early engagements. He won his DCM on 20 April, his citation reading: 'For conspicuous gallantry on 20th April, 1915, in holding by himself a crater on the hill, from which all others had been driven, and remaining in possession until supports arrived.'

Sergeant Walter Summerfield[128] won the fourth DCM, his citation reading: 'For conspicuous gallantry and ability in the trenches. On "Hill 60" he showed great courage and resource in the defence of a crater, after 30 out of his 35 men had been killed or wounded.'

Private Bob Pigg, whose cousin Private Albert Pigg[129] had arrived with the battalion just days earlier, was one of those who had not only survived every battle his battalion had been engaged in so far, but was also one of the few to come through Hill 60 unscathed. In a letter home, he wrote of the fighting:

No doubt everyone at home has read about the terrible fighting which we have just gone through. I am glad that God has brought me through the ordeal. I was at Hill 60 and it was the worst sight I have seen since the war began. The hill was blown up on Saturday night and then the bombardment started. The Germans were mowed down in thousands and they lay in heaps. There were many casualties in our regiment but it mattered not who you saw wounded or how bad their wounds, the first thing they asked for was a 'fag'. We were in the trenches for eleven days. We have just been relieved and General French has just been to see us and before we came up here we had the honour of being inspected by the King of the Belgians. ... There are not many of us left now that came out with the battalion. ... It is hard to see first one mate and then another either killed or wounded. When we come out of the trenches we ask for this one and that one and the answer is 'Oh he's killed', or 'he's wounded'. We all feel quite sure we shall beat the sausage men.

We were at 'Murder Hill'. ... Little did we think to see the hill blown up. Two

Companies of East Surreys and two of Bedfords charged the enemy not losing a single man, although we had been shelled for 24 hours. The Surreys ran short of ammunition and we had to retire. We afterwards charged the hill again and that was when we lost a lot of men, but the Germans lost a lot more. Thousands went down, It was a 'ding-dong' fight on that hill for four days. Lieut. Kennedy of our regiment had his leg shattered and a Captain of the Queen Victoria Rifles took his place and so won his V.C., and Bridgestock [sic], the heavyweight boxer of the 1st Beds, got his D.C.M. For what he did, we boys thought he ought to have had a V.C.[130]

In the event and despite the disbelief of the survivors from his company, Private George Brigstock (referred to as Bridgestock above),[131] the battalion's well-known heavyweight boxer, was not awarded a gallantry medal but would get the greater gift of surviving the war after transferring into the Machine Gun Corps.

The 'lucky' Lance Corporal William Webb had managed to come through the bitter fighting unscathed once more, but his luck had not extended to his brother who was fighting alongside him. In a letter from the end of April William wrote of several near misses, before concluding: 'I am sorry to say that my brother was seriously wounded in the same trench as me. He had his arm smashed above the elbow with a shell and a piece of shell entered his shoulder, three pieces in his left thigh and one in his right.' Although evacuated to receive medical treatment, Private Henry Webb[132] was among those who died from his wounds.

General Fergusson wrote of the fighting: 'I wish to record my opinion that the gallantry and endurance displayed by all ranks throughout the operations were beyond all praise. The concentration of hostile artillery fire on the small hill top was intense, continuous and devastating. Our infantry suffered many casualties also from hand grenades. Soldiers who refused to be terrified or thrown back by a bombardment of this fury can stand anything. They cannot be beaten.'

Sir John French even visited the surviving Bedfordshires on the afternoon of 22 April to personally congratulate them on their defence, but, while they were refitting and reorganising, events were unfolding north of Ypres and the battalion was issued urgent orders that evening to move to Ouderdom and maintain a 'ready to move' posture. As the 13th Brigade rushed north to help stem the German attacks, at 9.30 p.m. the exhausted Bedfordshires reached huts and grabbed what badly needed rest they could while waiting for orders that may take them into another desperate situation at any moment.

Over the coming months and years, those Bedfordshires at Hill 60 during the initial struggle would become understandably unhappy. Units to either side of them were credited with various accolades, even the four Victoria Crosses won on the hill going to the East Surreys and an officer from another unit who happened to be there during one of the Bedfords' numerous attacks. Yet incredibly the battalion was largely left out of the accounts of the vicious struggle for Murder Hill, despite having held firm against all the odds and having suffered such a dreadful, long casualty list.

The Battles of Ypres 1915 (the Second Battle of Ypres): 22 April–25 May 1915

At around 5 p.m. on 22 April, the German army launched its first massed use of gas on the Western Front. Some 168 tonnes of chlorine gas were released along a 6.5km frontage north of Ypres, against unprepared French territorial and colonial troops; 6,000 French soldiers died within the first ten minutes of what would be called the Battle of Gravenstafel, and thousands more were blinded. Those surviving were forced to evacuate their trenches and were mowed down by artillery and machine-gun fire as they appeared above ground. The disaster created a 6km-wide undefended gap in the Allied lines, but their success was not fully exploited as the German commanders had not foreseen just how effective their new weapon would be, so had no reserves nearby to exploit the opportunity.

A series of German assaults and counter-attacks followed over the coming days as both sides sought to gain supremacy over the strategic city of Ypres. Curiously, the British had still viewed their German counterparts as a generally fair adversary who stuck to the rules of engagement. So when it was realised what this new shock weapon actually was, initially there was concern and uncertainty in the British ranks – but this soon turned to a disgusted resolve to punish their enemies for using what they viewed as an unfair weapon. So as events unfolded and the British salient to the east of Ypres shrunk, those troops in the dangerously exposed bulge in the lines kept a vigilant watch to their front and an eye to the rear.

Then, between 24 April and 4 May, the Battle of St Julien (Sint-Juliaan) was fought north-east of Ypres, with both sides losing heavily, and it was in conjunction with this fighting that a fresh German attempt to regain Hill 60 was launched.

Although exhausted, at less than 40 per cent strength and having only been relieved from their ordeal on Hill 60 hours earlier, the Bedfordshires were placed on alert, ready to move at ten minutes' notice. After a day waiting in divisional reserve at Ouderdom with the similarly depleted East Surreys, on 24 April the battalion moved to support positions west of the Zillebeke Lake in response to the start of the Battle of St Julien. Over the previous two days, two drafts of ninety-nine and eighty-nine men had arrived in addition to Captain Hugh Courtenay and four further officers.

The next day they were moved into the front lines to the left of Hill 60 just as, thousands of kilometres to the south, British troops stormed the beaches at Cape Helles on Gallipoli. Consolidation of their new lines between the western edge of Zwarteleen and the western boundary of Armagh Wood continued. Four more officers arrived on the 24th as the battalion gradually tried to rebuild and reorganise before its next engagement which, given the ferocity of fighting unfolding to the north, was fully expected.

On the 26th Second Lieutenant Robert Fawcett, who had only been with the battalion for a matter of days, was killed and a further three men wounded as heavy fighting continued to the left and rear of their lines. Among those injured was 30-year-old Private Charles Jackson from Langford, Bedfordshire.[133] Charles had received his discharge papers

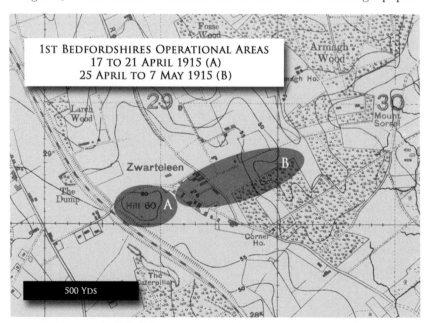

1ST BEDFORDSHIRES OPERATIONAL AREAS
17 TO 21 APRIL 1915 (A)
25 APRIL TO 7 MAY 1915 (B)

500 YDS

days before war broke out yet chose to offer himself for the task ahead, stating that 'it is my duty to'. He was moved back to the 13th General Hospital at Boulogne, only to die from his wounds on 27 April.

The following days saw several more men lost to the ongoing trench warfare, including Sergeant Reginald Fearn who was killed on 29 April, just nine days after he had won his Distinguished Conduct Medal on the same hill.

On the 30th, among a much-needed draft of 3 officers and 300 men arriving were Lieutenant William Harold Louis Barnett and Second Lieutenant Arthur Nugent Waldemar Powell, bringing the battalion's overall strength to over 800 once again. It was comprised almost entirely of men who had never experienced warfare before and included brothers Jim and Tom Neale from Aspenden,[134] who had been civilians before enlisting together in August 1914. They had trained together and would now face a shocking and harsh introduction into the realities of war as they marched headlong into the carnage that surrounded the hill. Only one would be left alive by the end of the war and the other would endure campaigns on the Western Front and in the Middle East, although not entirely unscathed.

By now, less than half of the battalion were veterans of the 1914 campaigns and many of those had already been wounded at least once. The rest had been civilians like the Neale brothers before war was declared nine long months earlier. As many of the new arrivals were completely untried in warfare, the battalion was organised carefully, as it was clear to all that they would soon be thrown headlong into their first taste of conflict. Although intimidating, those men new to the front lines must have taken some comfort from the sight of the soldiers who greeted them and who would stand beside them when things got tough. Aside from the experienced officer corps and the highly capable band of NCOs who ran the battalion, their new comrades included hardened young men like Private Fred 'Bruiser' Clifton,[135] a fighting man from Markyate who had run away from home while very young, lived with gypsies and spent some time at His Majesty's pleasure for fighting before joining the battalion at Ypres in 1914.

The date of 1 May was planned as their last day in the front trenches before a welcomed relief. It had been a relatively quiet day for the tired men, who had spent it making their positions more defensible and waiting for the relieving troops to arrive. As daylight started fading, sentries were placed and the companies took a short break before the night's work began.

Private Ted Warner[136] had been coming to the end of his twelve-year term of service in the regiment, serving in the reserves when war broke out. He had been due to complete his service in May 1915 but with dependants, 75-year-old widowed mother Charlotte and new fiancée Maud Burton, waiting at home, was doubtless contemplating whether to extend his service or take the well-earned, honourable discharge that would be offered to him in the coming weeks. Having come through the dreadful battle on Hill 60 in April, he had written to his mother days earlier: 'You will see in the papers that we have been in a tight corner. I think it's the hottest place I have ever been in but, thank the Lord, I have been spared to get through alright. We have lost a lot killed and wounded. It was a proper death trap. The dirty pigs could not have blown us to pieces fast enough so they tried to blind us but I am pleased to say I am safe.'[137]

Ted and Private Fred Brimm[138] were both St Albans' men in B Company and had seen the war through side by side. Ted had landed with the first wave in August and Fred had followed in the first reinforcement draft ten days later, so, other than a poisoned hand that had kept Ted from the fighting at Givenchy the previous October, the two pals had done well to come through unscathed.

Fred had already served in India with the battalion and was also coming to the end of his twelve years when he had been called from the reserves in August. With four other brothers serving the country, two of whom were in the 2nd Bedfordshires, Fred was certainly from military stock. He wrote home that they were sitting in the trench 'having a yarn together' about Ted's recent short home leave and how everyone back in St Albans was when the alarm went round that gas was being released to their right.[139] Ted rushed off to rejoin his platoon in trench 46, at the far right of the battalion lines, as Fred made his way to his own platoon.

At 6.30 p.m. the Germans launched a fresh gas attack, this time the victims being around 300 of the Dorsets to the right of the Bedford-shires, with some gas drifting into the Bedfords' trenches. A heavy bombardment followed but the full German infantry assault was not launched against the left half of the Bedfordshires' section, as some of their gas blew back into their own lines and made the assaulting troops hesitate. Initially, dozens of the Bedfordshires were violently sick but remained at their posts so the right-hand section was thought to have suffered very few casualties. However, as time passed more and more men reported in, threatening to render much of the battalion's right flank ineffective.

Private Ives of B Company wrote in a letter to his sister that Ted's 'platoon occupied a part of the trench about 50 yards on our right when they caught more of the gas than we did'.[140]

The entire platoon in trench 46 on the far right flank of the battalion lines had little choice but to retire, all of them instantly being struck down by the effects of gas. After running back a few metres, Ted Warner decided to return to his post and, despite being completely alone and with the uncertainty of how he could survive this new weapon's effects, held the trench. Single-handedly he fended off several attempts by German troops to gain a footing in his trench, although the gas was starting to take its toll on him. An attempt to reinforce Ted was foiled as the supports could not get through the impenetrable wall of gas and shell fragments, but once the chance arose, Ted made his way to them and the group followed him back to trench 46.

To Ted's left Fred Brimm's platoon were holding out, although they were losing men by the minute. Among those gassed in Fred's trenches were 'some half mad and nearly suffocated' who 'left their trench and were immediately cut down with bullets. Others with luck got away until they fell exhausted.'

The left section of the battalion lines held by A Company stood to and endured an inferno of German shells and a thick gas cloud, but no infantry came their way, their attentions being firmly fixed on the Dorsets to their right. William Quinton and his pal Petch were with C Company in the support trenches, 50m behind A Company. Quinton described how his section dropped what they were doing once the shelling started, threw their equipment on and were held at the ready for what seemed like hours while the unseen German attack raged out of sight, over the brow of Hill 60. All around them the intense bombardment destroyed all it came into contact with and several of his section fell wounded as they waited. 'Suddenly, through the communication trench came rushing a few khaki clad figures. Their eyes glaring out of their heads, their hands tearing at their throats, they came on. Some stumbled and fell and lay in the bottom of the trench, choking and gasping whilst those following trampled over them. If ever men were raving mad with terror, these were.'

Quint's section watched helplessly as the gas cloud drifted slowly towards them and, with the numbers of men who had just barged past them, they expected to find themselves faced with enemy troops advancing along the trench at any second. The cloud arrived, striking the entire section down instantly, despite wrapping the previously issued body belts around their mouths:

A large shell burst on the parapet just where we were sheltered. We were almost buried beneath the falling earth. Young Addington, a chap about my own age, was screaming at the top of his voice and trying to free his buried legs. … At last came the order to advance to the front line. Glad to move, whether it be backward or forward, we staggered through the trench leading to our objective but after a few yards were at a standstill again, for here the trench was absolutely blocked with dead and dying. We clambered over them … our feet sank into soft bodies. We struggled onwards, for we must reach the front line trench before the enemy got possession.

The section arrived at the front trench and found it empty of able-bodied men from either side. Spreading out, they opened fire at any moving shapes to their front, thereby discouraging the Germans from any thoughts of advancing. Once the immediate danger had passed, Quint made the mistake of looking around to become familiar with the position they found themselves in:

What was left of A Company, who had been holding this trench, lay in the bottom of it overcome by gas. Black in the face, their tunics and shirt fronts torn open at the necks in their last desperate fight for breath, many of them lay quite still while others were still wriggling and kicking in the agonies of the most awful death I have ever seen. Some were wounded in the bargain, and their gaping wounds lay open, blood still oozing from them. One poor devil was tearing at his throat with his hands. I doubt he knew, or felt, that he had only one hand and that the other was just a stump where the hand should have been. This stump worked around his throat as if the hand were still there and the blood from it was streaming over his bluish-black face and neck. A few minutes later he was still except for the occasional shudders as he breathed his last … we had other work to think about. It was a good job we had, for what human being could have stood by and seen such sights without wanting to end the sufferings of such poor devils, with a bullet.

By nightfall the trenches on the hill were shared by troops from both sides, separated by a series of hastily thrown-up sandbag barricades. Isolated bombing duels flared up but made no headway before fading into the growing darkness, leaving the hill's inhabitants edgy.

A localised, head-on counter-attack from D Company late that evening regained some of the lost Dorset trenches, bringing to a close the day's ferocious brawl on what had become nothing more than a desolate heap of churned-up earth.

The night quietened down and on the morning of 2 May Fred Brimm found his mortally wounded friend, Ted Warner, 'more dead than alive' at the nearby Regimental Aid Post. He wrote: 'Ted was quite sensible to within half an hour of his death. He knew he was going and only wanted another chance to get at them again. His last words were "They've gone and done for me, the cowards."'

Fred added that, 'Whenever I go near his grave, I see that it is alright.' Sadly, Ted's grave would be lost in the fighting that raged in the area for over three more years and today he is remembered on the Ypres (Menin Gate) Memorial to the missing.

Ted's elderly mother later remarked: 'There was never such a boy and his father thought there was no fault to be found with him except when he enlisted and he thought he was wrong then. But he pleased himself, poor boy. He was a very good boy – always a very good boy to me.'

Overnight the battalion set to burying the dead, moving the wounded back for treatment and generally organising their positions ready for the next day. Although no attacks came at them on the 2nd three more men were wounded in the sporadic shelling, with twenty-two more being treated for the effects of gas from the previous day's fighting. Quint's description of the day's events continued: 'Next morning we were all nerves, fearing another gas attack. We watched the wind anxiously. There is no doubt about it, every man jack of us were absolutely terrorised by the thoughts of it. I have seen the faces of men with iron nerves turn a sickly white when some fool hissed out "Gas!"' The chloride of lime used to sprinkle on the latrines even played havoc with the men's imaginations as the smell resembled gas, spurring more than one of their number to panic and start calling the gas warning as they visited the toilet areas.

With the resumption of German attentions against the hill, the battalion's relief was cancelled so the tired men had little choice but to keep going. The following days were relatively quiet so they set about repairing their damaged trenches during the day. Major Benjamin Roche, Lieutenant Edward Small and Lieutenant Frederick Whittemore joined the battalion late that evening. Frederick Whittemore brought nineteen years of experience with the regiment with him, including having fought in the South African wars in addition to having served in India, Gibraltar, and Bermuda before being commissioned the previous October.

Food was a problem because supplies could not be brought up as the enemy dominated the surrounding area. Most of the battalion survived on a ration of two biscuits per day, with water being even more of a problem. A small brook had been used for water, which appeared from the German lines, but overnight they had piled the water with dead bodies, thus polluting the supply. However, the battalion had no choice so drank it rather than endure the thirst, later suffering the consequences. Small, overnight parties were also raised from each company for the hazardous task of making their way back almost 4km to where the battalion transport wagons were to rendezvous with them. On a good night, the one or two-man parties would return with bags of biscuits, but on other nights they would return empty-handed if the wagons were unable to get through, or not at all if they had been caught out by snipers or artillery observers.

On 3 May gauze, mouth pads and bandages were hurriedly issued and doused with a solution of soda to prevent some of the gas penetrating. Despite being no use against sustained exposure, it at least provided some degree of immediate defence against the new weapon.

Lack of troops to man the line resulted in it being shortened by 700m on 4 May and the left half of the battalion shifted further left, with the far left flank forming a defensive dog-leg. Naturally, the German infantry took over the vacant trenches and the day became uncomfortable for the left section of the line as it suddenly found itself in a salient and subjected to heavy enfilade fire. Despite the volume of fire directed against them, the men were well dug in and suffered few casualties.

The morning of 5 May saw favourable weather conditions for a renewed gas attack and at 8.35 a.m. a fresh gas cloud was released onto Hill 60, most of it engulfing the sector held by the Dukes who had been loaned to the 15th Brigade only hours before. They lost heavily to the gas and were overwhelmed by the infantry assault that followed, the 450-strong Dorsets rushing forward from support in Larch Wood to retake the lost portion of the line. The Germans held on to the entire section between Hill 60 and Zwarteleen, thus enabling them to enfilade the Dorsets to their west and Bedfordshires to their east.

Private William Sherman[141] of C Company was among those on the front when the gas drifted into their lines:

We have had it a bit rough just lately on Hill 60 and just round about there. The other day I was nearly asleep when some of my mates came rushing to me and said there was a lot of smoke over the German lines. I got up and before I could look at the smoke it was all over us. It was poisonous gas and we soon had some pads over our mouths and noses. It gave us a good doing but we stuck it and the wind took it away in time. Ted Medlock had another narrow go. He had a bullet through his hat. It cut his hair off as it went through but did no other damage.[142]

The Bedfordshires had held their positions throughout the first attack, losing a few men to the gas but with around 100 others suffering to varying degrees from the effects. At 11 a.m. another gas cloud was released directly onto their section of the line, driving those in Zwarteleen from their trenches, breaking the battalion line and prising open more of the British front lines.

Re-forming on a new line running from 150m east of the Zillebeke to Zwarteleen road to the edge of Armagh Wood, the Bedfordshires held their positions and kept a heavy fire up against any German attempts to advance further, until a company of Cheshires moved forward to reinforce them after midday.

Private Bob Pigg was in the Zwarteleen sector when the gas clouds drifted towards them. In a letter home, he described the event:

I shall always remember my birthday (May 4th) and what the Germans gave me. It was our first experience of gas. You feel like a drunken man, it turns your face blue and your breath comes out in snatches. If you should fall down you would never get up again, so those who did not get the gas took hold of others who did and walked them about until the effects wore off. Later the wind turned and took the gas back to the Germans and they not being prepared with respirators, down they went and we had our own back.

The left flank of the Bedfordshires had already been shelled heavily since the previous morning and a series of assaults against them after the gas attack were repulsed with heavy loss each time.

B Company in the right trench had already been through the ringer over the last three weeks but there was more to come. Led by Captain Sheldon Gledstanes, they now found themselves sharing their lines with the German attackers, who had worked their way into the position from the yawning gap on their right, created earlier that morning. Coupled with the retirement of the battalion from Zwarteleen, Gledstanes's company found itself isolated and surrounded on three sides, with the ground to its rear being dominated by enemy fire. The Germans were desperate to drive their assault deep into the huge gap created around Hill 60, but for as long as Gledstanes's position was held, their plans were thwarted. Surrendering was unthinkable so with nowhere to go and no options open to B Company other than to stand their ground, this part of the line was to be the scene of some of the most desperate fighting that would continue unchecked all day.

The beleaguered Bedfordshires were assaulted with bombs, bayonets, machine guns and artillery, much of the fighting being at very close quarters. At length, German troops worked their way into the open rear of Gledstanes's band, surrounding them completely, and they even found themselves being shelled by their own artillery throughout the day as no one expected British troops to be holding on. German infantry worked their way into the shrinking lines several times that day, only to be thrown out by their immediate bombing and bayonet charges, the day developing into one long ferocious brawl. Both sides were 'using hand grenades fiercely' until it seemed that the ammunition would run out unless some form of relief was forthcoming.

Inevitably, the 25-year-old Captain Gledstanes was wounded in the shoulder leading the defence but remained at his post and continued fighting, while his servant, Private Harry Cox from Stotfold, was killed by a British shell.[143] Lieutenant Whittemore shot over fifty Germans alone during the day's fighting before being wounded by a bayonet in the hand and suffering from gas poisoning, a fate that he shared with Lieutenant Small. Curiously, Lieutenants Whittemore and Small had in common many experiences during the war: both had been NCOs in the 2nd Bedfordshires; were injured at Ypres on 29 October 1914; and had been commissioned together, arriving with the 1st Bedfordshires only a few days earlier. Now they were wounded in the same trench, would be loaded onto the same hospital train and would both recover in No. 4 General Hospital in Versailles. Whittemore would be awarded a Military Cross for his part in the defence and be back with the battalion at the end of the year.

The 29-year-old Lieutenant Eric Arthur Hopkins was killed in action during B Company's siege, having already been wounded once before during the 2nd Bedfordshires' heroic defence of Ypres in October 1914. The son of an organist, Eric was an art graduate from York and had been an assistant master at Elstow School before enlisting into the

3rd Bedfordshires on 3 August 1914.

Having become the senior officer on the spot, Second Lieutenant Alfred Cyril Curtis took over the defence of the hard-pressed trench 47 on the far right of their small portion of the line, personally leading his men despite being sick from the effects of gas himself and having been in the thick of things for several days by then. The young, 'thick set and heavy built' former Bedford Grammar School rugby forward held the flank together throughout the series of assaults and heavy bombardments, resisting each new attempt to capture their positions and personally leading several bombing attacks. For his outstanding leadership Alfred was mentioned in despatches and awarded the Military Cross.

Around 9 p.m. three worn and tired battalions from the 13th Brigade were moved in to retake the lost section of the line at Hill 60. Despite their gallant efforts, the counter-attack was a disaster but a continuous divisional line was re-formed to the east of the isolated and shrinking B Company.

The fighting did not ease the following day and a series of fresh assaults tried to dislodge Gledstanes's Bedfords, all being repulsed by Second Lieutenant Curtis and his exhausted men despite them still being completely cut off from any other British troops around them. No reinforcements, rations, ammunition or water could reach the trapped garrison yet incredibly they fought on. Exhaustion started to engulf the men, many of them unwittingly falling asleep despite the immense strain they were under, the urgency surrounding them, and their basic human instinct to survive.

Among the day's wounded was veteran Company Sergeant Major John Stapleton from Sawtry,[144] who had coolly led his men from the front throughout the fierce fighting. He would be back within a few weeks, along with scores of others whose injuries were not severe enough to return them to Blighty for treatment.

At dawn on 7 May a last counter-attack was launched by men from two fatigued companies of the King's Own Yorkshire Light Infantry, a badly weakened battalion of Cheshires, and supported by bombers from the Royal Irish Rifles. Although they did not retake the hill, and the entire Yorkshire contingent was lost, the Irishmen managed to reach and relieve Gledstanes's garrison at 8 a.m., after they had built a sandbag defilade to enable movement between the trapped garrison and supporting units. Not many of Gledstanes's band were unhurt and piles of dead and wounded men were found in the middle of their shrunken defensive cordon, so the task of getting them out began in earnest.

The now badly wounded Captain Gledstanes was among those evacuated, but he died from his wounds on 9 May, aged 25. In a letter to his parents, Lieutenant Colonel Griffith wrote of Gledstanes's defence that 'the authorities recognised the achievement as one of the finest episodes of the war' and he was mentioned in Sir John French's June despatch.

Despite the vastly superior numbers of German artillery and infantry being used in conjunction with gas, the outgunned and isolated British infantry stopped the threatened breakthrough by sheer determination and astounding gallantry, but paid heavily in the process. Between 1 and 7 May the 5th Division lost over 100 officers and 3,000 men. Of those, the casualties of the 15th Brigade amounted to 33 officers and 1,553 men, the Bedfordshires losing around 300 of that number, with many more suffering from mild exposure to gas but being unable to leave their battalion due to the urgency of their situation.

Private Alfred Mayes from Welwyn[145] had been with the battalion since early April and was among those who carried on fighting despite being gassed. He described the effects of gas poisoning in a letter to a friend of his:

A peculiarity of this gas is that one rarely loses consciousness. I will endeavour to describe the sensation. When the wind is right, the Germans fire a shell over us and you see a green cloud of smoke rolling along the ground towards you. When it envelopes you, all the air disappears and you start gasping for breath and as you gasp this stuff fills your lungs until you haven't strength to gasp at all, or move hand or foot. All the time one's brain is clear and you know what is going on all around you, but you cannot breathe and all your strength seems gone. If the gas does not blow away it is all up with you. When it does, some are too far gone and gradually sink. Personally, I could not walk ten yards without being 'done up'. I have seen fellows six feet high being fed with milk and having air pumped into them to keep them alive, I have seen them die two days afterwards with their faces as black as a nigger's.[146][147]

Many of those lost in the battalion had been among the drafts arriving just days earlier, such as Privates Charles Cleaver[148] and Frederick Dumpleton[149] who had lived in the same town. They had enlisted together, trained together, arrived in the 300-strong draft on 30 April together, and both would lose their lives on the hill. Charlie was posted as missing and later confirmed as having been killed, whereas Fred was found among the wounded of Gledstanes's garrison but died on 7 May.

Private Frederick Groom[150] had been a porter at St Albans' Midland Station until enlisting in the regiment early in September 1914 and had also been among those arriving in the 300-strong draft on 30 April. In a letter to his old work chums Fred wrote:

Well old boys, it is very exciting, I can tell you, especially when you first get under shell fire. When I arrived from over the water, we went straight up to the firing line and it very soon made us wish that we were back at Harwich, but when you get used to it, you don't take any notice of it. They say the Germans can't shoot, but give them the chance and see! We are doing very well but we cannot get the chance to get any of our clothes off. In fact we have not had a wash for a week so I bet I look pretty dour. Old chums, I think I shall get enough baccy and cigs without you sending me some, but we get short of tea and sugar, so if you could send me some cocoa and sugar instead, I should be much obliged. You might send me the 'St Albans Times' when you write, as I do miss it so.[151]

Fred had been sitting in the trenches writing early on 5 May and added the postscript: 'I am very sorry to say that just after I wrote this letter the Germans started attacking with poisonous gas. … I have got a lot of gas in my lungs and am wounded in the head with shrapnel.'

Even some of the luckier veterans who had come through many close calls did not get from the hill unscathed, Private Theodore Rowlett of St Neots[152] being one such man:

Twice he has been buried from the effects of a German shell; the back of his overcoat was burnt by some corrosive liquid emanating from a shell and had his collar not been turned up, his flesh must have suffered; his head has the marks left by a bullet; he has the scar of another wound on his right wrist; and a piece of the little finger of his left hand was taken off by a bullet. A fortunate turn of the head saved him from what would probably have been a serious wound. Another soldier called to him and as he turned his head to reply, a bullet came whistling along and just shaved the side of his face. Had he not turned he would have got it in the cheek. He has also experienced the unpleasant sensation of being in a shelter on top of which a bomb has burst. Once when he was carrying some tea along the trenches the man next to him had half his head blown off by a shell.[153]

Lieutenant Colonel Griffith was once again mentioned in the Commander-in-Chief's despatches in June for his leadership of the battalion throughout their difficult, stubborn defence, as was Private Benjamin Bosley[154] who carried several of his wounded comrades under heavy shellfire despite suffering from gas poisoning himself. Lieutenant Francis Hyde Edwards, who had been with the battalion from Mons and recovered from wounds received during the Battle of the Aisne, was also mentioned and awarded the Military Cross for his actions on Hill 60. Sergeant Frederick Spicer, too, was mentioned in despatches and awarded the Russian Cross of St George for his bravery during the battle and would go on to add several more awards to his name by the end of the war.

Trench life: May–July 1915

At home, although news of the British struggles around Ypres was reported on, outrage at the sinking of RMS *Lusitania* at 2.10 p.m. on 7 May dominated national headlines. Column inches in local newspapers throughout Bedfordshire and Hertfordshire were presided over by a mixture of long casualty lists and letters home describing conditions over the three weeks the battalion was engaged on the hill.

Back in Flanders, the 5th Division remained in the area around Hill 60 but the men were spared involvement in any of the actions that continued around Ypres throughout the month. In fact, it would be over a year until the division was engaged in any further set-piece battles, giving it valuable time in which to rebuild, reorganise and retrain their men.

Like the other battalions in their division, the Bedfordshires had been so heavily engaged since their arrival that they bore little resemblance to their pre-war structure. Even after the return of hundreds of men who had been wounded during the 1914 fighting, over half of their number had been civilians when war had broken out over nine months earlier.

While events developed around them, the depleted battalion spent a relatively quiet few weeks between reserve and support positions. However, with the destruction of all shelter within Ypres, new support and reserve locations were established and from late on 7 May they rested in huts near Ouderdom and reorganised. Training in the use of hand grenades was given a priority and their machine-gun sections were brought up to strength once again.

In Ouderdom, Second Lieutenant Richard Wynne reported sick and was found to be suffering from gas poisoning and German measles, so left the battalion.

Early on 12 May the soldiers marched back to dugouts near Hill 60 and a draft of thirty men joined them, although Lieutenant Colonel Griffith was moved to temporary command of the brigade until the 20th.

From the 14th until the 16th the battalion returned to Ouderdom, later moving on to huts at Rosenhil, near Reningelst until the 19th. While resting, a much-needed draft of reinforcement officers arrived: Second Lieutenants Bartle Stuart Frere, Rupert Edward Gascoyne-Cecil, Henry Patrick Claude Burton, Eric William Coulson-Mayne, Thomas Reginald Mulligan and William Rolfe Nottidge joined on the 15th; Captain Charles Ogden rejoined on the 19th, having recovered from his wounds received in March; and on the 20th Captain Richard Reuben Langstow Thom joined after recovering from injuries received in the 2nd Bedfordshires along with Second Lieutenant Mayne.

While visiting the support trenches at Hill 60 on the 20th in preparation for the battalion's move back into the line the following day, Second Lieutenant Leonard Johnston Jones was wounded, which would signal the start of a continuous tour in the front line or in close support that would last until mid-July. Once they were back in the trenches, the Bedfordshires were initially held in support of the rest of the brigade until the end of May, providing working parties by day and night, their base being in the railway embankments near Zillebeke Lake.

Captain Thom left to rejoin the 2nd Bedfordshires on the 21st, being replaced by Captain Harold Wilbraham Molyneux Tollemache on the 22nd. The date of 24 May saw another German attack thrown at the British lines north of the Menin Road and, although not directly involved, gas reached the battalion causing a few casualties. For many nervous hours that day a yawning gap in the British lines around Hooge existed, to the left flank of the brigade, which was finally re-established the following day.

During their ten-day tour in support, Second Lieutenant Gascoyne-Cecil was wounded on the 23rd and ten other ranks lost their lives with a further fifty-one being wounded by shelling, sniping and gas.

Lance Corporal William Webb,[155] a regular writer of letters featured in the *St Neots Advertiser*, had finished his day's fatigues on 24 May and dropped by to say hello to one of his pals, Albert Norman. Sitting in a dugout, William was updating Albert about his brother having died a month earlier at Hill 60 when a German shell scored a direct hit on their dugout, wounding all five inhabitants. His Company Sergeant Major, George Bull, was nearby when the shell tore into their shelter and rushed to help dig the men out. Bandaging William, he sent him on his way only to learn that he had died from his wounds the following day. CSM Bull's letter to William's fiancée made its way into the local papers as yet another local character's story came to a premature end.

Also dying as a result of the shelling was Private George Brewer from Oxfordshire. The 35-year-old had only been with the battalion a few weeks when the chance shell hit his dugout and he died the next day. Private Hayward of the South Staffordshires was passing George's grave some weeks later when a note inside a glass bottle, reverently laid beneath the wooden cross, caught his attention. Unravelling the note, he was so moved by its contents that he copied it down and posted it to his parents:

In memory of a good soldier of Christ.

A crescent moon, enough to shed
Upon this field, where lie our dead,
A shimmering ghostly light to show
Where Britain's heroes met their foe.
What need to tell of clash and din,
Of the deadly bayonet driven in;
The shrieks and cries of those in pain,
Of men becoming beasts again.
To see men fight and writhing die
And describe, like Zola, I'll not try;
But when all's over I could say
The best of mankind died today.
Ye British wives and daughters too,
Hold high your heads; it was for you
Those heroes made their last advance
To find a grave 'Somewhere in France'.[157]

Like so many others, Private Brewer's grave was later lost and he is remembered on the Ypres (Menin Gate) Memorial to the missing.

Among the wounded was Sergeant Frederick Howe of Baldock[158] whose war had been incredibly hectic so far, as he had been in the thick of the fighting since his arrival in France in August 1914 and had countless near misses. In spite of surviving the heavy fighting in 1914, he was picked off by a sniper on 10 January 1915 but returned on 12 April. Once again he came through the intense fighting on Hill 60 only to be caught by a chance shrapnel shell on 28 May, which saw him leave the

battalion entirely. He would be transferred into the 2nd Borders later
that year, and survive going over the top at Mametz and the horrors of
High Wood in July 1916 before being wounded at Ginchy in September,
and again when buried for two hours by a shell in 1917. Winning the
Military Medal the same year, Sergeant Howe's luck finally ran out soon
after his return from ten days' home leave in July 1917, when he was
killed in action on 26 October 1917. The 25-year-old's body was never
found and he is among those on the Tyne Cot Memorial to the missing.

Despite the lottery of life in the front lines, as many of the men as
possible continued to enjoy simple pleasures wherever they could, such
as Private Clark who wrote a letter to his sister in Lidlington: 'I am only
dressed in a pair of trousers and a vest. I don't wear a shirt now as it is
so hot. We are having glorious weather. I am not going to complain of
the heat because I know what it is to be cold. … At night I can hear a
nightingale quite plainly. We went out the other day in a wood and found
quite a lot of birds' nests but didn't touch the eggs. … Today we had to
wear our respirators for ten minutes to get used to breathing with them
on. We all looked like a lot of highwaymen let loose.'[159]

By the end of May, the brigades within the 5th Division had been
reorganised back into their formal structures and between 1 and 13 June
the Bedfordshires were back in the front line at the base of Hill 60, at the
southern flank of the 15th Brigade sector.

German shellfire dominated the next fortnight, with the battalion
losing men daily. By the time they were relieved at 9.30 p.m. on 13 June,
ninety-nine more men had become casualties, most being caught by the
sporadic but heavy shelling of their lines. By day the battalion went
about their fatigues and sheltered from shelling and sniper fire but at
night they left their havens to conduct repairs to trenches and patrol into
No Man's Land, keeping the battalion very busy.

Two days in close support around the railway embankment was spent
providing large working parties for the front line, before they returned to
the hill again on the 17th. On the 18th Second Lieutenant Gascoyne-
Cecil rejoined, having recovered from his leg wounds from almost a
month earlier, and the following day saw a German mine explode close
to the Bedfordshires' trenches, fortunately injuring just one man. Second
Lieutenants Coulson-Mayne and Mulligan were also wounded during
the period on the hill, neither officer returning to the battalion after
recovering.

Late on the 21st relief came and the Bedfordshires returned to the support area, providing continuous working parties for the Dorsets. Upon their return, those men not assigned duties instantly thought about eating before resting in readiness for the following night's fatigues. Although out of the front lines, they were still within the sight of German artillery spotters, as Corporal Alfred Hall explained:

In the morning, we were sitting around a fire in our billet taking breakfast when two shells dropped outside. I said 'I will sit back a bit' and just after I had moved away a shell crashed into the building, killing one man, wounding six and blowing me right through the window. I was stunned by the shock but I soon recovered and then I rushed to the assistance of the wounded. I dragged two of them outside and the others were also got into a place of safety, although for the whole of this time the deadly shell fire was kept up. One fellow had two fingers smashed and was badly hurt about his head and body, but he never murmured while his wounds were being bandaged. The building was more like a slaughter house than a place for British troops to live in and we were very glad when we left it.[160]

Brigadier General Northey was wounded on the 23rd, causing Lieutenant Colonel Griffith to leave the battalion until the end of June while assuming command of the brigade. Lieutenant Hugh Pearse, who had been with the battalion since mid-April, was injured on the 25th and a further five casualties were sustained before returning to the forward trenches on the 27th.

News arrived that five more men from the battalion had been mentioned in despatches on 18 June for their gallantry during the fighting in April and May: Quartermaster and Honorary Lieutenant A.E. Peirce; Regimental Sergeant Major Wombwell, who would be commissioned and receive the Order of the Bath in 1919; Acting Sergeant Joseph Cross,[161] who had served with the regiment through the South African wars and died from his wounds on 30 July 1915 in Norwich hospital; Sergeant William Humphries;[162] and Acting Corporal Albert Knight,[163] who was later transferred to the Machine Gun Corps.

As the month went on, three more Distinguished Conduct Medals were awarded to men of the battalion.

Acting Company Sergeant Major Alfred Hawkins[164] had already been mentioned in despatches in September and October 1914 before he was awarded the DCM 'for conspicuous devotion to duty throughout the war', having 'continuously set an example of gallantry, cheerfulness and zeal'.

Company Sergeant Major George Garrett[165] had been with the battalion since Ireland and was included in the King's birthday honours list. He was presented with his medal 'for conspicuous devotion to duty and gallantry under fire. He has set an example of cheerfulness and zeal under difficulties.'

Corporal Ernest Barnes's[166] citation on 21 June 1916 read: 'For conspicuous gallantry. He has frequently led bombing parties against the enemy and has done very good work on patrols and with wiring parties. He has set a fine example of coolness and courage.'

Between 27 June and 3 July sixteen more men were lost, including Lieutenant Percival Hart, who was wounded in the right ankle on 2 July, having been with the battalion for a few short weeks. Of those killed was Private Walter Warman from Ware,[167] who had arrived with the battalion just a month earlier. Before leaving for the front, the 24-year-old Walter had promised his mother that if anything happened to him and he was still able to, he would write to her. On the 27th Walter was fatally wounded, but 'with true soldier's courage he managed on the battlefield to write a post card, almost indecipherable, saying that he was badly wounded but was going on well'. Despite being found the next day and moved to No. 8 Casualty Clearing Station he died, but not before giving the card to the sister who cared for him in his final hours.

During their next spell in support, the stirring news reached the battalion that Private Ted Warner had been posthumously awarded the Victoria Cross for his gallantry on Hill 60 in May.[168]

By their return to the front on 9 July, a further thirteen men had fallen to shelling and sniping, but their coming tour in the front lines was to prove more costly. Before reaching the trenches that day there were many changes to the officer contingent. Major Benjamin Roche, Captain Harold Tollemache and Lieutenant Bartle Frere were all admitted to hospital with fever, while a draft of six officers arrived. Second Lieutenants Philip Vyvyan and Lindsay Austin Horne joined from the Queen's Regiment reserves, while Lieutenant C.H. Douglas, along with Second Lieutenants Frank Luckyn Williams, Alexander Harry Waddy, Westropp Orbell Payton Winmill, Harry Willans and Allan Oswald Rufus Beale, arrived from the Bedford reserves.

While the infantry held the churned-up wasteland around Hill 60, mining had been frantic below ground and the consequences showed on the surface from 11 July when a German mine blew close to trenches 38 and 39, creating a large crater. Although the Bedfordshires' main trench lines were practically unscathed by the initial explosion, the shower of debris and immediate German artillery bombardment that followed accounted for one officer and eight men killed, with over thirty more wounded. One of the listening posts established forward of the main line was almost obliterated in the blast, with all six men becoming casualties in an instant. One of the inhabitants was Private Frederick Miller,[169] who had only been with the battalion since the end of April and who would win the Distinguished Conduct Medal for his subsequent actions. His citation reads: 'For conspicuous gallantry. The enemy exploded a large mine near our trenches, and two men of a listening post were blown to pieces, and the remaining four were buried by debris. Private Miller, one of the four, succeeded in working himself free, and, although injured, managed to dig out the remaining men, working under considerable shell and rifle fire.' Frederick was recovered and moved back through the medical system for treatment. However, his wounds would be too severe for him to return to active service and in June 1916 he was discharged from the army.

Among the dead was the 20-year-old Lieutenant Rupert Edward Gascoyne-Cecil, who had been with the battalion since May and had already been wounded. Rupert was the youngest of four sons of the eccentric Right Reverend Lord William Gascoyne-Cecil (born Rupert Ernest William Gascoyne-Cecil), Rector of Hatfield and later Bishop of Exeter, and Lady Florence Gascoyne-Cecil (daughter of the 1st Earl of Lathom). By 1918 the family would lose two more sons to the war, John Arthur and Randle William, with only Victor Gascoyne-Cecil surviving, having been wounded several times.

The following day, another mine was exploded near trench 37, causing hardly any damage to the Bedfordshires' section of the line but wounding five men, and around midnight the 46th Division relieved the entire 5th Division, with the 1st/4th Lincolns taking over from the Bedfordshires at the base of the hill.

Once the 5th Division had concentrated on the morning of 13 July, they were removed from the Second Army and positioned in reserve between Poperinge and Hazebrouck, the Bedfordshires billeting in Boeschepe until 21 July. Great secrecy was maintained, with all moves being completed under cover of darkness, but the route marches and exercise proved welcome after their prolonged spell in the trenches.

Having moved to billets in Abeele, 3km north-west of Boeschepe on the 21st, the following day saw a visit from Major General Thomas David

Pilcher. Pilcher was the CO of the 17th Division so had no official reason to be there, but as he had served with the 2nd Bedfordshires during the South African wars, took the opportunity to drop in and see his old regiment while the chance allowed.

The next day the men of the battalion found themselves standing tall as the CO of II Corps inspected the brigade before they left his command for the newly formed x Corps, Third Army, complimenting them on their 'excellent record' during the inspection.

Private George Leonard Page of Godmanchester wrote home while enjoying the rest, describing the comparatively luxurious surroundings: 'We are still at rest and I am writing this in a big barn in a farmyard. The barn is our sleeping and dining compartment. There are probably about 50 fellows all together. We are happy as sand boys … when we go into the trenches again, we are going to another part of the country instead of our old position.'[170]

Bob Pigg of Royston was among the thousands of soldiers who chanced his arm at poetry as a way to eat up some of the tedious hours spent in trench warfare, or during rest periods while in reserve. Although he was never to be recognised as the equal of the likes of Siegfried Sassoon, Bob's amusing little ditty was a variation of a poem that turned up in many papers from the time. Written during their spell in reserve that July, it reflects the humour of many Tommies at the time:[171]

I've a little wet home in a trench,
Where the rain storms unceasingly drench.
There's the sky overhead,
Clay and mud for a bed,
And a stone that we use for a bench.

Bully beef and hard biscuit we chew,
It seems years since we tasted a stew.
Shells crackle and scare
Yet no place can compare
With my little wet home in the trench.

So hurrah for the mud and the clay
Which led to 'Der Tag' – that's the day
When we enter Berlin,
That city of sin

And make the black hearted ones pay.

Yes we'll think of the cold slush and stench,
While from Huns our just payment we wrench.
There'll be shed then, I fear,
Redder stuff than a tear
For my little wet home in the trench.

Chapter 9

The Somme Sector
July 1915 – January 1916

'Generally much quieter than the other areas
the battalion has hitherto been in.'

British presence in continental Europe had been slowly growing, with the arrival of the first of Kitchener's New Army divisions in May 1915. Initially they had been fed into the front lines piecemeal to familiarise them with life on the Western Front and, once the fresh divisions in France were ready, the British army took over a further section of the front lines from the French. Although some of the veterans from the retreat to Paris almost a year earlier had been around 40km east of the previously unheard-of area of France, many of the battalion had never so much as heard of places like Albert and the River Somme.

Late on 29 July the men of the battalion were loaded onto trains at Godewaersvelde, 9km south-west of Poperinge. After an all-night journey that took them around 100km south-west, the men detrained at Corbie next to the River Somme and marched to billets at Lahoussoye, 13km south-west of Albert.

As his men were organising themselves after their long move, Lieutenant Colonel Griffith visited the trenches his battalion was to take over on 31 July, to acquaint himself with the unfamiliar area and conditions. A 7km march to billets in Morlancourt followed on 1 August and, as the men prepared for a move to the front lines, their company captains inspected the front-line trenches 9km north-east, near Fricourt. On the 2nd the remaining officers visited the new front and that evening the Bedfordshires relieved the French 410th Regiment. The 1st Norfolks already held the line to their left and the 1st Cheshires came up overnight

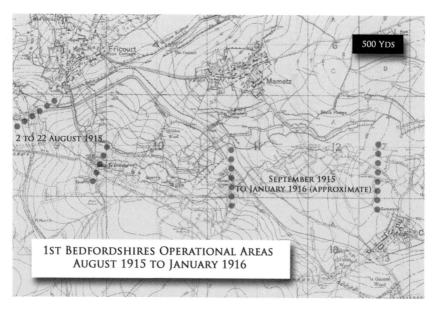

1ST BEDFORDSHIRES OPERATIONAL AREAS
AUGUST 1915 TO JANUARY 1916

and took over on their right, thus completing the 15th Brigade's deployment.

With the 51st Highland Division to their north and the French army to their south, the 5th Division formed the southernmost flank of the British army, but with no reserves other than those each division could pull off at a local level, the line was painfully thin.

It was instantly clear that setting their new positions up for their own style of defence was going to take an enormous effort, but arriving in the beautiful, quiet countryside in midsummer could not have been a more stark contrast for those men who had lived through the previous winter and survived the indescribable conditions on Hill 60 that spring. So, fatigues, rebuilding the trench system and random dangers of trench warfare aside, the battalion would settle into a comparatively luxurious summer on the Somme.

The 19-year-old William Quinton wrote of the contrast he saw between the Ypres salient and the Somme, remarking in amazement that 'one could often see a lone figure with a team of horses and a plough, busily engaged in the peaceful occupation of ploughing'. Some months later the lovely myth this image created was undone when the plough-man was found to be a German soldier acting as a spy. He was shot by firing squad and buried in the field he ploughed, marked by a wooden cross bearing the inscription 'Died for his Fatherland'.

Alongside preparing their lines for defence, the battalion tutored the recently arrived 7th East Surreys in trench warfare between 4 and 15 August. Sporadic shelling, sniping and the occasional clashes in No Man's Land in the dead of night still continued, but the soldiers' first tour on the Somme saw just two men killed and ten wounded in the first three weeks until relief came on the evening of 22 August. The adjutant was so surprised at the number of casualties that he even remarked in their war diary that it was 'very much lighter casualties than the Battn. has ever previously suffered in a corresponding period'.

Even with so little going on, rumours still formed a part of the daily lives of both the men and their worried families at home, as reported in one local paper. Concerns in Royston over one such rumour suggesting that a well-known local footballer called Kruger had been killed proved untrue when, in a letter dated 13 August 1915, he wrote asking his mother for a pork chop to be sent out to him.

Between 22 and 30 August the battalion rested in billets at Sailly-Laurette, 5km south of Morlancourt and astride the River Somme. Although large working parties were called on for digging duties, the men enjoyed bathing in the river in the height of summer, away from the gaze of German guns and snipers.

While resting, news arrived that Bandsman George Law from Ashwell in Hertfordshire[172] was to be recognised for his service during the war. George had served in the regiment since the spring of 1909 and had been with the battalion on the Western Front since it had first landed in August 1914. He was awarded the Russian Cross of the Order of St George, Third Class, for his distinguished services as a stretcher-bearer throughout the campaign and had incredibly survived the intense fighting despite his hazardous job.

In the same *London Gazette*, Company Sergeant Major George Garrett,[173] Sergeant Frederick Spicer and Corporal George Franklin[174] were all awarded the Russian Cross of the Order of St George, Fourth Class, for their gallantry.

At around the same time the first divisional band of the war was formed, which brought a welcome diversion to the men while resting as bands had been forbidden for the first year of the war, with impromptu mouth-organ players being the only musical sounds heard from any line of march. Within two months this grew and developed into an entire divisional concert troupe called the 'Whizz Bangs'.

A single officer replacement – Second Lieutenant Ernest Alfred Rex – joined them on 13 August and by the end of the month, the battalion boasted an impressive 23 officers and 952 men present at muster.

On the 29th the chilling news reached the battalion that Private A. Turner had been sentenced to death for being found asleep at his post three times.[175] In what would be the second and last event of its kind within the battalion, Private Turner's sentence was commuted, ensuring no men from the regiment were shot at dawn.

Late in August the 18th (Eastern) Division arrived on the front and took over between the 5th and 51st Divisions, enabling both to shorten their own lines considerably. As a result, the new divisional line ran from Mansel Copse, 800m south of Mametz, to the River Somme. Of the service battalions which formed the 18th Division were the 7th Bedfordshires, a fact that caused delight when men from either battalion accidentally ran into one another. Their arrival also allowed for only two of the division's brigades to be deployed in the front, the third always being held as reserve and thus providing valuable working parties in addition to a defensive depth not previously enjoyed.

The battalion's return to the trenches came on the evening of 2 September when the men moved to the area around Maricourt, 10km east of Albert, taking over trenches 28 to 25 from the 1st Devons. Although the overall condition of their trenches was good and the area was described as 'generally much quieter than the other areas the battalion has hitherto been in', much work was still needed, keeping the men ever busy. Sergeant Herbert Spencer, who had come through the entire campaign without a scratch, despite being involved in some extremely close-quarters fighting on Hill 60, even wrote in amazement how 'gramophones and pianos were heard' from Mametz. The main trench line was 300–400m from the German lines, although advanced posts were maintained that were just 50m from the enemy. A draft of twenty-five NCOs and men joined on the 8th and Lieutenants Alfred Curtis, Charles Reginald Glyn and Hogden, who had been attached from the Indian army, received sudden orders to return to England. The battalion would not see Lieutenant Curtis again during the war, although he went on to win the Distinguished Service Order, a Bar to his Military Cross, and was mentioned in despatches six times in all.

A spell in billets in Morlancourt between the 11th and 15th was followed by the battalion's return to the trenches south of Mametz. The 15th Brigade took over the line from Mansel Copse to the north-east of Carnoy, where the soldiers remained until moved away from the area in January 1916. The Bedfords' almost comfortable spell on the Somme came to an abrupt end once the battalion took over the lines between trench 69 at Mansel Copse and trench 62 at the western edge of Carnoy, as the trenches were badly incomplete. The parapets were not thick enough to stop a rifle bullet, leaving the inhabitants exposed; there were hardly any fire steps in place, which would enable the defenders to see over the parapets and fire their rifles if assaulted; and no lateral defence was possible along the lines of trench, so if an enemy took control of one section, those to either side were almost impossible to hold effectively. Added to this, the length of line they were to man was at the very limits of their capability, leaving very few men spare to carry supplies and complete the urgently needed work required to make their trenches defensible.

As if their job was not already challenging enough, German trenches were only around 130m away so aggressive patrolling and outposts were needed, draining their thinly spread resources even further. However, their counterparts seemed relatively disinterested in troubling them, so, despite the battalion's offensive posture, very few men were lost during the tour.

Second Lieutenants William Arthur Shaw and Herbert John West joined the battalion while in the line, the latter being wounded within a week. Second Lieutenants Gerald Sherry and Robert William Friend also joined on 25 September.

As the Battle of Loos opened almost 60km further north, the original intention had been for the 13th Brigade to assault and take Pommier Ridge in conjunction, but following the failure of the Loos offensive, the attack was called off. For their part in the offensive actions, the battalion was to demonstrate against the Germans opposite, supposedly to convince them of an imminent assault against their lines. To their amusement the Bedfords and their neighbours 'fixed their bayonets and waved them above the parapet of the trench, at the same time emitting lusty cheers'.[176]

The last few days of September saw patrols stepped up and dummy sniping posts established to draw the attention of German snipers. The posts worked and attracted a 'gratifying amount of attention from enemy's marksmen', some of whom were sniped once they revealed their own positions. Trench 61 at Carnoy was also added to the already stretched line by the end of the month and the division shook itself out into a line of three brigades once more, with the Bedfordshires' brigade on the left of the divisional lines.

A German bombardment fell onto their positions on 1 October and the soldiers of the battalion were enfiladed from east of Carnoy but no infantry assault came their way and just Second Lieutenant Herbert West and one man were wounded. After an edgy day wondering if their counterparts would throw any surprises at them, strong patrols were again sent into No Man's Land overnight. One sector in the Bedfordshires' line was not expecting any of the battalion's patrols to return to its section, so when a group of men were identified as approaching its lines stealthily, two groups of bombers ventured out to surround them. Second Lieutenants Allan Beale and William Shaw led their respective teams into action and ambushed the approaching raiders, only to discover they were Bedfords who had become disoriented and returned to the wrong part of the lines following a patrol. The sudden crack of bombs and rifle fire from the darkness shocked the German trenches into opening fire themselves and the sounds of nervous sentries unleashing salvos at imaginary enemies rattled along the lines for some time before dying down again. William Shaw and three other Bedfords were wounded during the ambush and rifle exchanges, although thankfully none lost their lives.

Their last few days in the line were very quiet as improvements to their positions continued in earnest, with just one man being lost in the period. In one of the war's many ironic twists, Sergeant Albert Sirrell of Shrewsbury[177] was killed on the last day of their tour, which was also to have been his last day in the line as he had completed his five-year term of service.

The rest of October was spent in reserve at Bray-sur-Somme, Chipilly and Étinehem supplying large working parties. Sergeant Spencer recalled how, while in Bray 'we could go to plays, buy anything and get a good bath. Civilians were very kind to us and we had some good times. The R. Somme ran through this town and we had some good swims, played football and cricket.' Second Lieutenants David Newbold Gaussen, Alexander Robert Charles Eaton, Ernest George Donnison, William George Courthope, Reginald Cumberland Green and Cecil Rees Thomas all joined early in their spell in reserve and a draft of twenty-five men also joined on the 15th.

Lance Corporal Bob Pigg wrote from his cosy billet while in reserve about the overall conditions they enjoyed: 'We have a Church of England Soldiers Club where we can go and spend a few hours at night; so you see it is quite different to what it was out here last winter. ... All of the Royston boys are quite well. Reg, Driscoll and "Kruger" are still at the old game (football), which we all enjoy when we are back resting.'[178]

With time on their hands, many of the young veterans turned their idle minds to various forms of distraction. Compared to their time at Ypres, the Somme was certainly quieter, but the ever-present danger of death naturally kept them from relaxing completely while in the front trenches. Private William Quinton was approaching his 20th birthday as October slipped by, having already tasted almost a year of front-line service and two costly battles. In an unguarded moment that belied the 'business as usual' attitude encouraged across the Empire, he wrote of the reality of life on the front: 'The papers at home made us sick with their twaddle about Tommy in the trenches being happy and in good spirits and never gambling and laughing at danger, etc., etc. We knew different and many times have wished that those editors could be dragged from their comfortable offices and be dumped among us, to share the happy life we were supposed to be leading.'

The wet trenches south of Mametz beckoned once more on 28 October as late autumn rainstorms battered the battalion's lines. The ground in the area was heavy with clay so, once waterlogged, the trench floors became sticky and cloying, often adding pounds of weight to the men's boots. Upon relief to brigade reserve at Bray on 3 November, large working parties and mining duties kept the battalion busy.

That autumn saw the arrival of both an antiquated-looking trench catapult that would not have been out of place in Caesar's legions, and later the West bomb thrower, which was ultimately a mechanically up-dated version of their wood and elastic catapults. More interestingly, the arrival of the first effective British trench mortar sparked interest in the front lines until it was realised that the accuracy of the $1\frac{1}{2}$in mortar attracted the attention of opposing German artillery, which still out-matched anything the British could offer in the area.

The well-known figure of Kruger was sent on a spell of leave early in November, once the battalion moved into reserve. While at Ypres almost a year earlier, he had taken a slight wound in the side but shrugged it off as many of his comrades did. However, that and a cold he caught in the trenches resulted in his health deteriorating so much that when he returned home on 2 November 1915 he got much worse and was hospitalised. After spending three weeks in Bedford hospital he returned home, but was discharged completely from the army in December 1915, his war and enthusiastic involvement in the lively games of football in reserve areas well and truly over.

Back in the Mametz trenches from 9 to 15 November, casualties remained low but the dreadful weather caused many landslides and it became a constant battle to maintain the shape and condition of the trenches. The workload involved in upkeeping just the front-line trench system was so heavy and fruitless that maintaining the communications trenches was abandoned throughout the entire division. The glue-like mud even clung determinedly to the men's shovels, so throwing it from the trenches became an exhausting job in itself and, despite all their efforts, the water level remained the same whether the mud was removed or not. As the battalion wrestled with Mother Nature, at home news broke of what was labelled the 'Derby Scheme', which was the first definitive move towards national conscription.

Company Sergeant Major John Stapleton, a veteran of over twenty years with the regiment, was promoted to Acting Regimental Sergeant Major on the 14th and early in the New Year would be recognised further for his unwavering commitment and reliable service since arriving with the battalion in August 1914.

Snipers were a constant problem as their presence often escalated the otherwise bearable existence below the ground. Once one was located a duel would break out between the opposing posts and, if not settled quickly, one side would find themselves supported by their mortars or artillery. Once the situation had developed to this point, the men on both sides knew what was to follow, as William Quinton explained: 'Some bad language was directed towards our gunners on these occasions as we made a dive for our dugouts to await the enemy response. These little exchanges of fire became known as the 'daily strafe' or the 'Hymn of Hate'. We would laugh about them before and after but they were really no laughing matter while they were actually in progress.'

During one of the many lengthy debates on the subject within their section, usually held in the confines of a dingy dugout where they 'filled the air with bad language and tobacco smoke', Quint's pal 'Pratty' summed it up: 'S'always the bloody same, our 'tillery starts strafing and us poor buggers have to stand the racket when Jerry has a bit of his own back.' After some time a 'grunt and a snore here and there' would usually signal that the debate had ended.

At 7 p.m. on the 15th relief came and the battalion returned to billets in Bray, providing constant working fatigues until returning to the front again between 21 and 26 November. By now, winter was arriving with heavy fog, frost and cold conditions becoming prevalent. Officer patrols ventured towards the German lines nightly, to generally harass and throw grenades into their lines, with trench catapults and West bomb throwers being used as the opportunity allowed. Just two men were wounded during the tour, and Lieutenants Andrew Cecil Thom-Postlethwaite and Frederick Arthur Sansom joined just before the next spell in reserve at Bray.

The last two days of November saw a thaw and heavy rain, causing massed trench cave-ins all along the lines, throughout the communication trench system and to numerous dugouts. Huge working parties were created to deal with the problems, leaving little room for rest.

On 1 December Lieutenants C.G. Thomson, Eric Chilver Wilson and Vincent Stanton Sanders joined, with Frederick Whittemore rejoining after recovering from his wounds sustained on Hill 60 in May. The same day saw an underground explosion kill Privates Charles Bettles and Henry King, as well as wounding two of their comrades while they worked with the brigade tunnelling company in trench 73.

An era came to an end on 3 December when Lieutenant Colonel Griffith left the battalion, having been promoted to command the 108th Brigade from the Ulster Division. He had led the battalion since October 1913, throughout their trying introduction to the war, and had earned himself a reputation as a fine combat leader. That night, under the temporary command of Captain William Harold Louis Barnett, the battalion returned to C sector near Mametz. Captain Francis Hyde Edwards returned to the battalion the following day, assuming command as the men struggled ceaselessly against landslides and torrential rain.

Lieutenant Colonel Benjamin Robert Roche arrived to take command of the battalion on 6 December 1915 as the quiet but extremely wet spell continued. That night every battalion in the division's front lines launched a simultaneous mortar barrage and trench raid on the German lines, with varying effects.

A return to billets in Bray and working parties from the 9th to the 13th saw Private James Brown from Northampton killed while on mining fatigues on the 10th, but was otherwise uneventful. After returning to C.1 subsector near Mametz on the evening of the 13th, rain made trench 69 almost unusable the following day, but the Germans seemed to be having the same problem as a group were fired on when they were seen leaving a communications trench near Mametz. A German deserter surrendered at trench 67 at around 5 a.m. on the 16th, having been wounded by his own men as he tried to escape. Half an hour later German troops made what the adjutant described as 'a feeble attempt to bomb The Mound (a salient from 62 trench)' but caused no damage or casualties.

Private William Quinton was in the section of trench that took the prisoner in and was impressed at how he had made it without being spotted and shot on sight: 'He was a pretty cool customer for now he had achieved his objective, his face was all smiles as he was led away to Hqrs to be interrogated.'

In a further reorganisation intended to strengthen the latest batch of New Army divisions with tried and tested regular units, the 14th Brigade was moved out of the division at the end of the year and replaced with the 95th Infantry Brigade, fresh from training in England. Before being transferred completely, the new brigade was split up and trained at platoon level within the division's veteran battalions. During this process, parties from the 16th Royal Warwicks were attached to the Bedfordshires for instruction, eventually taking over trenches 65 to 67 completely late on the 17th. The 16th Warwicks would entirely replace the 1st Dorsets from the 15th Brigade in the New Year.

After a few days in reserve at Bray the battalion returned to the same lines late on 22 December, ready to spend its second Christmas in the trenches. Two men were wounded on Christmas Eve, with Private Charles Garner of Sacombe dying from those wounds on Christmas Day.

Private William Quinton wrote that when in the front line 'washing and shaving were out of the question and we looked a queer lot after a week or so under such conditions. But at length, time would come for relief and back we would go with light hearts, looking forward to a good night's sleep, a clean up, a pay day and in all probability a good "booze up".'

Bob Pigg was back in the trenches for his second Christmas Day, writing: 'We had a little concert in the dug out on Christmas night, seven of us and I must say it [was] very strange that four of us came from Royston, two from Therfield and one from Barley. It was very quiet on Christmas Day but at about eleven our boys began to straff [sic] Fritz with some of Mr Lloyd George's shells but one thing I am glad to say that Fritz did not reply so we did not have to call for our stretcher bearers.'

Late on Boxing Day the Bedfordshires were relieved and saw the New Year in resting in reserve at Bray, Étinehem and Chipilly.

The year 1915 had been a difficult one for the Tommies on the ground, with shortages of many of the essentials needed for the type of warfare they were engaged in, uncomfortable conditions and meagre reserves.

The greatest military successes of 1915 belonged firmly with the Triple Alliance, which had driven the Russian armies from both Poland and Galicia in addition to having conquered Serbia. All in all, the Entente Cordiale's year had been one of largely failed offensives and disappointment, but the arrival of the British New Army had bolstered the remnants of their pre-war, professional army. The latter half of the year also saw the arrival of quantities of materiel that would enable the British armies to engage their enemy on a more even footing, including much more artillery, a significant increase in the production of shells and other essential material, and the arrival of new technologies which would include the now famous steel helmets making an appearance early in 1916.

Local roads were widened to support the movement of men and supplies more readily, more permanent structures were built for time spent in support and reserve, and trench design and stability were radically improved. Attempts to counter the unexpected effects of trench foot, frostbite and fevers, which had sprung up as a result of trench life, were also in full swing.

Despite Sir John French telegraphing as early as 21 December 1914 that the British army badly needed to be issued with munitions and supplies to the level their opponents were, and Sir Douglas Haig pursuing the same line since his promotion to the Commander-in-Chief of the entire British Expeditionary Force in December 1915, the Royal Engineers' army and ordinance workshops at Le Havre continued churning out all varieties of shells, grenades and munitions.

Back in Blighty, newspapers reported that almost a million Tommies were on the Western Front by the time 1916 opened and, with the Derby Scheme calling more and more groups to training as January developed, it was clear the British army was steadily building to a strength that would enable it to pursue a more aggressive stance.

The Bedfordshires had seen 1915 out in reserve, billeted in the now-familiar village of Bray-sur-Somme, while they provided large working parties for the front lines and the brigade's mining activities. During the last few hours of their mining fatigues on 2 January, two more Bedfords were killed underground in C.2 subsector, making their subterranean activities notably more hazardous than their duties above ground.

That evening the battalion resumed its tour on the front and the routines of shelling, sniping and patrols continued. The date of 5 January saw a marked increase in shelling from both sides of the front and

German rifle fire increased the following day, pre-war veteran Private Stephen Hare[179] being killed during the hail of bullets.

Four days on the front and four in reserve became the routine for January, with very few casualties and little activity over and above the usual game of chance being evident as the midwinter period stalled any thoughts of significant actions.

Lady Luck finally caught up with Sergeant Albert Higgins[180] of A Company on 14 January, when a sniper took his life as he repaired wire in front of his trench at 2 a.m. Although the pre-war veteran from East London was not aware at the time of his death, it transpired that later that day Albert's name would appear in the *London Gazette*, the soldier having been awarded the DCM for gallantry shown throughout the war. Three more Distinguished Conduct Medals were issued to men from the battalion in January.

Private Arthur Webb[181] of the transport section was awarded his for his dedication while at Hill 60 the previous year. Arthur's citation read that 'he succeeded in driving up by daylight, a wagon of supplies to "B" Company of his Regiment, which had been without rations for days along a road which was under heavy shell fire, and although warned that it would be impossible to get through'.

Acting Regimental Sergeant Major John Stapleton of Sawtry[182] won his 'for conspicuous gallantry and continuous good work at the front from the commencement of the war. He has invariably displayed great bravery and coolness, and has given to all ranks a fine example of ability, energy and devotion to duty.'

On 20 January, the 30th Division started relieving the 5th Division from the area, with the 13th and 95th Brigades being moved into reserve around Corbie. The 15th Brigade was held in the line under orders of the 30th Division for the rest of the month while the soldiers settled in. Unknown to the men their sister battalion, the 2nd Bedfordshires, was moved into the line less than 10km east of their own positions, and within days some of the officers and transport men would meet, exchanging greetings and stories as time allowed.

Although casualties had been light in recent months, tragedies continued and often came in the form of unusual events. Private Arthur Gray[183] of C Company had been a reservist who had arrived with the battalion late in April 1915, had survived Hill 60, and enjoyed a relatively quiet seven months since his shocking introduction to warfare. However, on 27 January it was discovered that, during the previous night's relief,

Arthur had unexpectedly shot and killed himself near the Citadel.

On 28 January a German assault was launched a few kilometres to the east and the Bedfords' C.1 subsector was shelled with around 2,000 shells, according to the adjutant, yet caused little damage and no casualties. The following day the weak remnants of a gas cloud drifted into their lines from Suzanne, again causing no casualties.

On what was to be their last day on the Somme for the time being, thick fog hid most movement from view, but one unlucky Bedford from A Company was killed at dawn by a sniper when the fog cleared just enough for him to be spotted. Battalion snipers similarly claimed fourteen Germans that day, all of whom were busily repairing their wire defences in the drifting fog.

At 9.40 p.m. relief came in the form of the 1st Norfolks and by 8 a.m. on 31 January 1916 the battalion had marched 12km south-west to billets in Sailly-Laurette on the Somme. This would mark the start of a welcomed break from the trenches that would last until March, when they would finally return to the line in a completely new section of the Western Front.

Chapter 10

The Arras Sector
January – July 1916

'For Christ's sake, hurry up Quint,
we're liable to blow up at any minute.'

The week spent resting by the River Somme was filled with cleaning, refitting, training and generally keeping busy. Lieutenant Colonel Roche was called back to duties in England on 1 February and was replaced by the highly experienced Lieutenant Colonel Cranley Charlton Onslow. After being wounded on the Aisne the previous September, Lieutenant Colonel Onslow had returned to lead the 2nd Bedfordshires in January and was greeted enthusiastically when he returned to his old comrades as they gathered themselves after their long spell in the front lines.

The following day Captain Francis Edwards was called to the Third Army School at Flixecourt to act as a temporary instructor, giving him a well-earned rest far from the sound of the guns.

On 6 February a move almost 9km due west left the battalion in improved billets at Corbie, but the next day a further march took the men back into filthy billets in Argoeuves, 6km north-west of Amiens centre. On arrival, Second Lieutenants Andrew Cecil Thom-Postlethwaite and Vincent Sanders left with three NCOs for training at the 5th Divisional School at Montigny. Almost a week went by, filled with company-level training, resting and general fatigues.

On the 11th they were marching once again, this time to Camps-en-Amiénois, 25km west of Amiens. Arriving just before sunset, they were greeted by more wet, dirty and cold billets.

In the two weeks the battalion remained in the area, training continued despite the uncomfortable winter weather. Around this time

Second Lieutenant Alfred Charles Hayhoe of Newmarket arrived, along with two reinforcement drafts. On the 13th C Company's CO, Captain William Nottidge, was posted to the Third Army School for instruction, being temporarily relieved by Lieutenant Henry Burton. Valentine's Day saw Second Lieutenant Sherry and three of his NCOs leave for the Sniper's School for instruction on the use of telescopic sights. Two days later a route march through heavy rain and gales was cut short after less than 1km as the weather was too unforgiving, an outcome that was repeated on the 18th in more atrocious weather.

New classes for the bombing and Lewis gun teams were started the next day, as was an inter-platoon football league, which kept the men amused and distracted.

While the battalion rested in billets on 21 February a massive German assault was launched 250km further south-east, against the fortified French positions around Verdun. Although not immediately obvious, this German attempt to 'bleed France white' would become one of the most notorious, prolonged battles of the war, would last all year, and would draw the British New Armies into their first set-piece battle before General Douglas Haig was sure they were ready.

After a route march in the snow the following day the boisterous first round of the battalion boxing tournament was launched to much anticipation, but further rounds would be postponed once urgent orders came that the division was being moved into VI Corps. The French armies were being drawn to the already ferocious fighting around Verdun, so a further section of the Western Front was being taken over by the British army to free up more French units.

Following several days of snow the weather eased and the battalion set off for its new post further north late on the morning of 24 February. A 15km march took the men across the River Somme around 1km from Picquigny, and they rested at La Chaussée that night. The next day's 19km march north became progressively more difficult as heavy snow and driving winds made the already slippery, undulating roads even more treacherous. Many British divisions were crammed along the inadequate and hazardous roads, with as many French units passing them heading the other way. Transport wagons regularly slid from the icy roads and the infantry spent many long hours trudging a few metres into the teeth of the north-easterly blizzard, halting, trudging a few more, then halting again. This particular march was later referred to as 'the retreat from Moscow' by those who took part. The entire division paused during the 26th, with the Bedfords billeted at Candas, 8km south-west of Doullens, while the weather settled. After several days the battalion was on the march once more, spending the night of the 29th at Doullens and the next two nights at Warluzel, 14km north-east of Doullens.

Two senior NCOs swapped posts on 28 February as the battalion reorganised. RQMS William Bartlett became the battalion's Acting Regimental Sergeant Major and the recently decorated Acting RSM John Stapleton moved into William's role as the RQMS, a post he would hold for the rest of the war. John had joined the regiment on 17 June 1895 and, other than the first four years spent with the 2nd Bedfordshires, had remained firmly in the 1st Bedfordshires throughout his career, aside from a brief spell recovering from wounds received at Hill 60 in May 1915. The square-jawed veteran was typical of the battalion's battle-hardened senior NCOs and would see the war out to the very end, completing twenty-three years with the regiment in 1919.

On 2 March the battalion moved through more atrocious weather to Dainville, 4km west of Arras centre, where the men would spend almost a week in billets as the 15th Brigade held divisional reserve. The 5th Division had taken over the section running from just north-east of Roclincourt to the River Scarpe, with the 14th (Light) Division to their south and the Highlanders of the 51st Division to their north. Here they would remain for around four months until more sudden orders would see them retracing their steps back to the Somme.

While in reserve, parties of officers reconnoitred the new area daily, in preparation for their own move to the unfamiliar trenches, while the battalion provided working parties for the front and support areas as the division set about preparing its lines for its own style of defence once more.

The Bedfordshires moved into the front-line trenches late on 9 March, holding the southern end of the divisional section and astride the River Scarpe. To the south of the river, outposts were manned among the ruins of Blagny, many just 10m from their German counterparts. To their north an isolated post of two Lewis guns and a supporting section of riflemen were stationed on the marshy river banks, between the two front lines, with the rest of the battalion lines running north from the river, facing the German positions among the ruins of Saint Laurent Blagny.

The snow continued falling for some days as the battalion set to preparing and draining its trenches, which were in a poor condition. Both sides were generally content with leaving one another alone

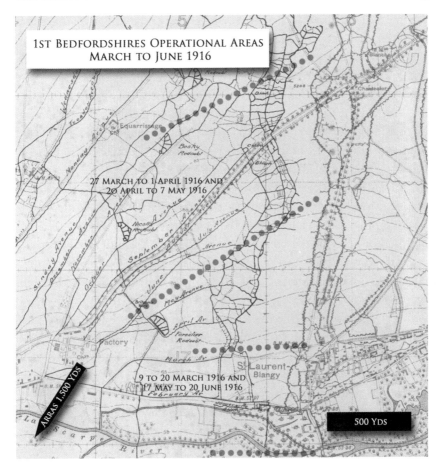

1ST BEDFORDSHIRES OPERATIONAL AREAS
MARCH TO JUNE 1916

27 MARCH TO 1 APRIL 1916 AND
20 APRIL TO 7 MAY 1916

9 TO 20 MARCH 1916 AND
17 MAY TO 20 JUNE 1916

500 YDS

throughout the bad weather, but on 11 March a German patrol stumbled across Second Lieutenant Beale's wiring party and wounded the officer and one of his men with a bomb. The ever-present menace of snipers threatening any unguarded movement cost the 24-year-old Second Lieutenant Charles Adam Cook his life that day when he was shot in the head and instantly killed. Charles had originally served as a private in the Hertfordshire Regiment until commissioned and was the first officer to be killed in the battalion since the previous July.

Other than much sniper activity, the rest of their spell on the front was quiet and Captain Nottidge rejoined the battalion from his training course. The battalion's first tour at Arras had cost it two officers and eleven men.

On 15 March A and B Companies were relieved and returned to billets in Arras, while C and D Companies were held in support trenches north-east of the town. Three days later the two halves of the battalion swapped positions and on the 21st the entire battalion withdrew 20km west to billets in Agnez-lès-Duisans. Lieutenant Colonel Onslow assumed temporary command as the brigade CO until 1 April, with Major Noel Lawder running the battalion in his absence.

Their return to the front lines on 27 March was to the trenches north of their original positions, 1km south-east of the centre of Roclincourt. This tour saw more mortar activity than before, with little chance to retaliate courtesy of the British ammunition shortage.

Lieutenant Frederick Whittemore, Sergeant Edward Quince[184] and Private Maurice Winch[185] from A Company went out on a night-time patrol on the 29th, which ended badly. Frederick Whittemore, a former 2nd Bedfordshires Company Sergeant Major and veteran of Ypres and Hill 60, who sported two wound stripes, was fatally injured in an exchange of fire in No Man's Land. His two comrades could not reach him but tried regardless, under extremely heavy rifle and grenade fire. Fresh efforts to recover his body the following night also proved fruitless and, as a result, the lieutenant is remembered on the Arras Memorial to the missing. For their determined efforts, Sergeant Quince and Private Winch were the first in the battalion to receive the recently introduced Military Medal in June 1916.

Overnight on 30/31 March, Second Lieutenant Philip Vyvyan was wounded and the following day the battalion withdrew from the trenches, half moving into brigade reserve in Arras, the other half moving to support positions in Roclincourt.

Lieutenant Colonel Onslow returned on 1 April and the Bedfordshires were held in reserve until returning to the front on the 4th. The following day Lieutenant Ernest Rex and three men were wounded by one of their own rifle grenades, but otherwise the tour was quiet until relieved to Roclincourt and Arras once more on the 8th. Captain Harold Tollemache commanded the brigade reserves at Arras, consisting of two companies of Bedfordshires and two of Norfolks.

Between 12 and 20 April the brigade was relieved completely, the Bedfordshires moving to their old billets in Agnez-lès-Duisans, 20km west of Arras. While there, Second Lieutenant Harold Bird joined from the 3rd Bedfordshires, although he was attached to the 13th Trench Mortar Battery almost immediately. Training took much of their time, when the torrential rain eased off enough to allow them to move outside, with daily trips from groups of officers visiting the sector of the front they would be manning once their rest period was over.

During one such reconnaissance trip on the 16th, Captain John Moyse was wounded by shrapnel in both legs and returned to England to recover; he was to spend some months in London hospitals. One medical report at the end of April remarked: 'The officer's general condition appears to be satisfactory but he has had 16 months continuous service at the front, which has been a severe strain.' While some men of the battalion had been through the worst the war could throw at them and not had a scratch, Captain Moyse had already recovered from influenza and a facial wound received on Hill 60, but would still rejoin the battalion later that year.

The Bedfordshires returned to the front lines on 20 April, taking over the J.2 sector astride the road running north-east from Saint-Nicolas to Bailleul-Sir-Berthoult. They were greeted by very wet and 'sloshy' trenches, but by the time they were relieved into support positions four days later, had completed a quiet tour. Their next tour was certainly warmer as the weather improved dramatically. However, it also marked the start of a considerably more cautious period as the local New Zealand miners reported German mining activity in their section, causing the lines to be evacuated between trenches 94 and 95. A wary but quiet few days followed, with two false gas alarms stretching the nerves of those in the front even further on 1 May.

On the 2nd the Bedfordshires moved back from the front-line trenches with B Company returning to Arras and C Company to Saint-Nicolas, both providing working parties for the front lines. D Company was posted to the Britannia Works redoubt, just south of the Saint-Nicolas road and A Company held the Nicholls and Bosky redoubts a few hundred metres further north. Two days of warnings followed as British miners were convinced the Germans were ready to explode their own mines, but by the time the battalion moved back into the trenches, nothing had happened.

At night on 5 May the relief was complete and A, B and D Companies held the front trenches with C in support in Britannia Works. Frantic underground activity had been taking place, with both sides busily preparing their own mineshafts and damaging their opponents' when the opportunity allowed. As a result, information on the preparedness of enemy shafts became confused and the entire front sector was warned as being in a 'dangerous' state, with mine explosions expected at any moment.

Among those engaged in the carrying parties that moved explosives to the end of the mineshafts were 'Quint'[186] and his pal 'Petch'[187] from C Company's No. 9 section. Understanding that the enemy were certainly doing exactly the same as they were and probably within a few metres, their nervousness would increase with each step that took them closer to the exposed end of the tunnel. Reaching the end after one of many trips, they paused to catch their breath among the tonnes of high explosives. 'Old Petch could see the humour in anything. Standing, or rather stooping in the tunnel, he stuck a fag in his mouth and asked me for a match. Perhaps I was not as quick handing him the matches as I should have been, for he suddenly said "For Christ's sake, hurry up Quint, we're liable to blow up at any minute" and then, realising what he had said, burst out laughing.'

Following two more quiet days, at 3 p.m. on 7 May a heavy German bombardment fell onto their lines and three German mines exploded, churning the ground and deafening the inhabitants. After ninety minutes the intensity increased, finally drawing to a sudden close at 6 p.m. All night the German gunners targeted the support and communication trenches intermittently but no further air, ground or subterranean activity followed the bombardment. Incredibly, considering the intensity of the shelling, the battalion lost just eight men. That night the brigadier congratulated the men for their behaviour and unflinching steadiness throughout the bombardment, and the bulk of the battalion stood down.

The 22-year-old Private Sidney Cox of Letchworth[188] was awarded the Military Medal for his actions that day, rushing to the aid of his comrades who had been buried by the explosion. Although three of the men he recovered were already dead, Sidney managed to save the lives of no less than fourteen men through his determined efforts. Within three months, he would find himself lying in a hospital bed in Cambridge recovering from wounds received at Longueval and would finish his war serving in the Labour Corps.

The three mine craters that now formed part of the divisional line were soon named accordingly. 'Cuthbert', 'Clarence' and 'Claude' were characters used in popular songs performed by the divisional concert party, the 'Whizz Bangs', at the time, so lent their names to the new features.

The artillery duel continued for the next few days, with the Bedfordshires spending several days between the 11th and 16th in the same support scheme as previously, split between the redoubts, the candle factory north-east of Saint-Nicolas, and support positions in Arras.

On their return to the front lines between 17 and 23 May, they moved one sector south of their old position, holding the front between the Saint-Nicolas road and the River Scarpe, as the new concept of Daylight Saving Time was introduced at home. The 31-year-old Lieutenant Reginald Green from Luton was shot at 3 a.m. on the 18th while examining a mine, dying before he reached the field ambulance. He had been with the battalion since the previous October.

Although rarely recorded officially as there were so many instances, overnight raids and skirmishes between the opposing troops were still regular occurrences. Some were a bloody business with bombs and bayonets being used freely, but others were more subtle and successful, as described by Bombing Sergeant Herbert Spencer who wrote of one such event during this tour in the lines:

A bombing party was formed and we were to go into the Germans' trenches. At about 9pm we walked over to the German trenches. German sentries were posted every 200 yards. We got into their trench and set to work to find how many were holding it. We disguised ourselves as Germans and waited for their patrol. It was quite dark, so that they couldn't recognise who we were. We got onto the parapet and the patrol passed right by us. All went well until one of them spoke to one of our bombers who could not speak German, but they could not get away and with two of our men the patrol were taken prisoners and led over to our trenches. The Germans were unaware of what had happened and one sniper kept having a pot at us. One of the bombers went up to him and spoke and demanded his rifle etc. and escorted him over to our trench. Shortly after a German officer came along and was caught like a rat in a trap; he too was sent over to the English lines. After two hours in the trench, orders were sent that we were to get back and after tearing up their barbed wire and breaking down their trench, we quietly walked back.

Two nights later a German raid was launched in retaliation but Spencer's bombers were waiting in ambush and 'caught them napping', capturing the entire party.

The Germans launched an attack against British positions 6km further north, near Vimy Ridge, on 21 May, with some of the gas barrage drifting into the Bedfordshires' lines. The entire line stood to but no assaults developed in their area, making the tour a relatively quiet one.

On the 23rd the brigade moved into divisional reserve once more, the Bedfordshires returning to their billets in Agnez-lès-Duisans. During this spell, Lieutenant Samuel Norrish joined the battalion. Training, marching and competitive activities resumed to keep the men occupied, with the battalion fairing well. In the 5th Division football tournament they beat the RFA 4–3 and the soldiers of the battalion transport took first place in the brigade's preliminary horse show, which saw them progress on to the very first divisional-level show. A church parade on the 28th signalled their last day in reserve, before returning to their old positions between the Saint-Nicolas road and River Scarpe again on 29 May.

Since their arrival at Arras, the division had taken an aggressive stance as fighting patrols were a regular nightly event and bombing raids were attempted almost every night. Reprisals often followed from the German lines and on 1 June came a German barrage, followed by three mines exploding in the Norfolks' section, to the left of the Bedfordshires. The German raid that followed was bloodily repulsed by the Norfolks, but the Germans facing the Bedfordshires chose not to leave their own trenches. On the right flank of the Bedfords' lines, the trenches were all but demolished and sixteen men were lost in the heavy bombardment, but things settled down into their quiet routines once again the next day.

During another spell between the 6th and 13th, in brigade support at Arras and spread throughout the redoubts behind the front lines, Lieutenant Colonel Onslow took command of the brigade and Major Lawder ran the battalion in his absence. The following week saw Lieutenant Colonel Onslow leave permanently to assume command of the 57th Brigade, with Major Lawder taking over for a month until the arrival of a new commanding officer. News also arrived that Captain Hugh Courtenay had been awarded the Military Cross in King George's birthday honours list and Corporal Charles Atkinson,[189] who had been with the battalion as a bandsman and stretcher-bearer since early 1910, had won the Military Medal. Also awarded the Military Medal in the same gazette were Sergeant James King,[190] Sergeant Edward Quince[191] and Private Maurice Winch.[192]

Back in the front lines from 14 to 20 June, the battalion continued with its aggressive posture and the casualties continued to mount. At 4 a.m. on the 18th the 28-year-old Second Lieutenant Edgar Millson was hit by a sniper and killed instantly while examining the German lines through his binoculars. A railway engineer in Colombia before war broke out, Edgar had rushed back to serve his country, initially enlisting in December 1914 as a private in the Royal Fusiliers. After being transferred to train as an officer and suffering from a bout of ill health, he had been in

France since the end of May and was only with the battalion a matter of days before his death.

The following day, Second Lieutenant Robert Wright was slightly wounded while leading a wiring party in the dark night and one of his men was severely wounded, but otherwise the tour was, once again, quiet.

During one of the many events from this period, Sergeant Spencer led his bombing section on yet another raid in mid-June, intent on finding and taking out a machine-gun post that had been 'mowing down a transverse'. His group of ten men made their way carefully through the belts of wire and laid up in front of the German trenches, inadvertently finding that the hidden gun was right in front of them. As Spencer remarked:

I had some very good bombers with me and two bombs were soon lobbed at it … the gun and gunners were soon blown to pieces. We got through the wire and into the trench. The German 2nd line was now staring at us. I posted a man to stop anyone coming up the trench from our left. I, with eight other men working our way up to the end. Soon after I heard a terrible scream and thought my sentry had been attacked, so I rushed back to see what was the matter but on reaching him, I heard him say 'It's alright Sergeant, he only ran into my bayonet' … the Germans soon realised something was wrong. Soon we were met by a party of German bombers. I was standing head and shoulders above the German parapet observing and had been doing so for several minutes. Two of our bombers were wounded. Not long after something seemed to mesmerise me. I could see a bomb with fuse burning coming straight at me but I could not move. A terrible crash sent me hurling backwards into the trench.

The raiding party fended off the German counter-attack and retired, carrying their six wounded bombers with them. However, Sergeant Herbert Spencer's war was well and truly over, having lost his eyesight and an arm while serving King and Country.

On 20 June the brigade was once again withdrawn into reserve, taking over its old billets 20km west of Arras. However, after just one day the men marched a further 10km west, into billets in Izel-les-Hameaux, and from there spent four days training in open warfare tactics, despite the rain and unhelpful weather. While training, news arrived that Captain Francis Edwards had been mentioned in despatches for the second time.

As the month drew to a close the battalion laboured away, split between Arras and Wailly to the south-west, oblivious of the events unfolding further south. It was well known that the French were under pressure around Verdun and the British were obliged to launch an offensive in support of the Allies, but news that trickled north to Arras through the army grapevine at the end of June suggested that although their offensive was imminent it was not clear when it would happen.

In support of the offensive a localised assault nicknamed the 'Wailly Stunt' was to be launched south of the River Scarpe. To this end, on the 27th the Bedfordshires and their fellow units returned to Arras and provided large working parties for the front lines on a daily basis, with the entire battalion other than transport, cooks and the headquarters section being used.

Early on 2 July, urgent orders arrived for the battalion to march in full daylight and concentrate at Givenchy-le-Noble, 21km due west of Arras. German artillery observers could not have believed what they were seeing as bodies of khaki troops assembled in plain view, but were quick to call down a barrage which fell on C and D Companies as they gathered in Wailly. Incredibly no casualties were sustained as the companies quickly dispersed into sections and headed west, but while the men were assembling an accidental bomb explosion killed Private Frederick Cain from Baldock[193] and wounded three others.[194]

The urgent orders had brought to an abrupt end the battalion's most relaxed spell since the beginning of the war, but training would continue in the relatively peaceful Givenchy-le-Noble area until fresh orders arrived on 12 July. That single piece of paper would start the battalion's move south and take the soldiers into the teeth of the largest set-piece battle the British army had been engaged in to date.

Chapter 11

High Wood and Longueval
July 1916

'Worthy of the best traditions of the British Army.'

Around Christmas 1915 the Allied generals had realised that with almost two million French soldiers already lost, the main weight of any actions in 1916 would be borne by the British and Commonwealth forces. The opening of the Verdun offensives had only hastened the need to launch a fresh assault on the Western Front, thus drawing Germany's gaze from the 'furnace' around Verdun. To this end, General Haig reluctantly succumbed to pressure to attack on the Somme, despite reservations that his New Army was not ready.

At 7.30 a.m. on 1 July 1916, eight French and sixteen British divisions had gone over the top and signalled the start of the Battles of the Somme (1916). By the end of the battle in November 1916, practically every British division on the Western Front had been engaged, and over one million men had become casualties.

While the 5th Division moved south towards the fighting, long route marches were interspersed with intense training to prepare the men for what was to come. Included in the division's preparation for the battle, new tactics were introduced into their training, such as how to liaise with aerial spotters above them during operations.

After the battalion officers had seen a demonstration on how aeroplanes and infantry communicate during offensive operations on 12 and 13 July, the soldiers set out on a 25km march south-west, taking them through Grand-Rullecourt, Lucheux, Grouches-Luchuel, Doullens and on to Hem Hardinval. Despite hot and dusty roads, their war diary proudly noted that not a single man fell out during the march, a feat that would be repeated throughout the equally testing treks during the next four days.

A further long, hot route march the following day initially saw the battalion move south-west to Candas, then march almost due east to Puchevillers, another 25km march in all. On St Swithen's Day they trekked 15km south-west before spending the next two nights at Lahoussoye, with the distant sounds of battle raging less than 30km to the east. Rumours of a cavalry breakthrough near Bazentin had surfaced during the march, but as they advanced nearer the front, the casualties being moved back past them increased and the news from the wounded told a completely different story. While billeted in the village Lieutenant Colonel Walter Allason took over from Major Lawder, having been commanding the 8th Bedfordshires since recovering from his wounds sustained on Hill 60 the previous year.

On the 17th a further march 10km east took them to Ville-sur-Ancre, 6km south-west of Albert, where the battalion started preparing for offensive operations over the next two days, and on the 18th a batch of nine officers arrived to bring them close to full complement.

So, with an almost complete establishment of officers and men and a well-trained and experienced battalion behind him, Lieutenant Colonel Allason ventured into the battle zone to understand more of what was expected of them over the coming days. For the first time in over a year, the Bedfords were about to go on the offensive.

High Wood: 20–25 July 1916

Orders arrived on 19 July for the 5th Division to move quickly and reinforce the men of the 7th Division, who were holding the hard-fought line between Longueval and the infamous High Wood. The 15th Brigade took up positions on the Pommier Ridge in divisional reserve, with the Bedfords east of Mametz and almost in the very trench system taken by the 7th Bedfordshires on 1 July.

Those Bedfords who had been in the area during the last half of 1915 hardly recognised it now. In place of little villages were smoking mounds of rubble, the green grass was now nothing more than a torn, brown scar of land, and the once dense woods were a tangle of shattered stumps. Littering this desolate landscape was an indiscriminate mass of un-exploded shells, discarded equipment and unburied bodies, some from assaults almost a fortnight earlier.

More than two weeks of piecemeal attacks had been launched in the area as the British prepared for a major assault on the second German line. The now-shattered remains of High Wood had been hotly disputed for over a week, with British troops gaining a foothold only to be driven out by counter-attacks delivered with a ferocity that highlighted the tactical importance of the position. German machine-gun placements in the wood were untouchable by artillery and dominated the ground for miles around, enabling the ever-efficient German gunners to take advancing British battalions in the flank. The position simply had to be cleared before any hope of breaking into the German second line could be realised.

Early on the 20th the offensive started, with the 5th, 7th, and 33rd Divisions assaulting German positions in and around the death trap that was High Wood, with additional divisions attacking the fortified village of Longueval to the south. The 13th and 95th Brigades of the 5th Division attacked to the south of the wood, drawing heavy fire from both flanks, yet capturing Wood Lane. Although on alert to move in support at short notice, the Bedfords' brigade was held in reserve on the ridge throughout the attacks.

Determined but costly British assaults by battalions from the 15th Brigade against Longueval and Delville Wood raged the following day, and on the 23rd the Bedfordshires themselves moved in to support the front lines between High Wood and Delville Wood. That night, C and D Companies advanced to the front line, taking over a long section running from the southern tip of High Wood, 750m along the road headed south-east towards Longueval, then following the side road due east for another 150m. Immediately they started advancing their forward posts 50–80m into No Man's Land, with B Company in support 250m further back and A Company in reserve an additional 250m south-west. Seven posts were completed overnight, all being well wired and with Lewis gun teams sited and ready by daybreak.

Among the battalion's casualties from their spell at High Wood was Lance Corporal Edwin Harvey[195]. An east Londoner by birth, Edwin had moved to Luton and joined the Bedfordshire Regiment early in September 1914. He was killed on the 24th and seven months later would be awarded the Military Medal for bravery.

Manchester-born, Second Lieutenant Gerald Sherry had been a pre-war Royal Engineer and had served in the original British Expeditionary Force in France since October 1914. Gerald was commissioned as an officer in September 1915, joining the 1st Bedfordshires the same month. During the work overnight, he was wounded in the thigh, dying at No. 39 Casualty Clearing Station on 26 July. Just six weeks earlier he had been mentioned in despatches for gallantry.

The 24th saw a marked increase in artillery fire, with Second Lieutenant Manning Milton and around thirty men being caught in the bombardment. Another of the Old Contemptibles was among the fallen, being Private John Rogers of Liverpool, a fifteen year regimental veteran.

Sudden orders came that relief was imminent and at around 4 a.m. the following morning, the Bedfordshires were relieved. They moved back to the area around the Pommier Redoubt and rested in bivouacs all day, but their rest was to be short-lived as the next day brought orders to prepare for offensive actions once again.

Longueval: 27–31 July 1916

Longueval was a fortified village just 4km north of the objectives set for capture during the opening day of the Battle of the Somme. It formed part of the well-sited German second defensive line, which Allied planners had expected to capture early in July, but as the month drew to a close it still eluded them. The village had been heavily disputed for days with control swinging wildly back and forth following attack and counter-attack. Now came the turn of the 15th Brigade, who were wound up to retake the positions in yet another assault.

The battalion's only interruption to an otherwise quiet spell on the Pommier Ridge was late on the 25th when an enormous explosion and firework display erupted from near Mametz, just west of the Bedfordshires in their bivouac area. Initial thoughts of a mine explosion were later quashed when it was learned that the divisional ammunition dump was hit, causing the impressive explosion. The next day, company officers inspected the ground around Longueval in preparation for the following day's operations, while the battalion readied itself for what was to come.

To those serving in the area, the German artillery barrage against the southern edges and approaches to Delville Wood, and to the west of Longueval, was so notorious and intense that it even earned its own name – the 'Longueval Barrage'. During the attack itself, communications between the assaulting battalions and their Brigade HQ were completely cut off for twelve hours by the barrage, with almost every man who attempted to find a way through being caught in the inferno.

With preparations complete, late on 26 July, 23 officers and 807 men from the 1st Bedfordshires set off for battle, leaving the transport and cadre behind. After dropping down into the valley north of Montauban, it became clear that the approaches to their jumping-off positions were being smothered with a German shrapnel and gas barrage, so a two-hour halt was called in the fringe of Caterpillar valley until a shifting wind created enough of a gap in the gas curtain to enable them to move through. A quick march eastwards along the dark valley floor was not the easiest of tasks and as they approached their destination the 'Longueval Barrage' increased even further, reaching a roaring crescendo. Undaunted and determined to follow orders, the Bedfords pushed on into a series of sunken roads and hastily dug communications trenches, Captain Frederick Parker being hit by shrapnel during the move. The battalion arrived in its positions in the old German second-line trench system just south of the village at 3.50 a.m.

At 5.10 a.m. a British bombardment opened on German positions in the village, which lasted for two hours while the assaulting battalions shook themselves into shape. Twenty minutes later, operational orders arrived and were filtered down to company level, keeping the men busy with preparations throughout the bombardment.

As per their timetable, A and B Companies left their positions at 7 a.m., moving north to take up the line being vacated by the 1st Norfolks, who had advanced across No Man's Land towards the German positions inside the village at 7.10 a.m., just as the bombardment descended onto a second, unseen line further north. B Company set up on the west of North Street, which ran north to south through the village, with A Company extending the line to the east. The next expected move was to have been at 8.10 a.m. but at 7.40 a.m. an urgent message was passed back to the Bedfordshires that the Norfolks had been held up by heavy shellfire near the centre of the village and needed immediate support. Lieutenant Colonel Allason took charge of the situation, ordering A and B Companies to advance to the Norfolks, finding them pinned down south of the village centre.

It became apparent that the original plans were doomed to failure as the assaulting Norfolks were already too thin on the ground. The Norfolks were initially assigned to take the second objective too, being the centre of the village, but with the arrival of their extra weight of numbers, plans were made by Allason for the two companies of Bedfords to join the Norfolks and take the advance on at 8.10 a.m., with C and D Companies moving into the trenches they would vacate. Once the second line was in their hands, C and D Companies would move through, taking the third and final line at the northern fringes of Longueval until relieved by the 16th Warwicks.

To their east the 2nd Division was advancing towards Delville Wood but the Royal Fusiliers on the Bedfords' eastern flank had been delayed. Despite leaving Allason's advance with an open flank, the decision was taken to continue anyway. Paying close attention to the orchard and open right flank, bayonets were fixed, bombers moved into position behind the leading waves, and the mixed Bedford and Norfolk band advanced into an instant storm of shrapnel and machine-gun bullets. Moving by short rushes between cover, the grim task of clearing each house by hand-to-hand fighting began, bombs and bayonets becoming the order of the day.

Among the early casualties was Private Arthur Reed of Letchworth[197] who had only been with the battalion a matter of days after recovering from a wound sustained in January while serving in the 8th Bedfordshires. He was hit in the abdomen by shrapnel as the soldiers advanced through the village. 'My chum, Lance Corporal Arthur Armishaw, at once dragged me to a shell hole and put my field dressing on; then he had to rejoin the platoon and I was left lying in this shell hole for five days. During these five days I lay there in agony ... I existed on Horlick's malted milk tablets. Old Fritz sent a lot of gas shells over just where I lay and I got partly buried time after time. All my teeth got loose and I went as yellow as a Chinaman.'[198] Arthur was eventually found and made it back home, being discharged in September 1917.

Although progress was being made, the infantry had been unable to keep up with the ambitious timetable. At 8.40 a.m. the British barrage was directed onto positions further north as arranged, but the Bedfordshires and Norfolks were still bogged down in close-quarters fighting, so were unable to follow up. This created a surreal situation, with the entire village disappearing from the sight of onlookers further back, being ringed by intense artillery barrages from both sides. Of more interest to those inside the ring of fire were the locally operated trench mortars that rained down their own shells into the village itself, often unsure of where the new front line was from moment to moment. With all this going on around them, the infantry could do no more than choose their moments to carry the fight to the next house, pile of rubble or hidden strongpoint, doing so to the exclusion of events surrounding them.

By the time C Company arrived with A Company at 9 a.m. and D Company moved into the new front lines to the west of North Street, no

artillery support was left. The new arrivals fixed their own bayonets as
A Company advanced into the western section of the village, clearing
each house in its turn as they went. With the section secured, they crossed
Princes Street that led east into Delville Wood, their eyes on two strongpoints that had been holding up the Norfolks. To the east of the village
and just outside the wood stood a heavily fortified redoubt, which the
company took at the point of the bayonet, capturing around 100 prisoners
in the process. While the position was being consolidated, Lieutenant
Arthur Fyson and his shrunken platoon turned their attentions to a
strongly held house 150yd to the west, which was stopping any movement around the centre of the village. They assaulted the garrison with
such ferocity that the surviving thirty-two defenders surrendered, be-
wildered at the determination of Fyson's small, outnumbered band.
Fyson would be mentioned in the Commander-in-Chief's despatches for
this feat of arms and come through the assault without a scratch.

The advance was temporarily held up by a stubborn German
machine-gun post in the centre of the village, sited to cover movement
in every direction. That position eventually fell after a series of carefully
planned rushes and individuals stalking their way forward to draw the
enemy fire, enabling Norfolk bombers to force their way in and over-
whelm the defenders. The same fate befell the supporting posts covering
it and, in a curious twist, prisoners captured revealed themselves to be
from the German 5th Division.

Meanwhile, two platoons from A Company had been busily working
their way north, along the eastern edge of North Street, having
completely bypassed the machine-gun nest while it was being engaged at
close quarters. With Delville Wood to their east and the largely German-
held side of North Street to their west, they had pressed on until
reaching the Flers Road, running north-east from the village. Here they
met with a group of Royal Fusiliers and the small band collectively
started consolidating their lines, waiting for reinforcements to show up
on either flank. Once the Norfolks took over the area north of Princes
Street, the rest of A Company moved north to support their comrades,
setting up a defensive line to the east of North Street. Facing the German
defenders on the opposite side of the road, they provided supporting fire
as the Norfolks carried their bayonets through the line of rubble running
north from the centre of the village.

Once the village centre had been consolidated, B Company tried to
push on, but German machine guns in Duke Street to the north-west

stopped any advance into the countryside so they strengthened the line and held the west half of Longueval with D Company in support. The Norfolks held the centre of the village while C Company moved to take over the south-eastern section of Longueval.

The forward sections of A and B Companies set up defensive perimeters facing north and west, lining the ruined houses. Pockets of enemy resistance were encountered as the day wore on, more Germans appearing from their shelters in well-concealed cellars and dugouts, often behind the front line of troops. Nevertheless, the British bayonets and bombs gradually overwhelmed the defenders until the entire village had fallen, an objective that had been fought hard for since 15 July.

Communications were now non-existent, with both the Norfolk HQ and Bedford HQ being cut off from anyone outside the village, as well as one another. Any attempts to lay telephone cables were almost immediately stopped, the signallers being killed or the cables being cut. Runners were assigned the hazardous task of carrying messages through the curtain of explosives and shrapnel, as even the brigade's carrier pigeons had all been killed by the afternoon.

Stokes mortars and heavy artillery had been called for to neutralise the German machine-gun post on Duke Street, but neither arrived, so the Bedfordshires and Norfolks remained pinned down in the village. Fortunately, some cover had been prepared when a German hurricane bombardment fell onto B and D Companies' positions late that morning, but Captain Barnett quickly understood that the heavy shelling and overcrowded trenches were causing serious problems. He quickly moved most of D Company back to the German second line, where they sheltered from the continuous bombardment. The officers' mess cook, Private Ashby, was among those rushed back to the old line further behind, which was being pounded into oblivion. He remarked: 'There was no room in the dugout, it was full of wounded,[199] so I just waited for death in the open for five long hours.' However, by the end of the afternoon B Company had lost 2 officers and 54 men of the 5 officers and 166 men they started the day with, while D Company suffered badly in the bombardment, finally losing 2 out of 5 officers and 106 of the 176 men who had marched in from the south that morning.

On the open eastern flank men found themselves under fire from those guarding defensive posts in Delville Wood who were not under pressure from their front, so looked for targets in the village. Corporal Thomas Harris of Luton[200] had become the senior officer in his

immediate vicinity and decided that enough men had been wounded or
pinned down by a particularly troublesome German machine-gun post.
As a result of his actions, he would be awarded the Distinguished
Conduct Medal, with the citation telling of how 'he attacked an enemy
post in a wood single-handed, and killed five of the enemy. He then
fetched up supports and 11 other enemy surrendered. He was wounded.'

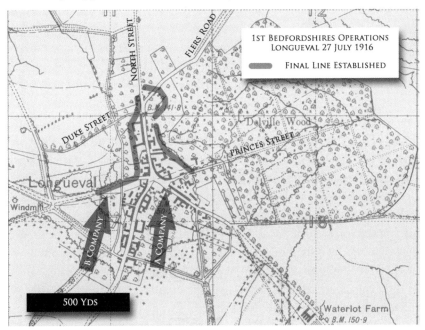

The 2nd Division had appeared in force that afternoon on the
vulnerable eastern flank and secured Delville Wood, which had been the
scene of some horrific fighting in the previous week and had earned the
inevitable nickname 'Devil's Wood'. So, with the line intact and the
survivors consolidating their gains with absolute urgency, lookouts were
posted to warn of the imminent counter-attack. It became clear that,
although the final objective lay around 250m to their north, further
advances were doomed to failure as several entrenched and heavily wired
machine-gun posts were spotted, looking down on them from the ridge.

That evening the expected German counter-attack came. It was as
determined and ferocious as ever but was repulsed with heavy enough
losses to keep the smouldering remains of Longueval in British hands.
When it seemed that the counter-attacks had petered off for the night, it
became clear that the defensive line was far from ideal. A thin outpost
line was left in place, with the bulk of those who had survived from each

company being withdrawn to a more tenable line among the rubble.

Some 9 officers and 303 men were lost during the battalion's assault against Longueval, with 14 officers and 504 men being relieved at 6 a.m. the following morning, when fresh troops arrived to take over. Four officers were killed, being the 23-year-old Captain Henry Patrick Claude Burton, 27-year-old Second Lieutenant Alfred Charles Hayhoe, 28-year-old Second Lieutenant Archibald Clare Holland, and the 20-year-old Second Lieutenant Norman Douglas Wemyss.

Among the wounded officers were Lieutenant Ernest Rex, who had been with the battalion for almost a year and had also been wounded in April; Lieutenant Frederick Illingworth, who would recover and return to the battalion in time for the Arras offensives the following April; Lieutenant Harry Willans, whose war had already been adventurous, having fought in numerous engagements and in several units since his arrival on the front in 1914; and Second Lieutenant Charles James Hunter, who had previously recovered from a wound with the 2nd Bedfordshires while at Loos the previous year.

Privates Arthur and George Boness,[201] cousins from Biggleswade, were among the long list of those killed at Longueval. George had been in a group buried by a shell during their advance and although dug out alive, he died half an hour later from blood loss as an artery had been severed in the explosion. Arthur's exact fate was unknown as no one was left to recount the story and the cousins' names sit side by side on the Thiepval Memorial to the missing.

While reorganising in their bivouacs back on the Pommier Redoubt the next day, the following message was relayed to the survivors:

15th Infy. Bde. 1st Bedfords. The Brigadier-General Commanding wishes to express to all ranks of the Brigade his great admiration at the magnificent manner in which they captured the Village of LONGUEVAL yesterday. To the 1st NORFOLK Regiment and the 1st BEDFORDSHIRE Regiment and some of the 16th ROYAL WARWICKSHIRE Regiment, who were able to get into the enemy with the bayonet, he offers his heartiest congratulations. He knows it is what they have been waiting and wishing for many months. The 1st CHESHIRE Regiment made a most gallant and determined effort to reach their objective and failed through no fault of their own. The way in which the Troops behaved under the subsequent heavy bombardment was worthy of the best traditions of the British Army. The Brigade captured 4 Officers and 159 other ranks 28/7/1916.

Following a quiet two days recovering and refitting, orders arrived at 6 p.m. on 30 July for the battalion to move urgently back to Longueval. Within an hour the battalion was organised and on its way, arriving in the village forty-five minutes later to reinforce the 13th Brigade, who had been heavily engaged while trying to capture the orchards north of the village.

The day had seen a localised British offensive launched, which included the Bedfords' sister battalion, the 2nd, assaulting Maltz Horn Farm just 3km south of Longueval. However, matters in their own vicinity were more pressing as reports had been received that the 2nd King's Own Scottish Borderers had been heavily counter-attacked and were retiring from their lines just north of the village, astride North Street. The Bedfords were rushed in to regain and hold the line regardless of whatever was causing the retirement. A and C Companies quickly moved north, although the Scottish guides were unable to find their companies in the dark so the Bedfords set up a line north of the village and sent their own patrols out to establish what had happened. B and D Companies set up a defensive line among the rubble west of North Street, facing west. The intention was to retire the Scots at dawn, leaving the Bedfords in place to continue the defence, but their whereabouts was unclear.

A confused night followed. In the darkness parties of Scots Borderers were discovered but no fixed line was apparent, as their assault had been brought to a bloody halt. In response to the uncertainty the Bedfordshires established their own firm line of resistance in readiness for further counter-attacks. Just before midnight a message arrived instructing bombers from the Borderers to move into the sunken road heading northeast towards Flers, as the Gordon Highlanders were in position there and a continuous line needed to be established. Within twenty minutes of them moving out, an intense German bombardment fell on the village, causing the defenders to seek what shelter they could in the low piles of rubble that were once houses.

By 2.30 a.m. on the 31st all companies reported heavy casualties from the barrage but the lines were intact, with contact having been made with the division to the east. Despite the mist, smoke, darkness and four hours of intense bombardment, by 6.25 a.m. a continuous battalion line was formed, running from 100m west of North Street on the northern boundary of Longueval, along the Flers Road, to the sunken section of road some 200m towards Flers. C Company on the eastern edge refused

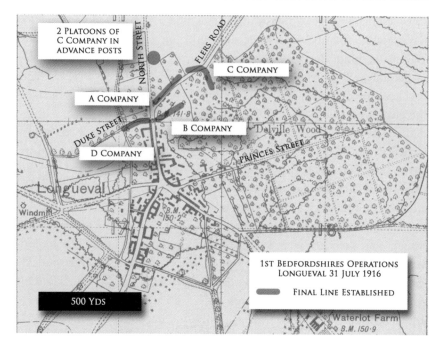

their flank as the situation in Delville Wood was still unclear and two platoons were moved 200m north of the main line to try to make contact with the 2nd Division. Any uncertainty surrounding the wood was soon cleared up once several German patrols stumbled into the Bedfordshires' lines in the pitch black night. Each successive patrol was broken up by bursts of rifle and machine-gun fire, the dark wood coming alive with fire from all directions with each fresh encounter.

Along the northern edge of C Company's sector a patrol moved north towards the German lines, intent on learning just who held the positions. A heavy burst of fire made it clear the occupants were unfriendly, so the patrol spent the next few hours playing cat and mouse with the enemy gunners as they slowly made their way back to their own lines.

With daybreak, patrolling ceased and all day German snipers and artillery observers plagued the Bedfords' lines. A sniping duel developed, each side goading their counterparts into revealing themselves, until at 6 p.m. the first phase of relief showed up. The Scots were relieved immediately and the forward sections from the Bedfords were also moved back to the centre of the village. Around 10.30 p.m. the Cheshires arrived to relieve the entire battalion and the companies withdrew independently to their bivouacs in the Pommier Redoubt.

By daylight on 1 August Longueval had claimed another 188 men, including 2 officers killed and 6 more wounded. The 23-year-old Second Lieutenant David Newbold Gaussen and 20-year-old Second Lieutenant Arthur Norris Marshall were both killed in the darkness. Among those wounded was Captain William Nottidge, who was mentioned in despatches for his behaviour at Longueval in January 1917, but having been knocked unconscious and buried by the same shell he would be among the numerous soldiers who spent many months recovering from shell shock and what was recorded as 'strain from prolonged service, including terrifying dreams' before returning to the 4th Bedfordshires early the following year. Also injured were: Lieutenant Sidney Gerald Mulligan, who would recover in time for the Arras offensives in April 1917, when he would fall in the 4th Bedfordshires' assault against Gavrelle; Lieutenant Leonard Johnstone Jones, who was wounded for a second time, the first having been on Hill 60 in May 1915; Lieutenant Ronald Johnstone Haye, who had been with the battalion since April; Lieutenant Charles Percival Mattey, who was wounded in the right fore-arm by shrapnel; and Lieutenant Oscar Dunsford Roeber, whose brother David was killed in the 7th Bedfordshires two weeks later. The Somme had caused many more cases of shell shock within the battalion than previously seen and 21-year-old Oscar Roeber was yet another. Having been buried in the intense shelling he was returned to England suffering from shell shock, where he would undergo many months of medical treatment for nervousness, headaches, palpitations, sleeplessness and a bad stammer. Eighteen months later he was fit for general service again and transferred into the Royal Flying Corps.

Two brothers from Yelling would also soon be receiving some dreadful news, telling how each of them had lost a son at Longueval. Privates Albert and William Currington[202] both fell during the battle and, as if that was not a high enough price to pay, a further three from the remaining four cousins would also be wounded before the war was over.

After three gruelling days assaulting and holding the heavily fortified and defended village, just over 300 men were left, including 8 officers.

The casualty list was certainly long, but among the sad news was the occasional tale of good luck and survival against the odds. Of those reported missing from the battalion, a tired, officer-less group of men who comprised the remnants of several platoons arrived back with the battalion days later, having been left holding the orchard and waiting for either relief or orders. Ambling back towards the battalion perimeter in tattered rags vaguely resembling uniforms and holding battered rifles, the bedraggled, filthy bunch were soon smiling from ear to ear once greeted with the usual torrent of banter from their chums.

Some days after the division had been relieved, a grubby, exhausted band of Scots Borderers arrived in the British lines, having been isolated in the final objective of their attack on the 30th. They had remained in place, fending off one assault after another, but had finally exhausted their water and ammunition supplies, so had retired back to their own lines.

Bob Pigg of Royston was still in D Company when the battalion advanced on Longueval. Bob's cousin, Albert, emerged without a scratch and although Bob himself had come through the war remarkably un-scathed so far, German gunners finally found him among the rubble. His local paper reported how 'he was buried twice and blown right out of the trench by a shell explosion'.[203] Bob spent a few weeks recovering at a con-valescent camp in Boulogne, but was soon back with his company, carrying on as if nothing had happened.

Thirteen-year veteran Private George Gazeley from Westoning[204] had joined the battalion as a 19-year-old groom and was one of the many wounded, having been hit in the right buttock during the fighting. One of the battalion since August 1914, he typified the service of many such men, as this was not his first wound and would not be his last. Hit in the chest in November 1914, he returned and became a sergeant in April 1915. George was wounded again in the left arm in May 1915, during the final few days of the defence of Hill 60, and was on the long casualty list for a third time after Longueval. George's leadership during the fighting would earn him the Military Medal and four months in Blighty recover-ing, but his time on the front lines with the battalion was not over yet as he would return again in the New Year.

Another veteran of Mons to win the Military Medal while being wounded at Longueval was Sergeant Oswald Gentle from Baldock,[205] who had served with the battalion since January 1913. George had been on the front constantly throughout the war and had certainly earned the respect of his comrades, his local papers reporting that he had not lived up to his name. Sergeant Gentle was hit in the foot by shrapnel, although he was back with the battalion before the end of the year.

Veterans of the fighting in Longueval recall it as being memorable for being the most intense concentration of shellfire that men from the 5th Division experienced during the war. Several letters home referred to highly experienced men 'going mad' from the shelling once their already frayed nerves were subjected to the unending blitz.

One such example was the cool-headed Sergeant Sidney Chamberlain.[206] Sidney had seen thirteen years in the regiment, had served through Mons and all of the early battles, had recovered from having been gassed on Hill 60, and had adapted to everything thrown at him by both the enemy and nature. In July 1916 he had become 'Time Expired' and had the option to finish his service with the colours but chose to remain with the battalion. Sergeant Chamberlain had survived the intensity of the fighting and barrage at Longueval, but by the time they returned to hold the village, shell shock took hold of his nervous system early in August. Despite his remonstrations, he was sent back from the lines to recover and would rejoin his chums some weeks later.

Chapter 12

Falfemont Farm and Morval

August and September 1916

'Well, now, you're the people who took
Falfemont Farm.'

A month's rest: August 1916

The Bedfords were held on the Pommier Ridge until move orders arrived, which took them 11km south-west to a billeting area north-west of Dernancourt, just south of Albert. As the division organised itself for a major relocation, the small battalion was kept busy with fatigues, inspections and marches. On the 4th a 5km march south-west to Méricourt was rewarded with a railway journey, which took them 40km west to Hangest-sur-Somme, 20km north-west of Amiens. A further 7km trek into overnight billets around Quesnoy-sur-Airaines finished the day's move, but the next morning the battalion marched 4km south-west to billets in Tailly, where they would remain for several weeks.

The entire 5th Division had been moved 70km west to rest areas south-east of Abbeville, 25km from the coast and well out of range of even the largest German guns. After a few days' rest, the battalion commenced training for their next operational tour, which included refamiliarising themselves with 'contact patrols' involving low-flying aircraft, with the infantry passing on information to the air-bound observers on their positions and condition.

Hastily erected rifle ranges were put to constant use and drills of all natures filled the men's days. Sporting tournaments were also well received and rowdily supported, with the battalion's heavyweight boxer, Sergeant George Brigstock[207] and the Cheshire's own heavyweight being the finalists in the brigade boxing tournament. Spectators described the bout as 'spectacular', although who won seems to have gone unrecorded. Horse shows, mischievous, loud sing-songs and the unexpected gift of forty-eight-hour passes to the seaside for those who had been in action at Longueval, balanced their rest period out well, ensuring the soldiers of the brigade were in good spirits by the time they were called on for active duty again.

Large drafts arrived while the battalion rested at Tailly, coming from the reserve battalion at home and being a mixture of returning veterans and untried recruits. One of the larger reinforcement drafts was drawn from the Hunts Cyclists and had been in France since 27 July.

Although several of the lightly wounded officers returned to the battalion during August, eleven new officers also arrived throughout the month. On the 14th Second Lieutenant Ernest Alfred Hague joined, having previously served in the 8th Bedfordshires, along with Second Lieutenant P.A. Gibbons from the Army Cyclists Corps. The next day Lieutenant Henry F. Graves, whose brother Walter had been killed in the 1st Bedfordshires in November 1914, and Second Lieutenant Hugh Cecil Covell joined from the 7th Bedfordshires, followed on the 16th by Second Lieutenant Vincent Stanton Sanders, who was returning from a month in hospital. On the 18th three more second lieutenants joined, namely James Hirst Banyard, Dion Albert Lardner and Horace John Everett, all arriving in France for the first time that month. A further officer draft of Second Lieutenants Addison James Howard and P.G. Smith appeared on the 27th. The final draft to arrive before the battalion's next action was at 8 p.m. on 2 September, when Second Lieutenants Christopher Blake and Basil Charles Williams joined from the 3rd and 10th Bedfordshires respectively, bringing thirty men with them as much-needed reinforcements.

Of the eleven new officer arrivals, by 4 September just Second Lieutenant Everett would be left standing.

The men of the battalion realised their comfortable spell in the summer sun was coming to a close when, on 23 August, the battalion transport set off on a 60km journey by road for Dernancourt, just south of Albert. Concentration and move orders arrived the next day, which made it clear they would be returning to the Somme battlefields and not to a new section of the lines further north.

A 10km march north on the 24th took the battalion to Longpré-les-Corps-Saints, where the infantry gathered and prepared for the 50km train journey. Early the next morning the Bedfords entrained, arriving at

Maricourt around 5.30 a.m. and marching to bivouacs north-east of Buire-sur-L'Ancre, then on to a tented area around the sandpits south-east of Méaulte.

A 7km move east to bivouacs 450m north at Bronfay Farm on the 26th was the battalion's final leg before going back into the trenches, and the next day, while senior staff inspected the area they were to be moving into, German shells started finding targets among the men.

Overnight on the 26th the 5th Division started relieving the 35th (Bantam) Division from the eastern slopes of the Maltz Horn Ridge. Once completed, the 15th Brigade would be holding the right half of the line, and the 95th the left, with the French continuing the line south from around Angle Wood.

Initially the Bedfordshires were held in divisional reserve around Billon Farm where, on 31 August, corps commander General Horne presented several gallantry medals to men from the battalion, for their actions at Longueval.

Sergeant Joe Afford from Offord D'Arcy[208] was awarded the Distinguished Conduct Medal, his citation reading: 'For conspicuous gallantry during operations. When his Company Commander was brought in wounded, he carried him back under heavy shell and machine gun fire. Believing that all his company officers had become casualties he took charge, and sent in a good report of the situation though suffering from shock, after being wounded and buried.'

'Afford from Offord', as he was known to his chums in the battalion, had first arrived on the Western Front as a private in the 2nd Bedfordshires and had been among their long casualty list from the First Battle of Ypres. Once recovered, he had served in the 1st Bedfordshires from May 1915, rising through the non-commissioned ranks until becoming Company Sergeant Major in July, when he had won his DCM.

Lance Corporal Bertie Pettengell[209] and Private Joseph King[210] were also awarded Military Medals for gallantry at Longueval.

After the ceremony the men fell out for a short rest before preparing to move into the reserve trenches that evening. At 8 p.m. the relief started, taking the Bedfords into Silesia Trench north of Maricourt – and straight into a cloud of tear gas. Among the casualties was the battalion adjutant, Captain Harry Willans, who was temporarily replaced by Major Noel Lawder as adjutant.

Other than the inevitable casualties and the unwelcomed addition of heavy rainstorms throughout 28–30 August, the sector was relatively quiet, the recent battle seemingly having run its course. Sporadic shelling continued from both sides, with patrols and sniping keeping the battalions in the line busy. In the run-up to their next operations, the Bedfords themselves provided large working parties for the front-line trenches and repaired the reserve lines, which had been subjected to intense bombardment during the previous battle.

After six days of intensive working parties the battalion had lost dozens of men to the German shelling of the rear and support areas, which included nine men of B Company falling to a single shell on the evening of the 2nd. The war diary remarks of this shell that it was 'of a peculiar type. It burst on the parapet and burst in a reddish light and formed no crater.'

As darkness fell on the 2nd the soldiers of the entire division took a deep breath, braced themselves and finalised the details for their next assault across the open fields of the Somme.

The Battle of Guillemont: 3–6 September 1916

The Guillemont sector lay at the southern edge of the British lines and a large, local offensive in mid-August had taken Guillemont station, but further progress had evaded the attacking armies. Several strongpoints and reinforced villages faced the Allied troops, each capable of support-ing their neighbours through extremely effective, carefully mapped-out fields of fire. As a result, the area was very much in German hands, but to enable the combined British and French offensives to move forwards, the sector had to be wrestled from the defenders once and for all.

On 3 September the 5th Division was set to go over the top once more, but before it could, the heavily fortified, highly engineered defensive position of Falfemont Farm had to be taken. This commanding position sat on the end of a high spur and would have decimated the division's assault if left in German hands, bristling with machine guns as it was. Reinforced buildings, deep bunkers, heavy belts of barbed-wire protec-tion and a complete, 360-degree enclosure stood between the assaulting battalions and their objective.

The plan to take Falfemont Farm was based on a heavy barrage softening up the defences and the infantry following up with a frontal assault. As usual, timing was critical and the soldiers would need to arrive at the farm before the numerous machine guns could be carried from their deep, protective shelters. If the barrage did not work, the German gunners would easily break up the waves of British infantry carrying their bayonets up the slope.

Things did not start well when, with no warning or explanation, the barrage failed to materialise, as it had been diverted to break up a German counter-attack further south. However, at 9 a.m. the Scots Borderers and Warwicks from the 13th Brigade who formed the right half of the divisional front, advanced nonetheless. German fire was nothing short of murderous and it was quickly realised that the assault was doomed. The remaining battalions from the 13th Brigade moved up in support, their intention being to attack alongside the main advance scheduled for just after midday.

Early afternoon and according to their timetable, the 95th Brigade advanced against Wedge Wood as the 20th (Light) Division supported by a brigade from the 16th (Irish) Division assaulted and captured Guillemont further north. The Gloucesters and DCLI from the 95th Brigade advanced on the heels of their barrage and carried almost all of their objectives despite heavy casualties, finally digging in on a line north of Wedge Wood, following the road line from Ginchy to Maurepas.

On the right, the fortress that was Falfemont Farm remained firmly in German hands and the 13th Brigade had suffered heavily during their attempts to reach it, unsupported by artillery once more.

At 1.55 p.m. orders arrived for the Bedfords to advance to Slit Trench, progress on to Maltz Horn Trench and finally to assemble in New Trench, just south of Angle Wood, which lay at the base of the hill dominated by Falfemont Farm. Despite narrow communications trenches, the 16th Warwicks advancing at the same time, and a heavy German barrage designed to restrict reserves moving forward, casualties were remarkably light. On arrival at New Trench, it became clear there was nowhere near enough room for two battalions, even though both were under strength. A second trench was hastily dug to provide a degree of shelter, the battalion losing about ten men during the frantic spell.

Around 6 p.m. orders arrived that the Bedfordshires were to assault from Wedge Wood to Falfemont Farm inclusive thirty minutes later, giving them inadequate time to prepare for such a task, as the entire battalion was strung out along a communication trench which headed away from the German lines. Company orders were scribbled furiously and runners dashed to their posts, so that within fifteen minutes the first squads of D Company were moving out. Despite their best efforts and with 900m of open ground to cover before reaching their positions, the British artillery barrage had already moved on before the Bedfords were anywhere near their jumping-off posts. Nevertheless, D Company advanced at the head of the strung-out battalion, but bore too much to the left and inadvertently advanced through the Warwicks and elements of the 95th Brigade in and around Wedge Wood. Although they had unwittingly secured the outstanding section of the 95th Brigade's objective, D Company had suffered as they moved forward across open ground, through artillery and machine-gun fire. Those left dug in along a line from north of the wood, through the sunken road heading north towards Ginchy, as the rest of the battalion arrived piecemeal alongside them and consolidated as best they could under heavy fire. Although the southern section of the circular trench system between the wood and the farm was in the Bedfords' hands, the northern part and the section running southeast to the farm remained in German control.

D Company had relieved thirty Warwicks from Wedge Wood once dusk arrived, setting their defensive line up north of the line of the trees. The rest of the battalion were in place, extending the line almost 1km south until they joined the Cheshires, who were set up facing Falfemont Farm. Plans to move the battalion into position ready for the morning's attacks were thwarted when the Gloucesters and DCLI announced they were unable to take over Wedge Wood from the Bedfords. This not only scuppered plans to bomb their way along the German-held section of

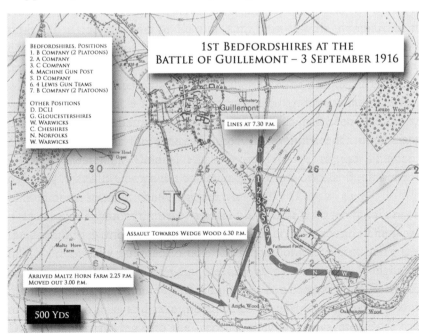

BEDFORDSHIRES, POSITIONS
1. B COMPANY (2 PLATOONS)
2. A COMPANY
3. C COMPANY
4. MACHINE GUN POST
5. D COMPANY
6. 4 LEWIS GUN TEAMS
7. B COMPANY (2 PLATOONS)

OTHER POSITIONS
D. DCLI
G. GLOUCESTERSHIRES
W. WARWICKS
C. CHESHIRES
N. NORFOLKS
W. WARWICKS

1ST BEDFORDSHIRES AT THE
BATTLE OF GUILLEMONT – 3 SEPTEMBER 1916

LINES AT 7.30 P.M.

ASSAULT TOWARDS WEDGE WOOD 6.30 P.M.

ARRIVED MALTZ HORN FARM 2.25 P.M.
MOVED OUT 3.00 P.M.

500 YDS

the circular trench between the wood and the farm but essentially held over half of the battalion in positions that would not influence the morning's fighting. With few options available, Captain Barnett's D Company pushed strong patrols out in the darkness and entrenched around 30m from the German trenches north-west of the farm despite opposition, with other companies following suit and ensuring they dominated No Man's Land.

Among the day's casualties was Second Lieutenant James Hirst Banyard who had been with the battalion just sixteen days when the advance against Wedge Wood went in, making the 29-year-old Cambridge-born solicitor the first of the battalion's officers to be killed during the battle.

Overnight the 13th Brigade was relieved by the 15th in front of the farm and, when coupled with the position of the Bedfords' advanced posts, an assault was obvious. No instructions arrived until 8 a.m. on the 4th, when a curious order was delivered demanding an immediate night-time assault against the farm. Closer inspection showed it was instigated just after midnight and had taken almost eight hours to reach them, the signaller having become lost in the unfamiliar, dark countryside.

Later that morning orders confirmed that the Bedfordshires would attack again the following afternoon, their objective being to complete the capture of the untaken portion of trench between the wood and the farm. The brigade advanced with all four battalions in line: the Bedfords on the left, the Cheshires in the middle, then the Norfolks, and the Warwicks on the eastern flank. The Cheshires and Norfolks were tasked with storming the farm itself.

D Company were in their assault positions just in front of the German trenches and A, B and C Companies sidestepped to their south, placing them behind the strung-out squads of D Company and ready to advance in direct support. As the morning wore on, British guns persistently shelled the Bedfords, apparently unaware the trenches they held were in British hands, with D Company coming under almost constant fire. Increasingly agitated messages to the gunners were lost, misunderstood or ignored until the Bedfordshires behind D Company had to evacuate the front trenches as too many men were being buried, wounded and killed in the bombardment. As the men rose and ran back, German gunners found tempting targets and many of the retiring Bedfords fell before making it to the safety of positions further behind. Captain Barnett's beleaguered company had little choice but to endure the bombardment, as the men were pinned down by defenders 30m to their front and the open expanse of No Man's Land to their rear. They spent the day being pounded, buried and having to dig one another out as their list of casualties grew ever longer. Barnett remained cool, joined his line of craters up as best he could, and held his men in place, waiting for the opportunity to advance and get them out of their impossible position.

At 3.10 p.m. the 15th Brigade assaulted the German lines between Wedge Wood and Falfemont Farm, also intent on carrying their advance north-east along the ridge if circumstances allowed. Despite a concentrated British barrage against the farm before the advance, the Cheshires and Norfolks could see German gunners mounting their machine guns onto their parapets before the push had really started. The result was inevitable, the two battalions doing their best across the bullet-swept slopes but having to go to ground.

While German attentions were fixed on the Cheshires and Norfolks hugging the grass slopes, two platoons from the Cheshires made it to the trench system and joined the Bedfordshires as they stormed and captured the trench line running between the wood and the farm. With their ears still ringing from enduring hours under a heavy bombardment, the soldiers of Captain Barnett's D Company launched themselves at the German lines with an incredible vigour, the rest of the battalion quickly advancing up the slopes. Within minutes Barnett's leading platoons had gained a foothold in the German trench, but they were forced to fight each man they met to the death as the German defenders simply refused to fold even when their plight was hopeless. Every last traverse and dug-out was hard fought for, with bombers, bayonet men and Lewis gun teams working together to overcome every fresh defensive pocket in their way. For 30m either side of the trench line the ground was a churned-up mass of craters, each capable of hiding a squad of defenders. Every last crater also had to be cleared to avoid a counter-attack from the flank or rear as the main party advanced along the trench, with Mills bombs being the most relied-upon weapon of the afternoon. On the odd occasions that a German section chose to retire instead of standing firm, the Lewis gunners and riflemen ensured none got away, as it was obvious that none of the staunch defenders intended to surrender.

C Company had moved quickly to support D Company, who had already lost every officer and a large proportion of the men. A Company under the battalion second in command, Major Lawder, followed suit but were soon without any officers too, the major having been killed by a shell. By the time B Company were also in the trench system, just two of their officers remained, but the NCOs were busily organising their companies and moving the assault forward.

With only 3 officers and around 200 fighting men left by this time, the arrival of 30 Cheshires on the right flank and 50 more on their left was warmly welcomed, just in time to meet the German counter-attacks. Company commander Captain Samuel Norrish, one of the few officers left, displayed 'great courage and determination' by quickly and coolly reorganising the survivors in each company into an effective defensive line and moving around ceaselessly while under heavy fire to check and encourage the perimeter. His actions would not only ensure the position was not lost in the coming counter-attacks but would also result in a well-earned Military Cross.

One of the companies without an officer was being ably led by Company Sergeant Major Frederick Spicer, a veteran of every engagement the battalion had been involved in over the past two years, and who had already been mentioned in despatches and presented with a Russian gallantry award in 1915. Sergeant Spicer was an NCO who was always in the thick of it and appeared in numerous letters published in newspapers from around Bedfordshire and Hertfordshire, writing messages to the next of kin of his fallen comrades. He led his men from the front, killing many defenders himself as they wrestled with the stubborn German garrison, and he worked constantly to ensure his perimeter was secure and the men alert. For his efforts, leadership and sheer determination Sergeant Spicer won the Military Cross and, although wounded before the battalion left the Somme, would go on to become a commissioned officer, serving in the opening battles of the Second World War over twenty years later.

German reinforcements arrived on both flanks to launch a strong, well-organised counter-attack and, as the battalion reserves were all committed, matters looked serious. With runners racing between battalions, each asking for reinforcements from one another as their own were already fully engaged, the outcome of the fighting was looking grim and all posts could do little more than hold on. A deadly mixture of Lewis gun fire, alongside British and German artillery bombardments, caused heavy casualties among the attacking waves, while those who made it into close contact with the Bedfords were seen off with bombs, rifle fire, bayonets and fists. Having paid so dearly to win the ground, the battalion was in no hurry to be forced from it.

Of the few prisoners taken during the fighting itself, two Germans emerged from a bombed dugout telling how their entire company had been caught in the dugout, which doubled up as a German bomb store. They had been trapped while the determined Bedfords bombed them to destruction, unaware of just how many German troops sheltered beneath them and the fact they were detonating a stockpile of German bombs at the same time. Fortunately for the Bedfords, not many of the company escaped; the result may have been very different if they had been able to emerge and counter-attack. Questioning the prisoners further, it became clear that an entire battalion, complete with machine-gun detachment, had held the position, explaining why each metre had been so hard won. Barnett's exhausted men were reorganising their newly captured positions when he realised there was an opportunity to break into the Falfemont Farm enclosure. No British troops had gained entry during the entire battle and he could see that the Norfolks and most of the Cheshires were pinned down in front of the farm. Forming sections of his own men and reinforcing them with nearby Cheshires, Barnett launched a fierce bombing attack along the line of the trench, heading directly for the stubborn defenders holding the farm. Metre by metre, traverse by traverse, Captain Barnett's band forced their way east until a foothold was gained in the northern and south-western corners of the enclosure, as the rest of the Bedfords consolidated a fresh defensive line running 200m north from the north-west corner of the farm.

Two companies of West Kents arrived at 4 p.m., strengthening the line and allowing for tactical thinking. As the bombers were engaged in close-quarters fighting in the farm enclosure, Lieutenant Colonel Onslow led a strong patrol of the Bedfordshires, Cheshires and West Kents north-east towards Leuze Wood, which had earned the nickname 'Lousy Wood', following the natural contour of a partially hidden valley. Aside from supporting the 95th Brigade's advance, which was to start to his left at 6.30 p.m., Onslow's intention was to isolate the farm from any possibility of German reinforcements. The next phase of a British barrage was due to be unleashed on the very ground he advanced over but, luckily, observers spotted them and called off the storm before they were caught in the open. The fifty Cheshires were positioned 200m north-east of the northern edge of the Bedfords' line, with the West Kents a further 150m towards the wood, both aligned on the reverse side of the ridge and protected from enemy artillery observers. As Onslow's Bedfords advanced into 'Lousy Wood', less and less resistance was met. Once their

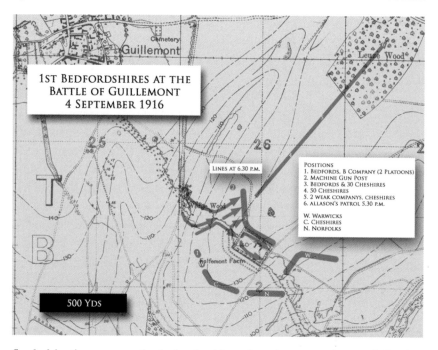

final objective was reached, the tired but victorious patrol started digging in along the Ginchy to Combles road and waited for the troops of the 95th Brigade.

Ferocious hand-to-hand fighting continued in and around the farm until signal flares finally declared it to be in British hands at 5.50 p.m. Almost instantly, a German barrage engulfed the enclosure, the gunners having their orders to level the position so it could not be used against them in the future.

By nightfall, the battalions had linked up and a continuous line was formed, which was held throughout the relatively quiet 5 September. Between the heavy German bombardments that day, the British troops buried their dead and prepared the position for defence as the fighting continued to their north. That morning the Bedfords also finally got a fresh supply of water for their bottles, the first for two days.

Communication between the battalions and Brigade HQ had been almost impossible for several days but the battalion Signalling Sergeant James Bush[211] kept the telephone cables intact despite them being constantly cut by shellfire and working under the most trying circumstances.

Regardless of the dreadful conditions,[212] German units fought to the death along the front-line trenches with an incredible ferocity until completely overwhelmed. Fusilier Regiment 73's diary remarks, 'Nobody from 3rd Company can provide a report – all the men were killed, as was every officer' and just five men from Infantry Regiment's 5th Company survived the onslaught. Once the position had been secured, defenders surrendered from their dugouts in groups, often already wounded. The Bedfords alone passed over 200 prisoners back to the divisional police, and accounts from survivors referred to many groups of wounded Germans simply being disarmed and left where they were until the divisional reserves could arrive to take care of them.

By the end of the four-day battle, the line from Guillemont, through Wedge Wood and Falfemont Farm, down to the French army boundary was in British hands. To the north, German defenders in Ginchy had repulsed the Irish Division and a further strongpoint between Ginchy and Leuze Wood also remained firmly in German hands. As a result, the division's left flank was wide open until the 95th Brigade angled their lines along the north-western fringes of Leuze Wood to meet any potential counter-attacks.

The German grip on the area was finally weakened and the British army could start looking to the next major German defensive line, between the fortified villages of Flers and Courcelette.

The Bedfordshires were relieved on the morning of 6 September, the battalion now being the size of two small companies. Four days earlier, they had advanced with 20 officers and 610 other ranks, but during the ferocious fighting around Falfemont Farm and Wedge Wood, they lost 17 officers and 289 men. Of the three officers remaining, only one could walk back without support.

On 4 September alone another five officers had been killed, including the battalion's second in command, Major and Adjutant Noel Wilfred Lawder. The experienced 29-year-old officer had served in the regiment on and off since 1906, having spent time in India, West Africa and Europe while in the British army. Company commander Lieutenant Addison James Howard was also killed, aged 23. He had joined the battalion just eight days earlier, having had a difficult time in England after a tonsillectomy had gone wrong in August 1915. Second Lieutenant Vincent Stanton Sanders was killed in the trench fighting, aged only 19. The former bank clerk had so impressed his peers with his remarkable coolness during a heavy bombardment in May that he was recommended for and granted a commission in the regular army almost immediately. The 24-year-old, Harpenden-born Second Lieutenant Christopher Blake had been with the battalion for just three days when he was killed. Second

Lieutenant Dion Albert Lardner had served as a Territorial Army rifle-man in the 16th London Regiment since February 1914, but the 20-year-old had only arrived in France for the first time in August 1916. He had joined the battalion with James Banyard and was killed a day later than James, having been on the front for just two weeks.

The list of wounded officers included the battalion's commanding officer, Lieutenant Colonel Allason, although his wounds were slight and he would not be removed from his battalion for treatment. Walter Allason would be awarded a Bar to his Distinguished Service Order for his skill, initiative and resourcefulness while handling the battalion during the assault. D Company's commanding officer Captain William Harold Louis Barnett was inevitably wounded during his superb advance and was recommended for an award, receiving the Distin-guished Service Order in recognition. Company CO Captain Herbert John West was severely wounded leading his company and was also recommended for an award, receiving his Military Cross from King George at Buckingham Palace in June 1917. Lieutenants Henry Graves and Arthur Topley, Second Lieutenants Hugh Cecil Covell, P.A. Gibbons, Ernest Alfred Hague, Douglas Frederick Howard and P.G. Smith had all been with the battalion for a maximum of two weeks and were all wounded during their first battle. Second Lieutenant Basil Charles Williams had spent less than forty-eight hours with the battalion before being wounded in the battle, and Second Lieutenant Ernest George Donnisson was also wounded while attached to the Machine Gun Corps during the fighting.

Among the long 'other ranks' casualty list was Bob Pigg's cousin, Private Albert Pigg from Royston. Within days of Bob's return to the battalion, having recovered from his own injuries, Albert was wounded in the chest and moved back to the Casualty Clearing Station in Corbie. Initial letters home from the hospital chaplain remarked how he would be 'released in a day or two', but this proved to be wrong as he died from his wounds around a week later.

Also killed were the 25-year-old Corporal Joseph Jarrett from Caterham in Surrey,[213] and Private Walter Neal of St Ives, Cambridgeshire,[214] who died from his wounds on the 12th at the Casualty Clearing Station in Amiens. Both of these men would be awarded the Military Medal.

Corporal Michael McGinn[215] was another battalion veteran who was lost during the assault. The son of a sergeant major, Michael's choice of career was made before he had even left school. Enlisting in the regiment in 1895 as a 13-year-old, he started with the rank of 'Boy'. Michael was mentioned in despatches for gallantry at La Bassée and the First Battle of Ypres in 1914 and earned promotion to company sergeant major. However, CSM McGinn was later reduced to corporal for misconduct and was wounded during the assault against the farm, dying as a result on 6 September.

Lieutenant Colonel Cranley Onslow also won the Distinguished Service Order for his personal gallantry and leadership, rising to command an infantry brigade as a result. He added the CMG, CBE and the French Croix de Guerre to his collection over the next few years, which already included campaign medals from his long career, including Isaza (1892) and Chitral (1895).

Preparation and reorganisation

After marching to Billon Farm, 3km south-west of Carnoy, on 6 September the battle-worn battalion rested and waited for orders until concentrating at the Citadel Camp near Carnoy on the evening of the 7th. A short spell of refitting, resting and parading followed while the division gathered. At Citadel on the 8th, Major General R.B. Stephens, the 5th Division's commanding officer, visited the brigade to congratulate them on their recent feat of arms. The brigadier general also stopped by the battalion later in the day, reading out the following message:

I have come here this morning to read to you a message that we have received from the Commander-in-Chief. He says, with reference to the late operations, 'The rapid advance on LEUZE WOOD, following on the capturing of FALFEMONT FARM, showed great judgement and determination, and has been of considerable assistance to the French Army on our right. I very warmly congratulate you and the Commanders and Staffs and the Troops under you on the results you have already achieved and on the energy and determination with which they were followed up. Well, now, you're the people who took FALFEMONT FARM, and I am very glad to be able to tell you that not only the Commander-in-Chief, but the Army Commander and the Corps Commander all realise what a great and glorious fight it was. It makes it all the better that you did it after there had been a failure; that always makes it more difficult. Nothing in the world could have been finer than the show you fellows put up by that Farm and the line up to WEDGE WOOD on the left of it. It was magnificent. I want to thank you all for what you have done and tell you that everybody thoroughly understands what a good show it was.

The Brigadier General Commanding feels he cannot too warmly express his admiration of the fine soldierly qualities again displayed by all ranks during the recent operations. The taking of FALFEMONT FARM, a most important and strongly defended post, was a magnificent performance and is one of the greatest successes accomplished during the war. This was made possible entirely by the good handling of their Battalions by Commanding Officers and the devoted conduct of all ranks. Heavy working parties were required when the Brigade was not in the Line and these did excellent work. The Brigadier-General thanks all ranks for their support and co-operation and trusts the Brigade will shortly enjoy a well earned rest.

From 9 to 15 September the Bedfords were billeted in Morlancourt, 6km south of Albert. Daily working parties were sent to Grovetown Station and smaller groups posted to fatigues at the Méaulte ammunition dump on the 13th and 14th, but otherwise the battalion rested, trained and refitted after their ordeal. Reinforcement drafts arrived, with sixty-seven other ranks joining on the 10th and thirty-seven on the 11th. Captain Montague Walter Halford arrived from the 1st Gloucesters on the 10th to assume the post of second in command and over the next week several more officers would join, including Second Lieutenants John William Sullivan, George Colby Sharpin, James Kenneth Hope, Geoffrey De Carteret Millais and Arthur Francis Woodford.

Among the new arrivals was Private Percy Craddock[216] who was posted to D Company. This determined young man had enlisted in 1914, aged just 15, and had already served on the Western Front in the Northamptonshire Regiment before his age was discovered. Undeterred, he enlisted in the Bedfordshire Regiment a month after his initial discharge, becoming a qualified Lewis and Vickers gunner within months. He would survive the coming battle but 'hammed' feet (i.e. trench feet) brought on by the wet, cold conditions in the line in October would see his removal from the battalion. His age would be discovered once more and he was discharged a second time for being underaged but still managed to return to the front again in 1918.

After their deserved rest, the front line beckoned the men back once more as the newest phase of the Battle of the Somme got under way. In a heavy rain, the 5th Division relieved the 6th Division in the line on the 18TH, which had just taken another strongpoint known as the Quadrilateral.

The divisional lines ran for around 1,800m from the northern edge of Bouleaux Wood, north along the eastern slopes of Telegraph Hill, an area that had only been captured by the 6th Division the day before. The 95th Brigade held the right half of the line with the 13th Brigade on the left, and the 15th Brigade initially formed the divisional reserve.

Marching back to the region around Longueval, the battalion fighting strength was still under 500 although the officer contingent was strong once more. After a pause at the Citadel on the 15th the battalion was under the orders of the 20th Division between 16 and 20 September, spending the rainy period on working fatigues in the run-up to the next phase of the battle. This was also the first time the men had seen any of the new 'land ships', as they passed several of the lumbering beasts on the 16th.

Casualties continued to mount despite their position in reserve, and on 15 September Private Archie Boness[217] was killed. He was the third cousin from the Boness family in Biggleswade to be killed in the battalion that summer and joined the column on the Thiepval Memorial, where all three can be seen in line today.

On the 18th the Bedfordshires left their billets around Waterlot Farm, on the Longueval to Guillemont road, and moved to the old German lines between Guillemont and Wedge Wood. During the relief the battalion bumped into the 8th Bedfordshires, who had been heavily engaged during the day's fighting, many men pausing to exchange greetings and news of shared friends. Here they spent two more uncomfortable days in the rain with little cover until recalled into the 5th Division on the 20th.

Between the 20th and 22nd the battalion was in position in the support lines 1km due east of Ginchy, occupying old German trenches as the soldiers provided working parties in preparation for the upcoming offensive. Parties from each battalion in the brigade were sent almost 1km north-east to dig assembly trenches north and east of the quarry.

On 22 September, the Bedfordshires were relieved by the Warwicks from the 13th Brigade and moved back 8km south-west to bivouacs in Oxford Copse, just west of Maricourt, with the battalion war diary remarking that the 'men greatly benefited by this rest. Weather fine.'

The Battle of Morval: 25 September 1916

The third major phase of the Battle of the Somme was launched on 15 September and became known as the Battle of Flers-Courcelette. Twelve British and Commonwealth divisions assaulted prepared German defensive positions on a 12km frontage, and the highly secret 'land ship' or 'tank' made its debut appearance on the battlefields. Forty-nine of these 28-ton metal beasts were assigned to support the opening day's attacks, but just fifteen made it to the front lines, the rest breaking down en route.

The Canadian Corps advanced on the left flank, taking their object-ives of Courcelette and the surrounding countryside and, in the centre, Martinpuich fell to the 15th (Scottish) Division and Flers was taken by the 41st Division, which famously progressed along the High Street alongside one of the few tanks that made it to the front. Further advances in the centre were impossible and their final objectives lay untouched some 1,800m further east. On the right, the 56th (London) and 6th Divisions were held up by the previously unseen Quadrilateral Redoubt, which had evaded detection due to poor visibility and caught the assaulting waves unawares, causing heavy casualties. The redoubt finally fell on the 18th after a desperate, bloody struggle and the advance continued up the steep, wooded hills until the Tommies were within striking distance of Morval.

To take the outstanding final objectives of the Flers-Courcelette offensives, the Battle of Morval was fought on 25 September. The object-ives were the fortified and heavily defended villages of Morval, Lesboeufs, which stood 1.5km to the north of Morval, and Gueudecourt, a further 2.5km north-west of Lesboeufs. To the south of Morval, the French Sixth Army was tasked with advancing their own lines east, taking Combles and flattening the salient which had formed at the boundary between the French and British armies.

Three tanks were allotted to the division's front, but planning went ahead based on them being as unreliable as they had been at Flers-Courcelette, so they were assigned to support the infantry rather than lead the way. In the event, these proved to be well-founded concerns as just one of them finally arrived after the infantry had already taken Morval, but did turn out to be invaluable when helping the 95th Brigade overcome a strongpoint south of Morval.

At 7 a.m. on 24 September an intensive British bombardment against Morval and surrounding positions began, signalling the start of a fresh operation. Early that afternoon, orders arrived that the 15th Brigade was moving forward in fighting order to relieve the 13th Brigade and at 4.30 p.m. the Bedfordshires marched out of their billets at Oxford Copse, heading north-east. After a pause for tea in Chimpanzee Trench, their route took them across the scarred battlefields, via Arrowhead

Copse, between the ruins of Trônes Wood and Guillemont. Marching through the rubble stacks that were once the heavily fortified village of Ginchy, they moved east, then headed north, following the communications trenches. A few men were lost to the German artillery that was sporadically probing the rear areas, knowing that British troops would be moving into their assault positions.

Around midnight the Bedfords arrived in the muddy assembly trenches they had been involved in digging a few days earlier, west of the quarry, as the barrage continued roaring overhead. The second line of trenches were not deep enough so the already tired men spent much of the night before battle digging, but given the intensity of the shelling in the area there was little option.

As daylight arrived, it transpired that the 15th Brigade had taken over the east-facing line around 1km west of the centre of Morval. The village was shielded from view by a slight rise in the ground, which sloped downhill from its right flank towards the remains of a road running into the village itself. The brigade's plan of attack was for the Norfolks to advance on the left, with the Cheshires to their right. Directly behind the Norfolks were the Bedfordshires, with the Warwicks behind the Cheshires. Each battalion frontage covered around 350m and all battalions would advance in four waves, with 150m between each wave.

At 12.35 p.m. on the 25th the British bombardment split into two parts. A stationary barrage fell directly onto the second objective, some 300m from the western fringe of Morval, while a creeping barrage started pounding across No Man's Land as the Norfolks advanced just behind it. Every minute the bombardment would extend 50m further east, enabling the infantry to move in behind it and clear out any remaining enemy posts that had survived the shelling.

German resistance was quickly overcome and the Norfolks secured their objectives, consolidating immediately. The Norfolks now held the first line of German trenches running north from the old chalk pit, while the Bedfords moved into the trenches they had vacated in support. Once the last of the Norfolks had left their jumping-off trenches, the Bedfords took them over. D Company moved into the line vacated by the Norfolks first and formed the left half of the line, with C Company behind them, taking up positions on the right half of the battalion line. B Company then moved into the second-line trench behind D Company, and A behind C.

At 1.35 p.m. the Bedfords started their own 700m advance, passing over the old German front line and through the German artillery and machine-gun barrage. The British bombardment had been pounding the area 200m east of the Norfolks' positions before it started moving eastwards. However, the 50m-per-minute rate of advance caused heavier casualties than expected, as the Bedfords found themselves waiting in the open for the next move forward under heavy machine-gun fire. The British creeping barrage also caught many men during the advance, as elements of it did not progress as one, catching out the advancing men who were keen to get into their objective and shelter from the attentions of enemy gunners.

By 1.40 p.m. the battalion had taken the second objective of the sunken lane running north, some 450m west of the centre of Morval, as the British barrage created an explosive curtain 200m further east of the road. Facing the small village, interspersed with mature trees and copses, Lewis guns were immediately set up and fired on the retiring Germans as the rest of the battalion improved their defensive cover under a combined German and British bombardment. When the British barrage was corrected, the men set to digging a series of forward posts to their front, ready for any counter-attacks. By 1.50 p.m. they had linked up with the 16th Brigade to their left, and at 2 p.m. the 95th Brigade to their right made contact. The line was now complete.

In their turn, the Cheshires advanced at 2.35 p.m., moving through the Bedfordshires to carry the third and final objective, being the central road in the village. Once in the western fringes of the village there was a short pause while the barrage intensified and focused on the central road running through Morval, before it lifted further east and the Cheshires moved in to finish the job. By 2.50 p.m. they were in among the rubble, gaining the upper hand against an overwhelmed garrison. Dugouts and cellars were stormed one by one and once a solid line was established along the main road, the final advance was started. In perfect alignment with their timetable, the Warwicks then passed through the Cheshires and, with little remaining resistance, it took just three minutes to reach a line 200m east of the fringes of Morval; the Warwicks started digging in, supported by additional elements of the brigade.

That afternoon a French aviator circling overhead gave a graphic description of the final phase of the assault:

A great calm befalls the battlefield. … The fight is without doubt finished for the day. But suddenly … the British artillery opens a tornado of fire on the German lines. The enemy, unable to discover the threatened point for this new attack, places a barrage at random behind the British lines. ... It is Morval; for it is here that the heavier shells are levelling the obstacles – it is there, too, that the B.E.s (the eyes of the Army) are circling.

The rain of shells has continued for half an hour when suddenly, without anything

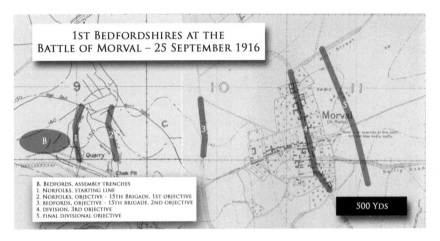

1ST BEDFORDSHIRES AT THE
BATTLE OF MORVAL – 25 SEPTEMBER 1916

B. BEDFORDS, ASSEMBLY TRENCHES
1. NORFOLKS, STARTING LINE
2. NORFOLKS, OBJECTIVE – 15TH BRIGADE, 1ST OBJECTIVE
3. BEDFORDS, OBJECTIVE – 15TH BRIGADE, 2ND OBJECTIVE
4. DIVISION, 3RD OBJECTIVE
5. FINAL DIVISIONAL OBJECTIVE

500 YDS

to warn the enemy of a change in the situation, the khaki line swarms forward as one man. Just as it reaches the curtain of fire, the latter, as if actuated by a single mind, moves forward in bounds, clears the village and establishes itself some hundred yards beyond it, forming a barrier under cover of which the assaulting waves gain mastery of the village and its outskirts. A few German signals of distress, a few bursting grenades around the dugouts, an attempt at defence rapidly overwhelmed and the khaki line, having gained almost a kilometre of ground, reforms beyond the objective.[218]

Once the brigade line was consolidated east of the village and the localised German counter-attacks were spent, sniping became the brigade's biggest nuisance. Annoyed by the attentions of one particular German sniper, Private Thomas 'Todger' Jones of the Cheshires set out across No Man's Land on his own initiative and stalked the culprit. Although he took a bullet through his helmet and another tore his coat, Private Jones located and silenced the sniper. As he was about to return to his own lines two more Germans raised a white flag from their shell hole but continued firing at him. Being an old hand to this kind of trickery, Jones also silenced this post. Deciding to investigate further, he made his way into the German trench and came across several dugouts full of the garrison. Jones single-handedly disarmed them all and held them captive until his comrades arrived. Some 4 officers and 102

Germans were escorted back to British lines, and for his incredible act Private Jones was awarded the Victoria Cross.

During the battle, the 5th, 6th and Guards Divisions had methodically advanced on their objectives, Morval and Lesboeufs both being occupied by 3.30 p.m. The attack had gone exactly to the timetable and not once had the infantry been left behind by an advancing line of shellfire, an event rare in the Somme offensives. By nightfall the objective running south from the Moulin de Morval was secured, and the following day was unusually free of counter-attacks in the Bedfords' sector although shelling continued unabated until relief arrived that evening in the form of the 6th Division.

Once again the 1st Bedfordshires had proven their ability in the field and would add Morval to their already long list of honours, but once again they had paid yet another high price. The battalion had advanced on the 25th with a fighting strength of around 500 officers and men but by its relief the following evening had lost almost a quarter of its number, with 114 casualties falling in and around the village.

Second Lieutenant Douglas Bowhill Candy was badly wounded by shrapnel during the advance, dying of his wounds on 25 September. He had only been with the battalion around a month and died in the XIV Corps' dressing station, aged 26. Among the effects returned to his parents were a silver cigarette case and three ten-centime coins, all of which were damaged by the shell that took his life.

By now, both of the Neale brothers from Aspenden had also been wounded during the battalion's campaign on the Somme. Private Tom Neale was hit at Morval and his brother Private Jim Neale[219] had also been wounded over the summer. Although Tom was back with the battalion soon enough, Jim found himself posted to the 5th Bedfordshires in the Middle East once recovered, and the war saw to it that the two brothers would never meet again.

The battalion's commissioned officers suffered. Five were wounded during the battle including Lieutenant Sydney Harold Draper, although he would return within days. However, the already badly thinned members of the sergeants' mess lost two more significant men at Morval. The ever-at-hand and highly influential Regimental Sergeant Major William Bartlett was killed, his body being lost during the fighting. William had served for around two decades in the regiment and having been present since Mons, had fought in every sector in which the battalion had seen service. He was mentioned in despatches in January

1917 for gallantry.

Company Sergeant Major Cecil Walker[220] took over as the Acting RSM, having recovered from a bullet wound at Longueval which was within millimetres of taking his eyesight and perhaps worse. With twelve years behind him in the regiment, including a tour in India and service as a policeman while on the regiment's reserves, Cecil was well placed to take over the battalion. A veteran of every engagement since Mons, he had risen through the ranks through his steady conduct under fire and had chosen to extend his service once his twelve years had expired. RSM Walker would continue in post until wounded a second time, also winning the DCM before the war was over.

Company Sergeant Major Joe Afford was wounded but survived. 'Afford from Offord' would be mentioned in despatches for gallantry at Morval, having become CSM only two weeks earlier. Joe received a commission in the field in February 1917, rising to the rank of captain in the Yorkshire Regiment, where his DCM from Longueval would be supplemented by a Military Cross before the war was done.

Final acts on the Somme battlefields

November and December also saw the issue of more gallantry medals for actions between March and October 1916.

November's *London Gazette* included three more Distinguished Conduct Medals for men from the 1st Bedfordshires, all won during the offensive actions on the Somme. Sergeant Charles Atkinson[221] had been awarded the Military Medal earlier that year, and added the DCM to his growing collection of medal ribbons by tending many wounded men under fire and rescuing two others who had been buried by a shell. Sergeant George Howlett[222] won his for taking charge of the company when all the officers had fallen, and for sticking to his post for two days despite being wounded. Private Percy Lewis[223] crept up to within 10m of a German trench and bombed them into silence, which enabled their advance to continue.

Almost thirty Military Medals were also added to the battalion's haul from the Somme offensives.

According to his local paper,[224] Sergeant Samuel Sheppard from Letchworth[225] won the Military Medal in March or April 1916. He had been with the battalion since November 1914 and had been wounded seven or eight times according to the report. Interviewed during a month's furlough around Christmas 1916, the reporter described him as 'unusually modest, even for a soldier', so he was not keen to reveal details of how he came to win his award.

Lance Corporal Sidney Wilson of Bourn in Cambridgeshire[226] had been with the battalion since September 1914 and had survived its many battles. His Military Medal was issued in November and he was mentioned in despatches on 2 January 1917, but Sidney was to lose his life the following July while attached to a trench mortar battery, aged 26.

Lance Corporal Harold McHugh[227] and Private Christopher Cross[228] were both presented with their Military Medal ribbons on 17 December. Harold was well known around Royston and had worked in Captain Whitaker's stables nearby before joining up early in September 1914. He had arrived in the battalion mid-May 1915, while it was being rebuilt following their losses on Hill 60. His local paper reported that Harold's medal was awarded 'for exposing himself to great danger in order to warn a number of men who were coming towards a gap in a trench and who would have been fired upon by the Germans'.[229] Harold was wounded at Morval while dressing the wounds of a colleague, and recovered at Rouen, rejoining the battalion within weeks and in time for his medal ribbon to be pinned onto his tunic. Christopher was from Broughton in Huntingdonshire and had initially enlisted into A Company of the 2nd/1st Huntingdonshire Cyclist Battalion in October 1914. After training he had been in a draft that arrived in France late in July 1916 and was among the reinforcements to join the 1st Bedfordshires after their losses at Longueval.

Acting Company Sergeant Major Reg Driscoll,[230] a Royston footballer, was awarded the Military Medal and granted a short period of home leave in October, but his local paper reported that 'his modesty had not allowed him to say exactly how the honour was won'.[231]

Private Albert Durham's[232] Military Medal was among the batch issued in November. A St Neots man who had served in the 2nd Bedfordshires from February 1910, Albert was wounded at Ypres in November 1914 and had served in the 1st Bedfordshires since May 1915. His 38-year-old brother, Private Thomas Durham, was killed in the 4th Bedfordshires at Arras in 1917, but Albert survived the war despite being wounded at Ypres again, in October 1917.

Several of the medals were won by the surviving Old Contemptibles from 1914: C Company platoon Sergeant Ernest Fox;[233] Sergeant Reginald Lansbury of Bromley in Kent,[234] who would go on to add a DCM to his collection; Sergeant Frank (Frederick) Stanley,[235] whose medals were forfeited in May 1918 when he disappeared while on leave; Sergeants Frank Butler,[236] Albert Johnson[237] and Fred Stubbings;[238] Corporal Charles Worboys;[239] Lance Corporal Clarence Mailing of Redbourn,[240] who recovered from being wounded on the Somme but was killed at Arras in the 4th Bedfordshires; Lance Corporals Robert Skipp[241] and Harry Steele;[242] and Privates Walter England,[243] Matthew Herring[244] and George Cotton.[245]

Two of the medal winners had been civilians in August 1914 and had joined the 1st Bedfordshires in May 1915, namely Privates Horace Scrivener[246] and Henry Shadbolt.[247]

The New Year's honours list would also see Lieutenants Allan Oswald Rufus Beale and Horace John Everett awarded the Military Cross for gallantry during the battalion's campaign on the Somme, with both going on to add further awards to their medals as the war continued. Lieutenant Colonel Allason and Lieutenant William Pottle were also mentioned in despatches in January 1917 for their leadership on the Somme, as was Sergeant Henry Guess from Aberdeen.[248] Henry became a second lieutenant in the Royal West Kents the following year and won the Military Cross for bravery during the 1918 German spring offensives.

By 11.30 p.m. on 26 September, the battalion arrived at bivouacs in Oxford Copse, and three days later would entrain for a new section of the Western Front, their tour of the Somme complete. While the battalion may have finished with the Somme, unfortunately the Somme had not finished with the battalion, as one last cruel, unexpected event awaited them.

On the 27th the battalion had marched back to the large hutted camp north of Bray called the Citadel, through a heavy shower that had soaked everyone. Once in the camp, large fires were built to dry clothes and equipment. In the pitch black night, a series of large explosions rocked the site, shocking everyone into action. The campfires were immediately doused but it was soon learned that a German bomber aircraft had flown overhead, dropping bombs on the fires. He was a regular visitor to the camp and one of his bombs hit the corner of a hut, killing three of the Bedfords and wounding eighteen more.

Two of those killed were pre-war reservists who had been with the battalion since the end of 1914: Private John Manning of Hitchin[249] had been on the front since just after Christmas 1914 and Private John Horne from Leighton Buzzard[250] had been with the battalion since November 1914. The third, Private Arthur Rayner from Therfield,[251] was a 38-year-old who had enlisted early in September 1914 and had been with the battalion since May 1915. All three lie in the Citadel Cemetery, Fricourt. Of those wounded, two would succumb at the local Casualty Clearing Station the following day: Lance Corporal Arthur Porter,[252] a 37-year-old who had only been out a matter of weeks, and Private Frederick Purdy[253] who had been fighting since Hill 60 in 1915.

Of the 500 or so battle-hardened men who formed up at Maricourt Station as the autumn rains set in, just a pitiful few of them were pre-war veterans who had survived the first two years of the campaign. Unbeknown to them, their campaign was only halfway through, despite it having already taken them down the 'long, long trail' from Mons to the Somme.

Notes

Compiling this story began with the source closest to the events, being the battalion, brigade and divisional war diaries. The resulting story was then developed using the sources listed below, including personal details from private letters, memoirs and diaries from those who were there.

Anyone who has researched a subject as complex as this will agree that the accuracy of sources cannot always be taken at face value. Laying out the parameters within which I have sought to verify facts is inappropriate here and would almost certainly result in a rather boring paragraph, so suffice to say that I have taken very little at face value as even the 'official histories' are prone to errors with the benefit of hindsight. When conflicts have occurred between facts, I have considered all angles and sought verification from other sources that did not themselves draw on any of the conflicting ones. Quotations from those who were there are given as they appeared at the time, regardless of any inconsistencies with the facts available with hindsight; to my mind, they should have the privilege of recalling their memories as they choose and it is not for me to correct them.

There is a mixture of metric and imperial units of measurement throughout, depending on the source and context. For example, a square on a 1/10,000-scale British trench map from the time is 1,000yd, so any reference to a map is made in yards, as are any quotations from the time which use miles or yards. In contrast, distances between locations on the Western Front are given in kilometres and metres, as that is the measurement adopted locally.

Names of towns are given using the local, modern spelling, with alternative, anglicised spellings included in brackets. The notable exception to this is Ieper (Ypres), which is shown throughout by the anglicised spelling to avoid confusion, as many official battles, memorials and other such titles are referred to using that spelling.

For those with a genealogical or personal interest to learn more, personally I am a huge advocate of physically standing on the sites where the events took place. Reading about them is one thing but standing on the very ground with the story in one hand and a map in the other while juggling a compass adds a dimension worth pursuing. Most of the aspects have not changed since our ancestors laid their eyes upon them, despite a century having passed. Many roads, woods and even buildings remain, so comparing features on a map from the war is often not as difficult as one may imagine. The difference, of course, is that we enjoy a landscape comprising green grass and farmers' fields instead of a vast swathe of grey-brown mud broken by shell holes and the litter of battle.

Sources

The following sources have been incorporated while producing this book:

The 1st Battalion war diaries, held at the National Archives under reference WO 95/1570 and at the Bedfordshire and Luton Archives and Records Service (BLARS) under reference X550/2/5. Much cross referencing was also undertaken from the National Archives WO 95/1570 collection, which includes diaries from other units within the 5th Division.

The History Committee, the Royal Anglian Regiment (Bedfordshire and Hertfordshire): Lieutenant Colonel T.J. Barrow, DSO, Major V.A. French and J. Seabrook Esq. (1986), *The Story of the Bedfordshire and Hertfordshire Regiment (The 16th Regiment of Foot). Volume II. 1914 to 1958.*

Hussey and Inman, *The 5th Division in the Great War* (reprint of 1921 edition), Naval and Military Press.

Gleichen, Brigadier General (1917), *The Doings of the Fifteenth Infantry Brigade, August 1914 to March 1915*, William Blackwood & Sons.

Hamilton, E.W. (1915), *The First Seven Divisions*, McClelland Goodchild & Stewart Ltd.

Edmonds, J.E. et al. (1925), *History of the Great War, Military Operations, France and Belgium 1914*, MacMillan & Co.

Edmonds, J.E. et al. (1927), *History of the Great War, Military Operations, France and Belgium 1915*, MacMillan & Co.

The Bedfordshire and Luton Archives and Records Service (BLARS) houses various records and information on the regiment over and above their local and family history collections.

The Wasp, the journal of the 16th Foot, the Bedfordshire and Hertfordshire Regiment, Gale & Polden.

Service records held at the National Archives under WO 339 and WO 374 (officers), WO 363, WO 364 and WO 97 (other ranks, including pre-war discharges).

The Imperial War Museum archives hold several personal diaries and memoirs of men who served within the battalion and whose memories have been quoted within this story.

Newspapers from the time, held by local, regional and national libraries and archives: *Ampthill News*; *Bedfordshire Times and Independent*; *Biggleswade Chronicle*; *Herts Advertiser and St Albans Times*; *Hunts County News*; *Hunts Post*; *Illustrated London News*; *Kettering Leader*; *Leighton Buzzard Observer*; *Letchworth Citizen*; *London Gazette*; *Luton News* and *Bedfordshire Chronicle/ Bedfordshire Advertiser*; *Royston Crow*; *St Neots Advertiser*; *St Neots and County Times*; *The Times*.

Acknowledgements

My personal thanks to the following people who have shared information from their own fields of research or who have provided moral support in some way:

First and foremost, my sincere thanks for the unwavering support extended by my wife Liz, who happily tramps around archives, battlefields, libraries, cemeteries and talks with me.

Fighting High's Steve Darlow, who was the one responsible for making me take this on after several years of just thinking about it.

To the individuals who have assisted with information from their own fields of interest: Steve Beeby; Barry Elkin; Nigel Lutt and those at BLARS; John Wainwright; Kenneth Wood; any others I may have inadvertently left out.

To the relatives of those whose diaries I have quoted from, or whose photographs I have included: Phillip Afford (CSM Joe Afford); Chris Barrett (RSM Bartlett); Mick Bonham (Private 'Bruiser' Clifton); Linda Caswell and Dermot Foley (Sergeant Walter Brazier); Dave Craddock (Private Percy Craddock); Jane Dobner (Lieutenant Colonel Onslow); Bill Guzek (the guardian of Captain Gledstanes's service dress jacket); Ron West (RSM Newbound).

Appendix 1

Old Contemptibles

On 19 August 1914, Kaiser Wilhelm was reported to have issued the following order of the day from his headquarters at Aix-la-Chapelle: 'It is my Royal and Imperial Command that you concentrate your energies, for the immediate present upon one single purpose, and that is that you address all your skill and all the valour of my soldiers to exterminate first the treacherous English; walk over General French's contemptible little Army.'

The regular, full-timers that comprised the British army were already a highly trained and effective force, with a high proportion of marksmen, and driven by both national and regimental traditions and pride. Numerically, they were vastly outnumbered by the relatively huge armies of Europe, but man for man they were certainly a match for any force that could be thrown at them.

The German Kaiser's contempt for the British army was widely reported on and the effect of hearing about this order not only stirred the British Tommies into an even more defiant frame of mind, but led directly to the honourable title the 'Old Contemptibles' that was adopted by the original soldiers who stood against their German opponents in the early battles of the war.

The tradition is that those men who served on the Western Front before the end of the First Battle of Ypres (22 November 1914) were regarded as Old Contemptibles. Officially, they were issued with a small silver rosette called a 'Clasp and Roses' to wear on their 1914 Star medal ribbon (also referred to as a 'Mons Star').

There appears to be no documentary evidence to confirm the Kaiser's order ever existed, so it is likely that the story was British propaganda unless the order has simply not survived over the years. Whether true or not, it certainly helped to stir General French's small army to achieve great feats at the time. It is also a phrase that has reverberated down the decades, signifying that anyone in that small band of Old Contemptibles holds a special place of honour in British military traditions.

Appendix 2

Regimental structure

The regiment was the overall 'administrative' body and was usually determined by a geographical area (for example, the Bedfordshire Regiment) or specialisation of some kind (such as the Grenadier Guards).

Because so many men were available from each area, regiments were split into battalions. Therefore, a highly populated area may have had over thirty battalions within its regiment, whereas a more rural and sparsely populated region may only have had five or six battalions. The largest areas, such as London and Cheshire/Lancashire formed more than one regiment to organise their resources more effectively.

Infantry regiments drawn from geographical areas typically had several distinct types of battalions. 'Regular' battalions comprised full-time, professional soldiers who served oversees or as required by the Crown; 'territorial' battalions were part-time, part-trained soldiers who were expected to defend the homeland when the regular army were fighting overseas; 'reserve' battalions provided drafts for the regular battalions serving overseas in addition to manning a geographical area of the UK; 'service' battalions were raised specifically for the duration of the war and were originally built around a cadre of experienced soldiers, although the structures changed as the war developed; 'garrison' battalions were raised to man and police specific areas of the Empire guarded by the regular army in peacetime.

Infantry battalions in the First World War

On average, a battalion spent between 10 and 20 days per year in intensive action and an additional 80 to 100 days holding the front line. Some battalions were extremely unlucky and spent over four times the average in battle conditions, while others were almost always moved to a quiet sector just before a major offensive hit the sector they had just left. The rest of their time was spent in 'support' (being between 50yd and half a mile behind the front line, depending on the theatre and terrain), 'reserve' (between 200yd and five miles behind the front line), or at 'rest' in billets. Rest did not necessarily mean a complete break, as the army always had something that needed to be rebuilt or repaired. As a result 90 per cent of rest periods were spent on construction, general fatigue duties or in training, whereas almost all the time in support or reserve was spent improving the defensive systems and training.

Although the composition changed as the war developed, in 1914 the battalion was the basic tactical infantry unit of the British army, and formed the bulk of the army in the field. When at full complement it comprised 1,007 men, including 30 commissioned officers, and was divided into a Battalion Headquarters and four companies.

Battalion headquarters

The battalion was usually commanded by a lieutenant colonel, with the second in command being a major. However, on occasions during the war a captain may have temporarily assumed command should the colonel and major have both been injured or temporarily attached elsewhere, for example. The Battalion HQ Company also had three other officers, being the adjutant (a captain or lieutenant in charge of the battalion's administration), a quartermaster (who ran the battalion's stores and transport), and a medical officer (usually attached from the Royal Army Medical Corps).

The non-commissioned officers (NCOs) of the HQ Company were responsible for the daily running of their respective duties and were directly in charge of the 'other ranks' as they went about their duties. The most senior NCO was the regimental sergeant major (RSM), who was ultimately in charge of all other NCOs and arguably the most influential individual in the battalion. Within the HQ Company a number of specialist sergeants filled the roles of quartermaster, drummer, cook, pioneer, shoemaker, transport, signaller, armourer and orderly room clerk.

Reporting to the sergeants were a range of corporals, lance corporals and privates. The basic structure was as follows: a corporal and four privates from the RAMC were attached for water duties and, in times of battle, for stretcher-bearing duties; a further sixteen privates were permanent stretcher-bearers and were often taken from the battalion's band; a corporal and fifteen privates acted as signallers; ten privates acted as pioneers, performing general engineering, repair and construction duties; eleven privates were drivers for the horse-drawn transport; six privates were used as the officers' 'batmen', effectively being their personal servants; and two privates were assigned to the medical officer as orderlies.

Collectively, this range of men took care of the duties required to support the battalion as it was in the line and ensured it had all it needed to perform its duties to the best of its potential.

For ease of command and tactical activities, battalions were divided into four companies over and above the Battalion HQ Company.

Companies

Companies in an infantry battalion were labelled 'A' through 'D', with the exception of the Guards battalions, which were numbered '1' through '4'. Some 227 men comprised a full company made up from: a major or captain in command of the company; a captain or lieutenant acting as second in command; four lieutenants and second lieutenants who ran the platoons within the company; the company sergeant major (CSM), who was in charge of the Company HQ and was the senior NCO within the company; a company quartermaster sergeant (CQMS), who ran the companies' stores and supplies; two privates who served as batmen, a further three as drivers, with the remaining 188 privates forming the main body of the company.

During times of attrition, in combat conditions or immediately after a battle, it was often the case that a second lieutenant (being the most junior of commissioned officers) temporarily ran a company when all other senior officers had been wounded or killed.

The company was further divided into platoons, in turn split into sections.

Platoons and sections

Four platoons made the company and comprised: a 'subaltern', being a lieutenant or second lieutenant in command of the platoon; eight sergeants (including one lance sergeant); ten corporals (including three lance corporals); four drummers; four batmen; and the privates without specialised roles who comprised the body of the platoon.

Each platoon was split into the smallest unit, being a section. Four sections made up a platoon and consisted of a commanding NCO and around a dozen men.

Soldiers recognised their regiment first of all, then their division. Above the divisional level, most soldiers were not especially interested as the unit became a bit of a blur and therefore less interesting to them. As an example, when asked to identify himself, a private would refer to himself as 'Private 4400 Kendall Herbert Charles, No. 10 Section, 2 Platoon, C Company of the 5th Battalion Bedfordshire Regiment'.

Endnotes

1   RSM 9482 Frederick Wombwell.

2   Lance Corporal 10265 Herbert Spencer. References to Herbert Spencer come from his memoirs held at the Imperial War Museum, reference 3762.

3   References to J. Macready during August and September 1914 are drawn from The History Committee, the Royal Anglian Regiment (Bedfordshire and Hertfordshire); Lieutenant Colonel T.J. Barrow, DSO, Major V.A. French and J. Seabrook Esq. (1986), *The Story of the Bedfordshire and Hertfordshire Regiment (The 16th Regiment of Foot)*, Volume II, Chapter II, which quotes extensively from a personal diary kept by him.

4   Private 7913 Arthur Basham.

5   Private 10333 Edwin James Bywaters.

6   References to J. Davenport between August and November 1914 are drawn from The History Committee, the Royal Anglian Regiment (Bedfordshire and Hertfordshire); Lieutenant Colonel T.J. Barrow, DSO, Major V.A. French and J. Seabrook Esq. (1986), *The Story of the Bedfordshire and Hertfordshire Regiment (The 16th Regiment of Foot)*, Volume II, Chapter II, which quotes extensively from a personal diary kept by him.

7   Sergeant 8087 Leonard Godfrey.

8   Sergeant 6394 Charles Kennedy.

9   Quotations from Major Onslow in August and September 1914 come from his 1914 memoirs, which are held by the Imperial War Museum, reference 86/9/1.

10 Bloem W. (2009), *Vormarsch* (1916), Kessinger Publishing LLC.

11 Private 8059 William Robert Pigg.

12 *Royston Crow*, 30 October 1914.

13 Corporal 9443 William Tucker.

14 Sergeant 9465 Percival Hunt.

15 Sergeant 8087 Leonard Godfrey.

16 Private 7246 Percy Green.

17 *St Neots Advertiser*, 12 December 1914.

18 *Royston Crow*, 9 October 1914.

19 Colour Sergeant Major 6466 Charles Hall.

20   Private 9213 Arthur Chandler.

21   *St Neots Advertiser*, 12 December 1914.

22   Regimental Quarter Master Sergeant 5710 William Bartlett.

23   Sergeant 9310 William Nolias.

24   Corporal 9113 Frederick Holloway.

25   Private 8598 Frank Cousins.

26   *St Neots Advertiser*, 23 October 1914.

27   *Royston Crow*, 30 October 1914

28   *Royston Crow*, 30 October 1914.

29   *Bedfordshire Times and Independent*, 16 October 1914.

30   Corporal 7074 Ernest Albert Higdon.

31   Private 10182 Samuel Seaman.

32   Private 8552 William Jackson.

33   Private 7937 Frederick Wagstaff.

34   *St Neots Advertiser*, 23 October 1914.

35   *Royston Crow*, 20 August 1915.

36   Lance Corporal 9284 Richard Wheeler.

37   *Bedfordshire Times and Independent*, 30 October 1914.

38   Drummer 7837 Herbert Henry Chequer.

39   Sergeant 7525 George Garrett.

40   *Bedfordshire Times and Independent*, 16 October 1914.

41   Sergeant 8237 Thomas Haycroft.

42   Corporal 7536 Ben Piggot.

43   Private 10234 Albert Bentley.

44   *Royston Crow*, 18 December 1914.

45   Company Sergeant Major 5559 William Sharpe.

46   Sergeant 7814 Alfred Mart.

47   Bandsman 9582 Albert Hodgson.

48   Private 9589 Herbert Brazier.

49   *Herts Advertiser and St Albans Times*, 7 November 1914.

50   *St Neots Advertiser*, 30 October 1914.

51   Sergeant 7867 Robert Burnage.

52   *Bedfordshire Times and Independent*, 30 October 1914.

53   Private 10091 Ernest Taylor.

54   Corporal 8074 Joseph Goodman.

55   Private 8178 William Medlock.

56   Sergeant 6792 Allen Cooper.

57   Corporal 3/6459 Jeffrey Tearle.

58   Corporal 10027 William Conrad Newbound.

59   Quartermaster Sergeant 4893 Thomas William Byford.

60   Private 8095 William Falla.

61   *St Neots Advertiser*, 4 December 1914.

62   *Harrovian War Supplement*, December 1914.

63   Company Sergeant Major 5316 Ernest Watson.

64   Sergeant 7633 Alfred Cogan.

65   Sergeant 7383 William Cogan.

66   Sergeant 7814 Alfred Mart.

67   Corporal 10129 Philip Cyster.

68   Private 3/6915 Alfred Hall.

69   *Bedfordshire Times and Independent*, 7 May 1915.

70   Private 8919 John Feary.

71   *Hunts County News*, 5 March 1915.

72   Privates 8178 Will Medlock and 3/6854 Ted Medlock.

73   *St Neots Advertiser*, 27 November 1914.

74   *Bedfordshire Times and Independent*, 7 May 1915.

75   *Royston Crow*, 22 January 1915.

76   Sergeant 8238 Richard William Allsopp.

77   Company Sergeant Major 5288 Michael Joseph McGinn.

78   Private 8389 Herbert Charles Cattle (Kettle).

79   Gleichen, Brigadier-General Count, *The Doings of the 15th Infantry Brigade*, William Blackwood and Sons 1917.

80   Private 10196 Herbert Hill.

81   *Bedfordshire Times and Independent*, 25 December 1914.

82   Private 8571 William Reed.

83   *Royston Crow*, 4 December 1914.

84   *St Neots Advertiser*, 4 December 1914.

85   Corporal 8976 Frederick Laird.

86   *Bedfordshire Times and Independent*, 4 December 1914.

87   *Bedfordshire Times and Independent*, 27 November 1914.

88   *Bedfordshire Gazette.The Mudlark* was the title adopted by the battalion's trench magazine, copies of which are held by the Bedfordshire and Luton Archive Service (BLARS) under the reference X550/21.

89   *Royston Crow*, 22 January 1915.

90   Lance Corporal 8189 Allan Brown.

91   Private 9398 Arthur Perry.

92   *Royston Crow*, 1 January 1915.

93   *Royston Crow*, 1 January 1915.

94   Sergeant 5160 William Blundell.

95   *Bedfordshire Times and Independent*, 8 January 1915.

96   Private 3/8066 Fred Ashwell, published in the *Beds Express*, 9 January 1915.

97   The National Archives, reference WO213/3.

98   The History Committee, the Royal Anglian Regiment (Bedfordshire and Hertfordshire); Lieutenant Colonel T.J. Barrow, DSO, Major V.A. French and J. Seabrook Esq. (1986), *The Story of the Bedfordshire and Hertfordshire Regiment (The 16th Regiment of Foot)*, Volume II, 1914 to 1958, page 123.

99   List created by the Bedford Regiment Prisoner of War Care Committee.

100 Private 10226 Fred Senior.

101 *Bedfordshire Times and Independent*, 15 January 1915.

102 Contrasts between official dates of death and those recalled by individuals were not uncommon.

103 Private 8328 George Franklin.

104 Private 8745 William Webb.

105 *St Neots Advertiser*, 12 March 1915.

106 Private 8847 Frank Wright.

107 *Bedfordshire Times and Independent*, 12 February 1915.

108 *Bedfordshire Times and Independent*, 26 March 1915.

109 The then Captain Griffith won the DSO while serving in the 2nd Battalion during the

South African wars in 1901.

110   Private 13848 Francis Brimicombe.

111   *St Neots and County Times*, 3 April 1915.

112   Company Sergeant Major 5316 Ernest Watson.

113   Company Sergeant Major 4893 Thomas Byford.

114   Company Sergeant Major 7312 Percy Chandler.

115   *Royston Crow*, 9 April 1915.

116   Sergeant 10004 Frederick Spicer.

117   Sergeant 9232 Joseph John Smith (known as John).

118   *The Times*, 13 April 1915.

119   Private 3/7322 William Quinton, from his memoirs held at the Imperial War Museum, reference 6705.

120   Private 10026 Albert Petchell.

121   The History Committee, the Royal Anglian Regiment (Bedfordshire and Hertfordshire); Lieutenant Colonel T.J. Barrow, DSO, Major V.A. French and J. Seabrook Esq. (1986), *The Story of the Bedfordshire and Hertfordshire Regiment (The 16th Regiment of Foot)*. Volume II, 1914 to 1958, page 125.

122   Drummer 8537 Charles Bellamy.

123   *St Neots Advertiser*, 30 April 1915.

124   Formerly Sergeant 6394 in the 1st Battalion.

125   Sergeant 8427 Reginald Arthur Rosamund Fearn is recorded as such on most official documentation, although the alternative name Richard appears on some of his military paperwork.

126   Sergeant 8341 Henry Trasler.

127   Private 10120 George Whiting.

128   Sergeant 9183 Walter James Summerfield.

129   Private 14099 Albert Pigg.

130   *Royston Crow*, 30 April 1915.

131   Private 8749 George Brigstock.

132   Private 8810 Henry (Harry) Webb.

133   Private 3/8605 Charles Jackson.

134   Privates 15472 Jim Neale and 15478 Tom Neale.

135   Private 10469 Fred Clifton.

136   Private 7602 Edward Warner, VC.

137   *Herts Advertiser and St Albans Times*, 3 July 1915.

138   Private 7309 Frederick Brimm.

139   *Herts Advertiser and St Albans Times*, 3 July 1915.

140   *Herts Advertiser and St Albans Times*, 24 July 1915.

141   Private 3/6853 William Sherman.

142   *St Neots Advertsier*, 28 May 1915.

143   Private 7898 Harry Cox, published in the *Bedfordshire Times and Independent*, 14 May 1915.

144   Company Sergeant Major 5362 John Stapleton.

145   Private 13579 Alfred Leonard Mayes.

146   Use of language such as this was commonplace at the time, so has been quoted in its original form.

147   *Herts Advertiser and St Albans Times*, 5 June 1915.

148   Private 14929 Charles Cleaver.

149   Private 14958 Frederick Dumpleton.

150   Private 16454 Frederick Groom.

151 *Herts Advertiser and St Albans Times*, 22 May 1915.

152 Private 3/7386 Theodore Rowlett.

153 *Hunts County News*, 26 June 1915.

154 Private 13618 Benjamin Bosley.

155 Lance Corporal 8745 William Webb.

156 Private 14194 George Brewer.

157 *Letchworth Citizen*, 20 August 1915.

158 Sergeant 10150 Frederick Howe.

159 *Bedfordshire Times and Independent*, 4 June 1916.

160 Corporal 3/6915 Alfred Hall, published in the *Bedfordshire Times and Independent*, 7 May 1915.

161 Acting Sergeant 6236 Joseph Cross.

162 Sergeant 3/3784 William Humphries.

163 Acting Corporal 8515 Albert Ernest Knight.

164 Acting Company Sergeant Major 9623 Alfred Hawkins.

165 Company Sergeant Major 7525 George Garrett.

166 Corporal 3/7676 Ernest Barnes.

167 Private 18734 Walter Warman.

168 Published in the *Royston Crow*, 16 November 1915.

169 Private 13825 Frederick Thomas Miller.

170 Private 16003 George Leonard Page, published in the *Hunts County News*, 30 July 1915.

171 *Royston Crow*, 20 August 1915.

172 Bandsman 9448 George Eli Law.

173 Company Sergeant Major 7525 George Garrett.

174 Corporal 8328 George Franklin.

175 The National Archives, reference WO 213/5.

176 Hussey, A.H. and Inman D.S. (reprint of 1921 edition), *The 5th Division in the Great War*, Naval and Military Press, page 87.

177 Sergeant 6395 Albert Sirrell.

178 *Royston Crow*, 29 October 1915.

179 Private 8426 Stephen Hare.

180 Sergeant 10094 Albert Higgins.

181 Private 8411 Arthur Webb.

182 Company Sergeant Major (Acting RSM) 5362 John Stapleton.

183 Private 4/7341 Arthur Gray.

184 Sergeant 8765 Edward Quince.

185 Private 13045 Maurice Winch.

186 William Quinton, now a lance corporal.

187 Private 10026 Albert Petchell from Cambridge.

188 Private 4/7036 Sidney Cox.

189 Corporal 9522 Charles Atkinson.

190 Sergeant 9277 James Percival King.

191 Sergeant 8765 Edward Quince.

192 Private 13045 Maurice Winch.

193 Private 19447 Frederick Cain.

194 *Letchworth Citizen*, 14 July 1916.

195 Lance Corporal 14925 Edwin Granville Harvey.

196 Private 14925 Edwin Harvey.

197 Private 16755 Arthur Reed.

198   *Letchworth Citizen*, 25 August 1916.

199   The History Committee, the Royal Anglian Regiment (Bedfordshire and Hertfordshire); Lieutenant Colonel T.J. Barrow, DSO, Major V.A. French and J. Seabrook Esq. (1986), *The Story of the Bedfordshire and Hertfordshire Regiment (The 16th Regiment of Foot)*, Volume II, 1914 to 1958, page 137.

200   Corporal 10145 Thomas Harris.

201   Privates 18787 Arthur Boness and 18484 George Boness.

202   Privates 18042 Albert Currington and 19384 William Currington.

203   *Royston Crow*, 20 April 1917.

204   Private 8081 George Gazeley.

205   Sergeant 10190 Oswald Gentle.

206   Sergeant 7623 Sidney Spott Chamberlain.

207   Sergeant 8749 George Brigstock.

208   Sergeant 8939 Joe Afford.

209   Lance Corporal 17568 Bertie Pettengell.

210   Private 9349 Joseph King.

211   Sergeant 8186 James Bush.

212   Jünger, Ernst (1920), *Storm of Steel* (2003 translation by Michael Hofmann), Penguin.

213   Corporal 13485 Joseph Churchill Jarrett.

214   Private 3/6701 Walter Neal.

215   Corporal 5288 Michael J. McGinn.

216   Private 11011 Percy Craddock.

217   Private 20619 Archie Boness.

218   Hussey A.H. and Inman D.S. (reprint of 1921 edition), *The 5th Division in the Great War*, Naval and Military Press, pages 126 and 127.

219   Privates 15478 Tom Neale and 15472 Jim Neale.

220   Company Sergeant Major 7521 Cecil Ford Walker.

221   Sergeant 9522 Charles Atkinson.

222   Sergeant 19255 George Howlett.

223   Private 22058 Percy Lewis.

224   *Royston Crow*, 5 January 1917.

225   Sergeant 4/6259 Samuel Sheppard.

226   Lance Corporal 3/6448 Sidney Wilson.

227   Lance Corporal 13610 Harold McHugh.

228   Private 43031 Christopher John Cross.

229   *Royston Crow*, 10 November 1916.

230   Acting Company Sergeant Major 14061 Reg Driscoll.

231   *Royston Crow*, 10 November 1916.

232   Privates 9560 Albert Durham and 23285 Thomas Durham.

233   Sergeant 9391 Ernest Fox.

234   Sergeant 8721 Reginald Thomas Lansbury.

235   Sergeant 8557 Frank (Frederick) George Stanley.

236   Sergeant 8367 Frank Butler.

237   Sergeant 8212 Albert E. Johnson.

238   Sergeant 3/6670 Fred Stubbings.

239   Corporal 14112 Charles Worboys.

240   Lance Corporal 13192 Clarence Mailing.

241   Lance Corporal 10447 Robert Skipp.

242   Lance Corporal 7932 Harry Steele.

243 Private 9361 Walter England.

244 Private 7180 Matthew Herring.

245 Private 4/7172 George Cotton.

246 Private 13306 Horace Scrivener.

247 Private 15133 Henry T. Shadbolt.

248 Sergeant 13039 Henry Guess.

249 Private 4/7302 John Manning.

250 Private 3/6929 John Horne.

251 Private 16507 Arthur Rayner.

252 Lance Corporal 27807 Arthur Joseph Porter.

253 Private 20132 Frederick William Purdy.

Index of Personnel